# A Soldier Supporting Soldiers

by

Joseph M. Heiser, Jr.
Lieutenant General
U. S. Army, Retired

Center of Military History
United States Army
Washington, D.C., 1991

**Library of Congress Cataloging-in-Publication Data**

Heiser, Joseph M. (Joseph Miller), 1914–
　A soldier supporting soldiers / by Joseph M. Heiser, Jr.
　　p.　cm.
　Includes bibliographical references.
　1. Heiser, Joseph M. (Joseph Miller), 1914–　　. 2. Generals—United States—Biography.　3. United States. Army—Biography. 4. Vietnamese Conflict, 1961–1965—Logistics.　5. United States. Army—Procurement—History—20th century.　I. Title.
E840.5.H45A3　1991
959.704'3373—dc20　　　　　　　　　　　　　　　　91-11388
　　　　　　　　　　　　　　　　　　　　　　　　　　　　CIP

CMH Pub 70–40

First Printing

For sale by the Superintendent of Documents, U.S. Government Printing Office
Washington, D.C. 20402

# Foreword

*A Soldier Supporting Soldiers* is the second in a series of works by distinguished U.S. Army logisticians that focus on firsthand experience in the organization of combat service support. These studies seek to describe and analyze problems still familiar to those who provide the materials and other support required by today's Army. Their authors also clearly underscore the challenges that their successors will face in an era of limited resources. With active careers that span the last half-century of Army history, General Carter B. Magruder, in the recently published *Recurring Logistic Problems As I Have Observed Them* and Lt. Gen. Joseph M. Heiser, Jr., in the pages that follow, have much to say to the student of military operations about what constitutes efficiency and effectiveness in military logistics.

General Heiser's study marks a clear departure from the Center of Military History's policy of refraining from publishing biographies or memoirs. Although we believe that the compelling reasons for establishing such a policy fifty years ago still pertain, we also think an exception should be made in this case. General Heiser has a unique skill in conveying important logistical lessons through personal anecdotes. Especially in his early chapters, he uses specific incidents from his own career to illuminate for his reader larger principles of logistics. Thus in this special instance our audience is treated to an extended, personal account that in some ways has just as much to say about military leadership and ethics as it does about logistics.

The logistical principles discussed in this study appear especially vital to today's military students, given the recent massive challenges to logisticians posed by operations in the Persian Gulf and possible future contingency operations. I urge them to study and reflect on the insights provided in the engaging chapters that follow.

Washington, D.C.  
December 1990

HAROLD W. NELSON  
Brigadier General, USA  
Chief of Military History

# The Author

A logistics consultant to the Department of Defense, the General Accounting Office, and other government agencies, Joseph M. Heiser, Jr., retired from the Army with the rank of lieutenant general in 1974. General Heiser has been engaged in planning and directing logistical support of U.S. soldiers since his commissioning as an officer in the Ordnance Corps in 1943. He served in the Southern Base Section Command in the European Theater of Operations during World War II; as division ordnance officer in the 7th Infantry Division during the Korean War; and as commanding general of the U.S. Communications Zone, Europe, and of the 1st Logistical Command in Vietnam. In 1969 he became the Deputy Chief of Staff for Logistics.

General Heiser was awarded a master's degree in business administration by the University of Chicago in 1956. He is also a graduate of the Command and General Staff College and of the National War College. In addition to numerous articles, he is the author of *Logistic Support* (1974).

# Preface

I did not expect to write this book. I was asked to do so by Perkins C. Pedrick, then president of the Logistics Management Institute. I agreed because he and others thought that my story would be of value. I can only justify their faith in such an enterprise by trying to fulfill three goals.

I want to outline for today's generation of military logisticians and military policy makers those lessons I believe can be learned from the evolution of logistical doctrine and training I have witnessed in the U.S. Army over the past half-century. To achieve this purpose I could have adopted a familiar approach, listing logistics principles and their application in combat zones and headquarters followed by a discussion of how deviations from those principles led to weakened combat readiness and to inefficiency and waste. But when reviewing logistics principles, I find myself most often connecting them to a particular incident in my career. I seem to work best by going from the particular to the general, from analyzing the personal incident or problem to finding the underlying logistics principle. The editors at the Logistics Management Institute (where this project began) and at the U.S. Army Center of Military History agreed that this approach might actually assist the reader in better understanding and remembering the logistics lessons I was trying to impart. I took their advice. The pages that follow are thus part textbook and part memoir, in effect one man's understanding of military logistics based on forty-eight years' experience.

A second purpose for writing this book transcends the subject of logistics and is concerned with leadership and opportunity in the military services. I want to emphasize those qualities that I believe critical to a military career: dedication, integrity, loyalty, hustle, and common sense. All are essential, and I have tried to offer many examples of how they affect careers. But to explain adequately what I mean by leadership and opportunity, I agreed to preface my survey of military logistics with a brief but very personal account of my early education and training. This account is meant to demonstrate that one can overcome a youth filled with problems to attain positions of leadership and responsibility in the

U.S. Army. In doing so I hope to pay tribute to the wealth of opportunity open to all Americans.

Finally, I want my story to underscore for the reader the logistician's responsibility for providing support to the combat soldier. It has been my privilege to be involved in this support effort for many years, and what follows shows the many facets of a career devoted to "supporting the soldier."

I dictated this account, which is based primarily on my recollections. Since I never planned on being an author, I saved few documents, and although I have done my best to be accurate, I apologize for any errors or embarrassments a faulty memory may cause.

Many people appear in this logistics history. I would like to acknowledge here the impact that they have had on me personally and on the progress of logistics in the Department of Defense. In truth, if my career is accounted any special worth it is because of the unfailing support and encouragement this large group of exceptional men and women in and outside the military have given me. People like Charles Fyfe, Gus Muscaro, and Father Dillon—who nurtured a lonely youth's emerging character—and noteworthy soldiers of all ranks such as Leo Dillon, Ferdinand Chesarek, and especially Creighton Abrams—who were my principal mentors during my military career—personify this support. I was thinking of them, of all those other colleagues who appear in the pages below, and of many other great friends when I observed at my retirement from the Army that "I have gained much credit in my career when I merely was reflecting the image of those with and for whom it has been my privilege to serve."

I also thank all of my colleagues at the Logistics Management Institute, especially my editor, Ted Watts, and Mrs. Dorothy A. West and Mrs. Miriam W. Parsons, for their valuable assistance. In 1989 the Department of the Army decided to publish this manuscript as one in a series of works dedicated to issues of historical interest to logisticians. My thanks go to Brig. Gen. Harold W. Nelson, the Chief of Military History, to historians Joel D. Meyerson, Lt. Col. Clayton R. Newell, and Morris J. MacGregor, to editor John W. Elsberg, and to graphics artist Linda Cajka.

My wife, Edith ("Sug") Cox Heiser appears frequently in the following pages. I want to acknowledge publicly my deepest gratitude to her, to our children, Annette, Joel, and Joan, and to my ten grandchildren for their constant inspiration and support.

December 1990                                        JOSEPH M. HEISER, JR.

# Contents

| Chapter | Page |
|---|---|
| Prologue: Lonesome Boy's Blues. . . . . . . . . . . . . . . | 3 |

### Part I: Journeyman Logistician

| | |
|---|---|
| 1. Joining Up. . . . . . . . . . . . . . . . . . . . . . . . . . . | 17 |
| 2. Preparation in England. . . . . . . . . . . . . . . . . . | 25 |
| 3. War in Europe. . . . . . . . . . . . . . . . . . . . . . . . | 39 |
| 4. War in Korea . . . . . . . . . . . . . . . . . . . . . . . . | 56 |

### Part II: Transition to High Command

| | |
|---|---|
| 5. Teacher and Student . . . . . . . . . . . . . . . . . . . | 91 |
| 6. Reorganization of Logistics, 1962 . . . . . . . . . . . | 101 |
| 7. Europe in the 1960s. . . . . . . . . . . . . . . . . . . . | 113 |

### Part III: Senior Logistician

| | |
|---|---|
| 8. Transition to Vietnam . . . . . . . . . . . . . . . . . . | 127 |
| 9. War in Vietnam . . . . . . . . . . . . . . . . . . . . . . | 141 |
| 10. Chief of Army Logistics. . . . . . . . . . . . . . . . . | 168 |

### Part IV: A Continuing Commitment

| | |
|---|---|
| 11. Retirement . . . . . . . . . . . . . . . . . . . . . . . . . | 201 |
| 12. Coalition Logistics . . . . . . . . . . . . . . . . . . . . | 217 |
| 13. A Point of View . . . . . . . . . . . . . . . . . . . . . . | 235 |
| 14. The Logistics Imperatives. . . . . . . . . . . . . . . . | 260 |

| | |
|---|---|
| Epilogue: Polishing the Mirror. . . . . . . . . . . . . . . . | 265 |

## APPENDIXES

Page

| | |
|---|---|
| A. "Economy of Force: Application in Combat Logistics". | 273 |
| B. Hqs, 1st Logistical Command, Commander's Letter 7–1, 1 July 1969 | 281 |
| C. DCSLOG Guidance Bulletin #24, 29 October 1969 | 284 |
| D. "The Logistics Offensive" | 288 |
| E. "Answer to a Challenge—The Logistics Offensive" | 294 |
| F. "The Long-Term Defence Programme: Crucial to Credible Deterrence" | 302 |
| G. Spreading the Word | 309 |

BIBLIOGRAPHIC NOTE . . . . . . . . . . . . . . . . . . . . 313

INDEX . . . . . . . . . . . . . . . . . . . . . . . . . . . . . 317

## ILLUSTRATIONS

*The following illustrations appear between pages 80 and 89:*

St. Charles Preparatory School Baseball Team
Basic Training, Camp Sutton
The Heiser Family, 1942
First Sergeant Heiser Calls the Roll
Red Ball Express Trucks
Lieutenant Heiser at SHAEF Headquarters
General Eisenhower Inspecting in Cherbourg
Brig. Gen. Benjamin O. Davis
Collecting Supplies Behind the Hedgerows, Normandy
Piers 1 and 2 at Pusan
7th Infantry Division Ordnance Support Base
The Port of Pusan
Loading Wounded on a C–54 Transport
Rekindling the Eternal Flame at the Arc de Triomphe

*The following illustrations appear between pages 186 and 199:*

POL Fire at Tan Son Nhut
The Fish Market
Thu Duc Storage Area
General Creighton Abrams at the 1st Log Command
Repairing T–53 Helicopter Engine
Cleaning Rifles for Retrograde
Sea-Land Vans Used for Transporting Supplies
Artist's Rendering of Mountain Resupply Routes in Vietnam
Assistant Secretary of Defense Thomas Morris
Repairing a 5-Ton Truck Engine
Cartoonist's Solution to Excess Materiel
General Heiser Reviews Logistics Operations
Computers Used in Inventory Accountability
CH–47 Chinook Helicopter Airlifting Supplies
Artillery Ammunition Prepared for Sling Loading
M551 Sheridan Tank Arrives in Vietnam
Armored Gun Truck Provides Logistics Security
Archbishop Terence Cooke
Bob Hope
Martha Raye
Billy Graham
Ethel Kennedy
Off-Loading Lumber and Steel at Newport
1st Log Command Soldier of the Month, April 1969

*The following illustrations appear between pages 266 and 271:*

"Spreading the Word"
DCSLOG Heiser with Assistant Secretary J. Ronald Fox
"Kicking Boxes"
Visiting Vietnam, 1971
Generals and Mrs. Abrams and Heiser
The 1st Logistical Command Vietnam Memorial

Illustrations courtesy of Lt. Gen. Joseph M. Heiser, Jr. (USA, Retired), or from the files of the Department of Defense.

# A Soldier
Supporting Soldiers

# PROLOGUE

# Lonesome Boy's Blues

> Oh lonesome's a bad place
> To get crowded into
> 
> Kenneth Patchen

In reviewing my career as an Army logistician, it is clear to me that good fortune and opportunity played a significant role in many of my successes. I have also become even more firmly convinced that my early years—to the age of twenty-two—were critical in shaping my later understanding of such personal values as self-reliance, perseverance, candor, and loyalty to others, under the general principle of the Golden Rule. These values are those our society expects a young man to learn. But in my case they were learned in an atmosphere of loneliness, parental indifference, and aimlessness. The fact that I was able to overcome this background is a tribute to the opportunities open to all Americans, but in the process the lessons and values I learned from others took hold with a particular firmness. In a real sense what I learned became the basis of what I have understood leadership to be.

From my birth in Charleston, South Carolina, in 1914 until my twenty-second birthday, my life was turmoil, without an objective, without a sense of "belonging" anywhere or to anyone. When my mother divorced my father because of his violent alcholic abuse, became terminally ill, and died—all before I was six years old—I was left to live with my grandaunt, whom I called Tante (the German word for aunt). Tante replaced my parents as well as she could. I was raised listening to continuous references to the havoc my father had caused under the influence of alcohol. I was told of the night when my father chased my mother out into the snow and ice, which led to her contracting the pneumonia that caused her death. His guilt always lay in the back of my mind when he would make one of his infrequent visits to Tante's home in unsuccessful attempts to become friendly with me.

My father, when sober, was a fine individual and a respected citizen of Washington, D.C. Before home rule, the community associations that represented the city's various neighborhoods were the only organizations that conveyed the feelings of Washington's citizens to the federally appointed District Commissioners, and my father, at one time, was the elected president of the city's combined citizens associations. He was able to get along with people, but his problem was that he was altogether a different individual when under the influence.

While I was living in South Carolina, my father remarried. My stepmother tried to bring my father and me together but without success. Later she became the object of the same drunken abuse that my mother had experienced. In January 1926, when I was twelve, my father paid us a visit in Charleston. His object, unknown to us at the time, was to take me back to Washington to live with him and my stepmother. He arranged for me to go with him for a ride, but instead we started out of Charleston along Route 52.

My mother's people owned a poultry farm at Ten Mile Hill along this dirt road. The word was passed that my father was kidnapping me and heading out this main road. As we approached Ten Mile Hill, a half dozen or so of my mother's relatives were waiting. I remember the picture very clearly. My relatives threw rocks at the car as we approached, but my father never stopped. Just as we passed, one relative fired several pistol shots, hitting the back of the car at least once. Meanwhile, I had ducked down onto the floorboard in the back. My father had turned the steering wheel over to my stepmother and, standing on the running board on the driver's side of the car and holding on with one arm, he was firing a pistol back at my relatives. We then continued north as fast as possible.

A new life began for me in Washington, a metropolitan area much larger than I had ever been in before. I was entered immediately in Sacred Heart Academy at 16th Street and Park Road, Northwest. I guess I got along very well at school. I remember that I soon made many friends, largely because I was able to drive in runs and play good basketball. In fact, school time became my refuge. I was, from the beginning, very unhappy at home. I had little or nothing in common with my parents except a last name.

Their one-bedroom apartment became crowded when I joined the family. I slept on a "Murphy" bed in the living room, and I remember that frequently I was told to go down and sit in the park, which was about a block away at 16th Street and Columbia Road, because I was in the way. Indeed, for much of the next decade, I was a "street" person free of any parental guidance.

# PROLOGUE

I avoided being at home with my parents whenever possible. I do not remember even participating in meals with my parents on any routine basis. I was usually sent out to eat somewhere on credit. In my idle time I would sit on the benches on the Ellipse behind the White House and watch the people go by or play ball on one of the four ball fields there. Often other boys took me to the Washington Boys' Club to play ball. Later I attended boarding school, but even then on days off and during summer vacations I slept in odd places—on benches on the Ellipse, in Union Station, in hotel lobbies, and at the Boys' Club. Despite the friendships developed in school and on the playground, I was truly a loner, with sports as my only joy in life.

I learned some important lessons about honesty and kindness during these experiences. I remember one cold and snowy week, for example, when I slept on the benches in Union Station. I discovered a fine restaurant in the station called the Savarin. I found that I could go in one entrance, order a meal, eat it, and then go out another entrance. If I left that way I could avoid the cashier. I did this each of the nights that I stayed in Union Station, although I did leave a dime tip. After I got a job at the Boys' Club of Washington and my first paycheck, I went back to the Savarin and asked for the manager. I showed him my unpaid checks for each of the meals I had eaten. I told him now that I had earned some money, I wanted to pay them. He asked me how I did it, and I told him. He said, "I should have seen that myself. Besides, I don't want any money, you've just paid me for the meals you ate, and in addition, let's you and I both go and have the best steak we've got in the house." So we did.

I also noticed that the Washington Hotel, which is still operating at 15th Street and Pennsylvania Avenue, turned out the lights in the large lobby about midnight. I found that if I went in then, I could find a couch way over in a dark corner where I could go to sleep. I did that several times until one night the night manager came over and shook me awake. Because I was looking for a job—I tried to look halfway decent in my one suit and in a clean white shirt that I bought for twenty-five cents at Woolworths—I was not treated with any disrespect. I explained to the manager that I did not have a room, that that was my problem. He said, "Well, we'll fix that up tonight." And he promptly took me up to a room and set me up for breakfast the next morning. Incidentally, Vice President John Nance Garner lived in the hotel at the time. He had to pay for his room.

But getting back to my story, after my first winter in Washington, I was allowed to go back to my people in Charleston for the summer. By this time I had come to appreciate what a home could be with people like Tante. In fact, after I moved to Washington she took on the job of raising my first cousin Marion when my Aunt Chris died. He later went on to a distinguished career in the Navy. That summer of 1926 was a great and happy time for me. However, August soon came, and I had to return to my father. That was the very lowest point in my life. I begged to be allowed to remain in Charleston but was told that this was impossible. I felt abandoned and completely alone in the world. Upon arriving in Washington, I learned that I was not going back to Sacred Heart where I had made friends, but to my father's old boarding school in New Jersey. This news certainly did not cheer me up.

St. Joseph's Academy at Convent Station, New Jersey, was a small, semimilitary school for elementary and junior high students. We wore uniforms and did a certain amount of drilling and marching in formation. By excelling in athletics, I gained some notice, which led to my being placed in leadership positions such as the cadet captain of my class and later school captain. These were relatively happy times except when I faced the prospect of having to go home for holidays and summer vacations, normally a happy prospect for students. When I could, I just stayed alone at the school.

Because I had mentioned the fact that I had been at the Boys' Club of Washington a few times, my father decided to send me to its camp during the summer of 1927. He felt that I needed toughening up, and since these were mostly boys off the street, he believed that this would be a good place for me to get some sense pounded into me. So I went off to the Boys' Club camp for eight weeks in southern Maryland near La Plata.

I recall having several fights of one kind or another. Apparently, however, the club director, Charles M. Fyfe, saw some good in the young troublemaker. At the end of the summer, he asked me if I would like to help close up the camp and then stay at his home until it was time for me to go off to school. I jumped at the chance, and thus began my close association with Mr. Fyfe and his family, who practically adopted me from time to time when I was in some kind of trouble at home.

Early that summer the camp baseball team had played an adult black team. In those days most small towns in the region were represented by semipro black teams who played one another on weekends. Because I was large for my age and threw a fair fastball, the manager of the black team asked me to play on his team on Sundays. I obtained permission, and for the rest of the summer of 1927 I was the only white player in that semipro baseball league. I actually earned a little money and learned a valuable lesson on a personal level about racial integration.

The school year of 1927–1928 was my last at St. Joseph's. Encouraged by the Sisters of Charity, I began to feel that I had a vocation to become a priest. They introduced me to various church authorities as someone interested in training for the priesthood. It was at that time that I met Fulton J. Sheen, the inspiring preacher and theologian who later went on to national prominence. I never did lose interest in becoming a priest until I met my wife in 1936.

After graduation from St. Joseph's, I became a summer camp counselor for the Washington Boys' Club. I was responsible for between twelve and fifteen campers. After a couple of weeks the camp director decided to put the roughest boys in my squad because I was physically a match for any of them, and they seemed to get along better with me. A new contingent of campers arrived every week, and the toughest in each new group were always assigned to my squad. Although rough and tough, they were usually very capable, and we generally won all the squad competitions, not only in athletics, but even in such things as washing the dishes, cleaning the table, and policing our cabins.

Gus Muscaro, Charles Fyfe's assistant, was the camp director. Muscaro had been with the Boys' Club at Mount Vernon and New Rochelle, New York, and really cared about training boys to become useful adults. He befriended me and gave me good advice throughout those formative years. I owe him and Fyfe a great deal. Men like these devote their lives to helping youths who normally would be found on street corners by providing guidance and leadership. Such work does not provide much monetary reward. Rather, their lives are enriched because they can see the good that they do.

High school was yet another boarding school, St. Charles College, a prep school in Catonsville, Maryland. I received a scholarship, and my four years there turned out to be the best years of my boyhood. Although the discipline was strict, the values instilled have had a lasting effect on me. I was especially helped by several priests at St. Charles who taught the elements of leadership to their students. At that time, when I was trying to understand what life was all about, these devoted men gave me special attention. I was left at school with the few foreign students during the lonely Christmas vacations, and I remember, for example, that Father Dillon would leave an envelope with $5.00 on the Christmas tree for me. That was a lot of money in those days, and it was also the only present I recall getting. As a result of this sort of parental-type attention and guidance, I began to realize what was really important in life. I learned that we had to have basic beliefs and principles based upon those beliefs, and I became disciplined in my dealings with other people, including my schoolmates.

After I finished high school at St. Charles, I spent two years at Providence College in Providence, Rhode Island, on another scholarship. Then I had a chance to try out with Clark Griffith's Washington Senators. It didn't work out; I wasn't able to crack the big leagues. But I got close. I met Walter Johnson when he managed the Senators, and Lou Gehrig had already taught me how to play first base when I was at school in New Jersey. Each summer I also continued to be a part of camp supervision at the Boys' Club of Washington camp.

These six years from 1928 to 1934 were spent at fine schools that provided unusual discipline, excellent learning, and perhaps most of all, permanent moral standards. I was fortunate to be placed in leadership positions that allowed me to learn early how to get along with people. A part of this was because of my ability to excel in athletics as well as to do fairly well in my academics. But I have searched into my past many times to try to discover the exact causes of my being chosen by peers and by teachers for these various leadership positions, and I can honestly say that I don't think that I was any different than my classmates. Certainly I was no smarter than my contemporaries, so I will have to put it down to the fact that I hustled in everything that I was asked to do. By nature I am something of an introvert, but as a young man I discovered that by hustle I could at least compete with my peers and earn their friendship. The more I hustled, the more I tended to have the opportunity to excel. Because of hustling and because of having learned to get along, I was repeatedly chosen to lead in such roles as team captain or class president.

Following the repeal of Prohibition, alcohol had again taken hold of the lives of my father and my stepmother. My stepmother was very patient, loving, and loyal to my father, but she suffered at his hands, and his return to drinking did nothing to improve my relationship with him. It worsened, in fact, into abusive confrontations in which I found myself many times in physical difficulty because I did not feel that I could fight my father. I just took it. During the summer of 1934 we attempted to come to a truce in which all three of us would make amends and try to live as a happy family. It did not work because of the alcohol and the lack of any really loving relationship. As a result at the age of twenty, going on twenty-one, I

## PROLOGUE

permanently separated from my parents. In many ways I clearly had been an abused child. My only satisfaction in saying this is that my own experience, at least, shows that an abused child is not necessarily condemned to hopelessly repeating a parent's behavior.

During late 1934 and early 1935 I thus once again wandered the streets of Washington, looking for permanent work. I was a homeless person, not unlike those people who spend winter nights in the parks and on the grates of Washington today. In some ways it was worse because during the Depression so many thousands were unemployed, living in empty buildings and forming long bread lines to eat. I managed to get by in part by being paid to form a baseball team among the homeless.

Earlier I had played for the baseball team that was created for the recreation of the thousands of World War I veterans who descended on Washington in 1932 to demand their promised bonus for wartime service. Frankly, if stone throwing had been in vogue in those days, I probably would have joined in when the Army, under the personal command of Chief of Staff Douglas MacArthur, was sent in to disperse the Bonus Marchers.

Work was unavailable in 1935, even though every day I tried to find some kind of job to support myself. Once again, Charles Fyfe came to my rescue. The job of coaching at the Boys' Club that Fyfe offered me was a lifesaver. I not only coached at the club, I even slept up in the attic. This job continued throughout the winter, and then I had full-time employment as the assistant camp director and aquatics director at summer camp.

At the end of the camp session I was faced with the decision of what to do with my life. It occurred to me to get in touch with my mother's people. Tante was still alive, and I took a bus to Charleston to see her. The family decided that they could use me as a helper on the family poultry farm, where some nine years earlier the family had tried to stop my father from taking me away. So, for that winter and into early spring, I worked at the poultry farm. Although I was treated very well by my relatives, I still had a feeling that I was an intruder.

Sports led me to a new life. During the Depression there was no television, of course, and many industries established athletic programs to provide recreation for their employees, especially in the southern and southwestern United States. These industrial, semipro baseball and basketball teams actually competed for players with the professional ball teams because industry could offer jobs, really for playing ball, that provided players steady, year-round income. They didn't have to work; they just punched the time clock and played on the company teams. In many cases it was better employment than playing six months of the year for a professional team. As a result, some industrial teams really were better than the minor leagues, and a few were competitive with the majors.

In the spring of 1936, while still working at the poultry farm, I learned that a Charleston baseball team sponsored by a national brewery was looking for recruits. I showed up as an unknown "walk-on," but quickly made the team. Once again, my baseball skills pulled me through. I even hit .400. I ended my farm work and moved into the YMCA in downtown Charleston. Since the salary was rather meager, I also began looking for another job.

Then I received an offer to play ball for the Boston Red Sox farm team in Columbia, South Carolina. I had just about decided to go to Columbia, when on the Fourth of July 1936, a Mr. Bolick contacted me and asked me to accept a position playing ball for the Adams-Millis Hosiery Company at High Point, North Carolina, to replace his injured son. Bolick was a fan who lived across the street from the Charleston ball park, where he had seen me play. So I decided to go to High Point instead of Columbia. I was put on the company payroll and played first base, and later basketball, for the company-sponsored teams.

Sports, in fact, have proved of great value to me all my life. When I was a small boy in Charleston, we didn't have little leagues. We played on any empty lot we could find, using worn-out balls wrapped with friction tape. Everyone seemed glad to have me on their team because I could play pretty well. It seems to me that what I learned in playing ball throughout my youth I unconsciously applied in working with others all during my life. This, I believe, is how I got the reputation for being a good team player in the Army.

Certainly, looking ahead, I can see a link between my involvement in sports and my military career. A baseball game at Camp Sutton, North Carolina, while I was a new recruit in World War II, led to my being noticed for the first time in the Army. I happened to get some hits to the opposite field which led to a review of my background and to my becoming a corporal. In Officer Candidate School, I believe excelling on the class baseball team caused me to be elected as an Honor Board member, an important mark in a young officer candidate's career. Much later I got along very well with some South Vietnamese military leaders because I played a tennis match with them during one of their High Command conferences. Because of my activities on the tennis court, I also got to know several Secretaries of the Army and Defense far better than if I had only faced them in a conference room or across a desk. This shared

PROLOGUE                                                                  11

interest in tennis applied to people like General William C. Westmoreland and Congressman C. V. "Sonny" Montgomery as well.

Athletic ability also helped break the ice with soldiers. For example, at almost every location in Vietnam where even a small number of soldiers were assigned, someone had installed a basketball backboard and net. On most occasions as I entered these compounds, large or small, invariably I would take a shot or two at the basket just because I like the sport. Every now and then I would make a hook shot on my first try. This would so amaze the troops who saw me do it that I decided to keep doing it whenever I had the opportunity. I was very nonchalant when I would try a first shot, and if it went in, I would stop right then and move on. The men observing could only guess that I could have done it that easily as often as I wanted to. They didn't know I was lucky. If I didn't make the first shot, I kept trying, and generally on my second or third, I would luck out. This still left me looking pretty good. So I became known and respected among troops to some extent because of my ability to make a hook shot. It was a small but meaningful reason for troops to develop some respect for an officer, especially if that officer was older, white, and wore stars on his uniform. It was often the only close contact they ever had with a general officer.

But back in 1936, going to High Point to play for the company teams had a much more immediate and practical utility. It meant a salary in the midst of the Depression. It also proved to be the most important decision that I ever made in my life. Most of the baseball team was living in a small hotel, but several of us decided to move into a boardinghouse, which would provide us not only with nice rooms but, more important, with three good meals a day when we were not away from home.

One evening just before the normal supper hour, we heard some unauthorized loud noises downstairs. It turned out to be two young women, one strumming a guitar and both singing country music. The lady who ran the boardinghouse had agreed to let these musicians earn their supper by providing dinner entertainment. We ball players didn't think very much of this idea. However, they soon won us over. Dorothy and Edith Cox were sisters from Randolph County, about 30 miles from High Point. I soon decided that maybe I should offer to take Edith, the younger and unattached sister, to a movie. This first movie led to a permanent attachment, to my asking Edith to become my wife, and to our getting married in 1937. Edith Cox (or Sug, short for Sugar, as I call her) gave me my first feeling of truly belonging to anyone, anywhere.

We had much in common. My wife enjoyed athletics, both as a participant and a spectator, as much as I did. We have played tennis together throughout our marriage. Sug had never held a tennis racket in her hand until I suggested that we should play tennis at a court on a hill just below the High Point Hospital. At first, she had the idea that hitting the ball over the wirefence backstop was the object of the game, like baseball. When she hit it over the fence at the hospital tennis court, it went into a street on a steep hill that ended at a sewer opening. I had to catch up with the ball or lose the only tennis ball we owned. (We didn't have enough money to buy balls by the can.) But she very quickly became a skilled player who has won many matches. Our relationship has been improved by tennis, not only because we both love the game, but also because we learned to control our tempers when one or the other played a lousy game against someone we wanted to beat.

With the increased responsibility of a wife, I felt I needed to improve my job situation. I began a correspondence course to become a certified public accountant, and at the same time I began to pressure Adams-Millis to consider me for a management position. Shortly after that, the company began to expand, and I was offered a position in its new plant at Tryon, North Carolina, to train new employees and organize their athletics. I had started to referee, especially basketball, at High Point, and I continued this in the Tryon-Hendersonville-Asheville area. Thus in addition to my salary at the plant, I was also making a small amount officiating at basketball and other sports on the side.

We stayed at Tryon almost three years, but in March 1940 I was offered a management intern position if I would play baseball and basketball for the General Asbestos and Rubber Company in North Charleston, South Carolina. This plant was owned by the Raybestos-Manhattan Corporation of Connecticut. We were expecting our second child (our daughter Annette had been born in Tryon the previous June; our son Joel would arrive in the fall of 1941), and because this seemed to be my best opportunity, I accepted their offer. I took a pay cut to $15 a week, but I was promised every opportunity to learn the business.

Alvin "Rock" Heinsohn, the general manager of Raybestos-Manhattan, kept his word. I played ball, but I was also given a real opportunity for advancement. Because I was a ballplayer, the other employees did not object when I was promoted quickly. First, I was put in the inspection department as a trainee; within months I became an inspector; within the year I became chief inspector. During the company's prewar expansion I was given increased responsibilities, becoming assistant superintendent for the second and third shifts. And since most of the new employees were assigned to these two shifts, I became personnel manager during the first shift as well. I also was able to squeeze in some management courses at the Citadel. Needless to say, this left me very little time for sleep.

As personnel manager I had been the Raybestos-Manhattan representative to the North Charleston Draft Board since the draft began in 1940. This board was responsible for evaluating local draft deferments. Managing company athletics and playing on both the baseball and basketball teams made me close to the team members, most of whom were single and subject to the draft. They were all drafted in 1941 and early 1942. Although not subject to the draft, I was trying to join up at the same time.

Raybestos-Manhattan played many exhibition games at the Marine base at Parris Island, South Carolina. In the fall of 1941 the commanding general, who attended the games, had offered me a commission as a Marine lieutenant to be the athletic director at Parris Island. I said that I was interested since it appeared we were headed for war. I filled out the necessary forms and took the physical examination, but since I could not meet the 20/20 vision requirement, I needed a waiver from Washington. However, by 7 December and the announcement of the attack on Pearl Harbor, no word had been received concerning the waiver and my commission. I immediately got in touch with the commanding general's office at Parris Island to find out what they could do to get approval for the commission. I was told that Washington was too busy. This delay persisted into January 1942.

PART I

Journeyman Logistician

# CHAPTER 1

# Joining Up

By early 1942 most of my friends had been drafted, and I couldn't wait any longer for the Marine Corps' offer of a commission. I applied to the Coast Guard and the Navy, in addition to the Marines, but nearsightedness caused my rejection by all of them. So I decided simply to enlist in the Army as soon as I could.

I must say that this decision to enlist was not greeted with much encouragement. Many of my friends told me that I needed my head examined. I was promised a considerable increase in pay and a bright future in management if I remained on the job with Raybestos-Manhattan. My wife and I had established ourselves in the community. I was the secretary and treasurer of the local credit union. I had become friends with the local congressman, L. Mendel Rivers, whom I had known in sports earlier, and I had obtained the governor's approval to be a notary public, a prestigious appointment in those days. I was also taking night courses in personnel management and in safety engineering at the Citadel, which were directly related to my job at Raybestos-Manhattan. But my wife supported me in my determination to enlist, and I did not waver. We often think about the decision we made then. It could have been a terrible decision from a family point of view because we really were not well established financially. In fact, we were poor, in relatively serious debt.

Then a notice appeared in the Charleston newspapers announcing that the Army was looking for skilled people to serve as combat support troops. Experienced personnel were needed to form an ordnance regiment that was being organized to support Maj. Gen. George S. Patton, Jr.'s combat units, which were just finishing training maneuvers in Tennessee and Louisiana. The National Automobile Dealers Association was recruiting men for commissions and for noncommissioned and other enlisted billets based upon their skills and background. Approximately 3,000 such skilled personnel were needed. The general idea was to start with experienced people, give them sixty days of military training, and thus avoid time-consuming advanced technical training. Such an ordnance regiment would be formed and ready to leave with Patton's troops within sixty to ninety days.

When I told Rock Heinsohn that I had obtained my wife's agreement to join the Army to do what I could as an ordnance support soldier, he agreed to give Sug a job operating an asbestos loom and also to allow my family to continue to live in the company house. He agreed to this reluctantly because, as he said, "I don't think they'll take you; in the first place you're 3F in the draft, and we need you here, and it would be foolish anyhow—you'd only be making $21 a month." But I wasn't making a great deal of money with Raybestos-Manhattan, something like $100 a month and a house to live in. There wasn't much money involved either way, especially with my wife now about to earn a little money.

As it worked out, I thumbed a ride to Columbia, South Carolina, and walked out to Camp Jackson to enlist. I went through a rather easy enlistment process and was told at the end of the day that I was now an enlisted reservist and that I should go back home and expect orders in a few weeks. Thus began a career that would occupy the rest of my life, a career in which I would serve in ranks from private through lieutenant general and in which I would meet chiefs of state, sports greats, film stars, religious leaders, and literally thousands of Americans dedicated to serving their country.

I returned home and told Heinsohn that I was now an enlistee and would be leaving in a few weeks. He didn't really believe me. I received orders about two weeks later to report for active duty, and when I showed them to him, he cussed me out more than I have ever been in my whole life. He was upset because he thought I had an important national defense job and because he was going to have to find a replacement for me. But when he finally realized that I was actually leaving, he stuck to his word and employed Sug as an asbestos loom operator. He also allowed us to retain the company house in which we were living.

As a member of the Enlisted Reserve, I was ordered to a place called Camp Sutton, North Carolina, and told to report to the fairgrounds at Monroe, North Carolina, about 35 miles south of Charlotte. I took the bus to Monroe the day before I was due to report and stayed in the only hotel in town. When I asked how I could get to the fairgrounds early in the morning, I was told the only way was by taxi. I didn't have the money for a taxi; I barely had the money to pay the hotel bill for one night. So the next morning I got up about 4:00 and walked down the dark road leading to the fairgrounds. It turned out to be quite a walk, about six miles.

# JOINING UP

I was the first one there and went to the grandstand at the small racetrack used during fair days. Soon other men began arriving until finally a great crowd had gathered. All of us reported, as ordered, with only the clothes we were wearing. The man who took the seat next to me had been given a direct commission as a lieutenant colonel. He had temporarily given up his position as the highway commissioner of North Carolina, and, unknown to me, he was slated to be commander of the battalion to which I was later assigned. Three thousand men had been expected, but double that number of volunteers were recruited. The automotive association had simply done its job too well, but the Army happily formed two regiments instead of one.

When they took us out to Camp Sutton from the fairgrounds, we discovered that Camp Sutton had just been created. I had thought it odd that we were told to report to the Monroe fairgrounds rather than to a military post. It turned out that Camp Sutton, until our arrival, had been the local prison farm. While we civilians were going in the gate that morning, the chain-ganged prisoners were coming out.

I emerged as somewhat of a leader my first day in the Army. Camp Sutton proved to be farmland with a pile of folded-up pyramidal tents. It was pouring down rain when we were emptied out of trucks and told to "raise the tent, that's where you live." After all my years at the Boys' Club camp I at least knew how to put up a tent! So I got a crew of guys together, and we quickly raised a tent to get out of the rain.

In its zeal to match the backgrounds of the recruits with technical billets, the Army made some mistakes that now seem amusing. For example, my unit was assigned to repair artillery and fire-control instruments. The technical sergeant in charge of this work had been a city fireman in Louisville, Kentucky, an altogether different kind of fire control. He spent several uncomfortable months completely out of his element before he was accepted for Adjutant General Officer Candidate School. But despite occasional errors such as this, the new soldiers did a great job. The few that were found to be physically unfit, including alcoholics (we had a few enlisted men who couldn't be put on KP because of access to the vanilla extract), were transferred as appropriate. Even though as a group we were older than most other units in an Army filled with draftees, we really worked hard at getting ready. We took our physical conditioning very seriously. We took special pride in being able to complete 20-mile marches in less time and to march at double time longer and faster than a neighboring Ranger battalion could do.

On the other hand, there were no uniforms and no equipment except for kitchen and mess gear. In fact, when I was put in charge of the company supply tent, I found it empty of any supplies except shovels for digging latrines. We eventually wore out the clothing we arrived in, and before long we were training in pajamas and underwear and replacing our shoe soles with cardboard. We pulled guard duty with sticks. I found a smooth broom handle to practice the Manual of Arms.

I found that I excelled at throwing hand grenades. This pleased my company commander, who was something of a gambler. He would arrange matches with such outfits as the Rangers, and I discovered unofficially that he was making bets on our outfit. We usually won, but in throwing those grenades for distance and accuracy, I threw my arm away, as ballplayers say. I never recovered the ability to throw a ball as far and as fast as I could earlier.

One day the Chicago White Sox stopped to play a pickup team from our camp on their way back north from spring training in Florida. The game had a good effect on morale, and my playing also caused our regimental commander to look up my records. When he found I had been a supervisor in industry before I enlisted, he sent for me and told me that some of the troops would be leaving the next day for New York to learn to maintain 90-mm. antiaircraft guns at Otis Elevator, the manufacturer. He said, "If they don't get uniforms they're going to look like a bunch of gypsies. If you take some men and trucks and go up to Charlotte and find some uniforms, which I understand are in a boxcar somewhere, and get them here before they leave tomorrow at noon, I'll promote you to corporal."

I know what follows violates most of what I later preached as a logistician about inventory control, but at the time I had what seemed a noble cause. I assembled a party from among my fellow ballplayers. We drove to Charlotte, found the railroad classification yards, broke the seals on all the boxcars we could find, and early next morning located a car full of uniforms. We loaded them onto our trucks and hurried back to Monroe. The troops were already in the railway coaches about to leave for New York. We pushed the uniforms and shoes, still in burlap bags, through windows and doors as the train pulled out. I never did hear how they sorted out the sizes, but we trusted that they all were in uniform with shoes on their feet when they arrived in New York. True to his word, the colonel promoted me and made the orders effective from my first day of active duty. This was my first logistics experience in the Army. It may seem

JOINING UP                                                              21

trivial, but the seeds of many later efforts to ensure adequate levels of supply are present in this tale of shoeless "rag-tag" soldiers.

From Monroe, we were sent on maneuvers in Tennessee. By this time I had been promoted to first sergeant. Suddenly one weekend we were alerted to proceed to the port at Norfolk. About 30 percent of our men were on leave or on pass, but we could not wait until they reported in. We had to contact them along the way, picking up men from Tennessee to Norfolk. We were temporarily placed in Camp Pickett, just outside Norfolk. Then we were loaded aboard ship, but for some reason we were just as quickly unloaded and sent to nearby Camp Patrick Henry. Somebody said that submarines were sinking ships leaving Norfolk, so we did not sail.

Rumor had it that the first three grades (which included first sergeants) of the 302d Ordnance Regiment were going to be pulled out of their companies and used as cadre for other combat service support units. At that point I certainly did not want to leave my outfit, and so I received a promise from my battalion commander that he would attempt to keep me. If he couldn't prevent my departure, he said he would put in my papers for Officer Candidate School (OCS). I valued his offer, but to be honest I had no desire to go to OCS.

As it worked out, my outfit was alerted one evening to leave camp at midnight. All of our plans had been made, so we all tried to get a quick nap before we marched to the railhead. I was awakened and told that I was wanted in regimental headquarters. There I learned that I would not be going with my outfit but would remain behind because my orders for OCS had come in. I was to report to Aberdeen Proving Ground, Maryland. So at midnight that night I had to say good-bye to my company. I followed them all the way to the railhead and watched them pull out as I stood in the dark with real tears in my eyes, wishing that I was going with them.

On my first day in OCS I made the mistake of reporting in uniform, sporting my first sergeant's stripes. The company commander and his small staff greeted me kindly and told me that since I was a first sergeant, they would appreciate my becoming the OCS officer of the day (the equivalent of the cadet company commander) for the formal beginning of OCS. I thought in a way that this was an honor until the next day began. From the moment I called the 360 men of the new OCS company to attention, I became the butt of criticism from every member of the staff, beginning with the company commander, Capt. Medwyn D. Sloan, who really proceeded to give me a lot of trouble in front of the entire company.

It was January 1943 and snowing a blizzard in Aberdeen. Sloan ordered me to form the company of 360 men in a column of twos and take it around to the post theater for orientation. We marched out of the company area to the first turn. At my order of column left, he allowed the company to go halfway around; then he told me to halt the company. He yelled, "Mister, where in the hell did you ever learn to drill a company? You're all wrong. Turn the company around and do it over again." That was the beginning of a torturous day. Everything I did was criticized publicly. I had to take the company around that turn four times; we were stopped halfway around each time. Finally we were allowed to proceed to the theater. In all that snow, I was sure that I was the most unpopular candidate in all of OCS. I got through OCS without too much trouble, but I never forgot that day.

While I did not have "too much trouble," the fact is that any OCS student does not have an easy time. We were continually under stress and being told to do things that we would rather not do. We were never sure that we would graduate successfully. I had many moments when I would have gladly remained as first sergeant of my old company. But the men of my OCS Class—No. 41—were truly outstanding. Quite a few had graduated from Texas A&M, but because of the condensed three-year wartime curriculum they could not act as commissioned officers until they completed the officer candidate course. Among this group was Homer Smith, a man who has been like a brother ever since we graduated together and were assigned to the European Theater of Operations. Promoted through the ranks to major general, he was the defense attache in the American embassy in Saigon responsible for the evacuation from the roof of the embassy and Tan Son Nhut Air Base in the last days of our presence in South Vietnam. He has written an account of this period, "Last 45 Days of Vietnam," that should be mandatory reading for all officers in the armed forces.* More recently he served as the first director of logistics on the staff of the Secretary General of NATO. In our class, in addition to Homer Smith and myself, at least three others completed thirty years or more of active duty, and at least two members of the Ordnance Hall of Fame came from our class. It was a great group of guys, one of the best group of officer candidates ever assembled.

Years later, after I returned home from Korea, I was assigned to Aberdeen Proving Ground as a member of the faculty of the Senior Officers' Preventive Maintenance Course. When I reported to Aberdeen, I ran into my old OCS company commander, the former Captain Sloan, again. Now a major called back to active duty,

---

*Homer Smith, Last 45 Days of Vietnam, unpublished ms, copy in CMH files.

# JOINING UP

Sloan, I had been told, was the course administrative officer. When I walked into his office he was sitting with his feet up on the desk reading a paper. I said to him as he looked up, "Is this the proper place for me to report? I am Lieutenant Colonel Heiser," with emphasis on the lieutenant colonel. He answered, "Yes, that's right." But he continued to lay back in his chair with his feet on the desk. I said, "Do I correctly ascertain that you're a major in the Army?" He said, "Yes, sir," beginning to feel something was up. I said, "You recognize that I'm a lieutenant colonel?" He said, "Yes, sir." I said, "You recognize that a major is junior to a lieutenant colonel and that when he enters an office, the major should come to attention?" And by this time, Major Sloan was really showing his embarrassment by the red in his face and neck. He took his feet off the desk and came to attention. I let him stay in that position just long enough so that he knew that I was really "pulling rank." Then I said to him, "Major Sloan, do you remember when you were the company commander of OCS?" He answered, "Yes, sir." I said, "Well, I happen to be the man you assigned as the candidate officer of the day on the first day that Class 41 reported in to OCS. You gave me holy hell. Now I've had the opportunity to even the score, and I may even have done a little better job of it than I expected I could do. You may now stand at ease." Red Sloan and I later served together in the United States and overseas, and we have been close friends ever since. He is now a colonel, U.S. Army, retired.

After considerable mental and physical stress, I graduated as a second lieutenant in May 1943. I was assigned to an ordnance company that was on maneuvers in Tennessee at the time, but due to be shipped overseas shortly. Sug and the family moved to Lynchburg, Virginia, where she could be close to her sister and brother. The family remained in Lynchburg until the war ended, and then a further year while I searched to find them a place to stay in Washington, D.C. From 1942 to late 1946, including my two years in the European theater, we were separated almost full time.

When I reported to my new ordnance company in Tennessee, I was told there must be some mistake. They checked the matter out and discovered that I had been reassigned to an ordnance ammunition company then training at Seneca Ordnance Depot in Romulus, New York. I retraced my steps by train and reported to the 699th Ordnance Ammunition Company at Seneca. We all had to learn how to handle ammunition by actually loading out ammunition from the depot. During that time we also took Army unit training and went through Army training tests that finally showed that we were ready for overseas duty. We received our "port call" in July 1943.

Looking back on this period, I now see that I had entered an Army that offered all kinds of opportunities for anyone showing leadership potential. This was the beginning of a trail of opportunities that led to significant assignments during my career. Although I hustled all the way, the fact is that I had very little to do with the opportunities made available to me. I worked with people who gave me these opportunities. At this beginning stage of my Army life I had not set any firm objectives; I just knew I had to get ahead not only because I had family responsibilities to meet, but also because I was sincerely dedicated to my country and its ideals.

CHAPTER 2

# Preparation in England

In August 1943 I once again reported to Camp Patrick Henry for embarkation. After finally boarding, we faced another delay while our already full ship loaded on another outfit. As we left Norfolk, we had about 3,000 men on board, which meant that some had to sleep on outside decks and under tables in ward rooms. Because there was no deck room on which to empty out the holds where companies of men were billeted, there were no safety drills or other training exercises during the voyage, and discipline was very poor. We sailed unescorted except for some aircraft that flew over us near Iceland. The seas were so rough that we lost half of our lifeboats and all the life rafts. We learned that twenty-six men had been washed overboard before we finally arrived at Greenock, Scotland.

From Scotland my unit, the 699th Ammunition Company, took the train to southern England for assignment to an ammunition depot headquartered at Stow-on-the-Wold, a small town some 20 miles from Oxford. The headquarters was in a castle that contained the officers' mess and billets. The enlisted men were quartered in tents surrounding the castle. Although the depot had been established almost a year earlier and had been receiving American ammunition for six to eight months, it and six or seven others like it in southern England were being operated by the British Ordnance Corps under lend-lease arrangements because there were no American ammunition troops available, evidence of the shortage of combat service support.

An ammunition depot in southern England in those days was really a headquarters with some staff doing the storage, accounting, and inventory management. The ammunition itself was stored along the verges of the highways 50 miles in every direction from the depot headquarters. I was responsible for one of these storage areas, as were the other company officers. The ten-ton stacks of ammunition were stored about 20 feet from each other and covered by metal semicircular shelters. Actually, before we stored our ammunition, the shoulders on these highways had been beautiful green roadsides to a depth of about 20 to 25 feet on each side. This area was called the "Queen's verge" to emphasize the sanctity of the grass.

The property lines of the private farms in that area began at that same distance from the road. Once another newly arrived officer and I were riding in a jeep when we saw smoke apparently coming from a fire close to the edge of a farm. As we approached the spot, we could see a farmer raking grass within his fence and burning it. He was on his property, but actually only about 3 feet from one of the ammunition storage stacks. When I stopped, the lieutenant with me quickly got out of the jeep, ran over to the fence, and told the farmer to put out the fire. The farmer paid him no mind until about the time I arrived alongside, when he calmly looked up and said, "The farm was here before the ammunition." In other words, if you want to prevent the ammunition from blowing up, move your ammunition; I've got a right to have this fire on my property.

Because we didn't have enough jeeps to go around, we were issued bicycles. Usually we put in 25 to 50 miles a day on our bicycles supervising the storage of ammunition in our areas. I can remember two noteworthy interruptions to this generally quiet country exercise. Once while I was supervising the unloading of ammunition at one of our storage sites, two women who were taking a walk along the country road with escorts engaged me in conversation. They turned out to be Queen Wilhelmina of the Netherlands and her daughter, Princess Juliana. They invited me and a soldier to tea at their home in exile. This encounter impressed on me the fact that even a person of junior rank must be ready and open for any possible experience in wartime. Another time I was bicycling around a curve when a command car with the top down went speeding by. I had to maneuver to get out of its way on the narrow road. It turned out that the command car belonged to Maj. Gen. (later Lt. Gen.) John Charles Henry "Court House" Lee, who commanded the Services of Supply in England from headquarters in Cheltenham. When I returned to the depot headquarters that evening, I was called on the mat because it had been reported that I had passed a command car without saluting the general. I explained that I did not salute because I was having trouble getting my bicycle out of the way of the car. Certainly I did not intend to miss a salute, but I thought it was more important to avoid an accident.

Although I didn't recognize it at the time, that incident was the beginning of a significant relationship that would affect my career. General Lee, a deputy to General Dwight D. Eisenhower and commander of all the logistics preparation for D-Day and combat on the Continent, was intent on several objectives, one of the most important being to maintain good Anglo-American relations. He wanted no trouble from the American troops in England.

But troubles occurred in the form of serious racial violence. The ammunition companies assigned to the American depots in southern England were, for the most part, manned by segregated black troops. Before some of the black units disembarked from their troopship, a British general had announced to them that there was no segregation in the United Kingdom. But men of the 29th Division, an all-white outfit that had been in England for almost a year, thought otherwise. Its troops, who had practically taken over the neighborhood pubs, felt they had a special claim on southern England and all the available single women who lived there. The ammunition depots were generally in rural areas because of safety requirements, but when our ammunition troops went into the towns on pass, the 29th's men did not take kindly to their going into pubs that the 29th considered more or less part of the division by that time. Significant problems began to occur between black and white troops on pass in the British towns.

One black ammunition company had been on the same overcrowded ship that my company came over on. Because of the cramped conditions, security was limited, and Thompson submachine guns issued to combat units had been left carelessly around the ship. It turned out that some of the black soldiers had brought some of the guns to the ammunition depots in their barracks bags. In one town in southern England, the MPs of the 29th Division broke up a fight between black ammunition troops and white soldiers from the 29th Division by running the blacks out of town. Some of these black troops went back to their barracks to get their unauthorized Tommy guns, and, returning to town, started a firefight with the MPs. Over twenty men were wounded or killed.

Needless to say, this incident caused considerable unrest among the American forces and a major uproar in the British press. An upset General Lee ordered that the men who participated in this racial incident be punished immediately. He also ordered that the officers responsible for their supervision be court-martialed. It was fortunate that Lee had at that time as his inspector general Brig. Gen. Benjamin O. Davis, the Army's senior black officer and first black general. With great wisdom and judgment Davis prevented a stampede that would have unnecessarily hurt individuals as well as the Army. He made sure that blanket courts-martial were avoided and that any action ordered was appropriate for the individuals responsible.

General Lee felt that bad race relations in the U.S. forces were partially the result of bad leadership—in this case, among the white officers in command of black ammunition units. As a result, the records of officers then in England were checked to locate anyone who was experienced in dealing with black personnel. Someone in personnel must have noticed that I had worked with black people in industry. I was ordered to proceed to the Southern Base Section (SBS) headquarters at Salisbury and report to the ordnance officer of that command, Col. Leo J. Dillon. When it looked like I might be transferred to the SBS, I pleaded that I be allowed to stay with my company. Colonel Dillon said that if he could, he would allow me to remain with my company, but several days after I returned to my unit, I was handed a scrap of paper while unloading ammunition. I quote the complete orders: "LT. HEISER—REPORT TO COL. DILLON SBS FOR D.S. [detail service] DO NOT WAIT."

These orders were the first of many which had a great effect on my career. It is also an example of how little someone like myself can know of what is best to do. As I explained to Colonel Dillon, I did not want to leave my ammunition company. I had gotten to know the men, and they had gotten to know me; we got along. I would have spent the whole war with these men if it had been left up to me. But it wasn't, and I did what I was directed to do. There were at least six or more important orders for duty like this one throughout my career which, if I had my way, I would have ignored. But I didn't have my way. I was ordered to a new duty, and in each case, although not pleased, I set about doing the new task as earnestly as I could. I learned from each experience, and they turned out for my own good.

It turned out that I was really being ordered to the SBS ammunition staff office responsible for supervising all the ammunition operations in southern England. Almost all of the ammunition for the Allied invasion of the Continent was being stored there. Later I would be involved in loading ammunition out for the landings, but my immediate assignment was primarily to act as a liaison officer representing SBS with General Davis. As a result of this I was able to see firsthand how, in spite of pressure, he put fairness above everything else.

Colonel Dillon had provided me with a letter instructing all commanders to cooperate with me in my investigation of the racial problem. As an unknown lieutenant, I was forced to use this letter at every interview. After those officers and men directly involved in the riot had been dealt with, I was told to make a complete round of all ammunition units, interview each officer assigned to a black ammunition company or battalion, and determine whether he should remain with the unit.

I must say that there was, not surprisingly, a certain resentment to a second lieutenant like me coming into a depot, reporting to the commander, who was in every case a colonel or a senior lieutenant colonel, and telling him that it was my task to interview all the officers in his depot, including himself, in order to determine what my recommendations would be pertaining to their future. One such investigation involved Col. John Abner Meeks. Meeks was a West Pointer of the old school who demanded that this new second lieutenant show identification as well as Dillon's letter. It turned out that a murder with an unauthorized weapon had recently occurred in his unit. He was actively considering whether to resign or face court-martial. Meeks was really a decent man, and before we were finished he was asking me, a young, inexperienced shavetail, for advice. These experiences taught me a great deal about how to get a job done in spite of the difficulty of working with senior officers who did not know me and resented my assignment.

Here I must pay well-deserved tribute to a man who happened to arrive in southern England at just the right time to have great influence on the racial situation. I spent much of my time in telephoning across southern England in the early morning hours because, as a junior officer, I could not get access to a telephone line at any other time—and even then it was tough. One morning around 0200 hours, I was sitting on the stoop of my Nissen hut waiting for a phone line, when two men approached the next hut. One of them was the special service officer responsible for entertainment and morale of troops. Because of the blackout, I could not tell who the other person was. The captain said, "Joe, I think you'd like to meet this fellow." I got up to shake hands with him, and I quickly discovered that he was a giant of a man. It turned out that I was about to shake hands with Joe Louis, one of the greatest boxers that the world has ever seen. He was in southern England on a personal appearance tour meeting the troops individually to build up morale.

The presence of this famous young black man was very important. Many of our visitors of varying ranks and callings, while well meaning, did not understand what the local racial problems were all about, and their dealings with the troops tended to cause considerable trouble. Louis, because of his prestige, was a great influence for good. He won my respect and the respect of everyone with whom he came in contact, both white and black. Before the war Billy Conn was my boxing hero, but when he came to entertain the troops he got into fights with some of the GIs. Joe Louis, on the other hand, was a true gentleman who did better work for us than some chaplains. I was proud to count him among my friends.

As a result of my working with General Davis, I became known as somewhat of an expert on racial matters, and whenever such matters came up within the command from then on, I was interrupted in whatever I was doing in ammunition operations and sent to take whatever action was appropriate. After a while I found myself gaining considerable experience in dealing with men of all races under crisis conditions because I often was detailed as temporary commander until the problems could be straightened out. This put me on the spot as a young lieutenant, but it also gave me valuable experience. During this period I learned that the best thing to do was to treat each and every person as I would like to have been treated in his position. I probably learned this more from General Davis than from any other man with whom I had served.

My experience with the racial problems that occurred during the early arrival of black troops into southern England gave me, if I didn't already have it, the firm conviction that integration, rather than segregation, in Army units was best for the individual and for the Army. I became an active proponent of integration from that point on. Later in Korea I had the opportunity to influence racial integration directly.

One of those whose career was caught up in the racial violence that broke out in a small town near Plymouth was the newly arrived executive officer of the ammunition battalion involved, Maj. Walt Partin. In the investigation following the killings, Partin was court-martialed for neglect of duty because his troops possessed unauthorized Tommy guns. Partin was acquitted, but this did not sit well with higher headquarters, and he was closely watched in his future assignments. Actually, Walt was a very dynamic officer with a great determination to carry out his part of the mission. He performed many courageous actions as an ammunition supply troubleshooter both on the D-Day beaches and in the hedgerows just beyond the landing areas. He fought several fires in ammunition dumps at the beach area. Because of his courage, he was awarded the Soldier's Medal and the Legion of Merit and was promoted to the rank of lieutenant colonel, all during the first sixty days after leaving southern England and after having narrowly avoided conviction in a court-martial.

Following the breakout from Normandy and liberation of Paris, Partin commanded a key depot in northern France at Soissons. Once again his dynamism and determination set him apart. His actions in a railhead fire and explosion at Soissons proved essential in saving more than two-thirds of the 1,500 ammunition cars in that vast depot. His leadership gained the support of the men needed to move the cars as well as of the commanders of nearby tanks that were used in place of locomotives. He personally supervised the movement of loaded rail cars away from those which were burning and exploding. In fact, Walt Partin was with me in the temporary command post in the railroad station when that brick building collapsed on us. The troops thought we had been buried and were trying to find us beneath the rubble when we came around from the railhead to see what was going on. We had fortunately managed to escape when the roof collapsed.

Word got to Supreme Headquarters, Allied Expeditionary Force (SHAEF), that there were two outstanding leaders at Soissons. General Eisenhower had been told of Partin's exploits, and he was planning to decorate him. He had also learned of the fine efforts of Maj. James McHugh, who commanded a battalion under Partin. He decided to visit Soissons to take a look at what was going on in this very vital ammunition setup and to personally decorate Partin and promote McHugh. Eisenhower was so impressed with what he saw during his visit that he suddenly asked a colonel in his inspecting group for his "eagles." Turning to Partin, he pinned the eagles on his shoulders saying, "You've done a great job; you're now a colonel."

Actually, it is believed that Eisenhower, while greatly impressed with what had been done under Partin's leadership, may have been confused about the promotion that was to be made. McHugh's promotion was welcomed by the local authorities, but Partin's sudden elevation was not. Brig. Gen. Charles O. Thrasher, the section commander, interposed saying, "General, we don't have a vacancy for a full colonel in the ammunition setup here." Eisenhower replied, "Partin is a full colonel. The rest is your problem." As it turned out, a provisional group was created to provide a command position for Partin as a full colonel to supervise not only Soissons, but other ammunition supply activities in northern France.

Walt Partin was recommended highly for one of the Regular Army commissions being given to outstanding officers after the war. However, he was also a very controversial officer who would never win a popularity contest. He cared very little about what people thought of him, and he had earned the animosity of many senior officers. I think it was this opposition, as well as his not having a formal college education, that caused Partin's application for a Regular Army commission to be rejected. Because of his value to the Army, there was a later effort to get him promoted to brigadier general as a reservist, but this recommendation was never approved. He remained on active duty and among other assignments became the commanding officer of the Pueblo Army Ordnance

Depot, which had an important role in early missile activities. Later, as a civilian Army employee, he played a key role in the establishment of the logistic support structure in Korea. After the Korean War, he became an expert in the application of computers to logistic support. Toward the end of the Vietnam War I persuaded him to help Maj. Gen. Homer D. Smith with the withdrawal of U.S. support from Vietnam.

When I think of Walt Partin, I realize that it's by putting together the efforts of many different kinds of personalities that you come up with the best results. I have many times said to myself as well as to others, "We need these so-called mavericks. You're saying get rid of them, and I say we can't do without them. You've got to accept the things you don't like in order to take advantage of the things you do like." I can name literally hundreds of people that this applies to, loners who while brave and productive nevertheless seemed to march to a different drummer. I would include John Harbert, another maverick, in this group. He was decorated with the Distinguished Service Cross for courage in World War II, an award seldom made to a logistician. Walt Partin has been nominated for the U.S. Army Ordnance Hall of Fame. He should clearly be honored to inspire those who may feel that there are no opportunities for heroism in logistic support. His heroism was based not only on displaying courage under fire, but also on demonstrating the dynamic leadership necessary to accomplish "impossible tasks."

I would also like to pay tribute to Leo Dillon. The example he set as my superior officer is one that I have always tried to emulate. By ordering me to his staff during the war and continuing his interest in my later assignments, he ranks among the three or four officers who most affected my career. In wartime England Dillon was really a hard worker, spending somewhere between eighteen and twenty hours a day supervising the support required by the combat troops who were going across on D-Day. He hadn't had any time off in months when his boss ordered him to take a day off. He loved golf, so he tried out a local course. Lo and behold, he hit a hole in one, the first in his whole life. I remember that he was so worried that the word would get out and be reported in *Stars and Stripes*: "Colonel Dillon Makes Hole in One!" He realized that most of the readers would not know that this was his first and only day off the job in almost a year, so he squelched any hint of his luck.

By early January 1944 the supplies needed for the D-Day troops had pretty well arrived and were stored. The tempo increased tremendously from that point. We began exercising loading and unloading landing craft and doing the many things necessary to prepare for such a great invasion. In fact, we practiced everything that would be executed on D-Day, except going over the French beaches. We used evacuated areas in southern England instead. The ammunition officer under whom I worked was a major who was definitely not a ball of fire. Soon after I arrived in SBS, Colonel Dillon decided that he should be transferred, and so he called him in and asked him how he liked Ireland. The major said he had never been there but he hoped some day to be able to visit since he was of Irish descent. Dillon told him, "You've got it made, you are now assigned there."

That left me without a boss. Dillon said, "Joe, you need some help, so I think you ought to choose a senior officer to be your boss." I proposed a candidate and Dillon said, "All right, get orders cut. Who is he?" He was Maj. Lebus C. Johnson, who commanded the ammunition depot near Oxford. Johnson was a country boy who took eight years to graduate from the University of Kentucky. He would work a year and take care of his mother, then go to school a year, work a year and take care of his mother, go to school a year. He was going to graduate no matter what. Johnson was one of the wisest men with whom I have served. He supervised the loading out of all the ammunition that went over for the invasion and the European campaign from our sector in southern England. He trained me to look ahead and see the problems that we could expect, what the bottlenecks would be, and what alternatives existed to open up those bottlenecks. We faced some difficult situations, but his foresight saved the day in many crises.

For example, we were ordered to strap onto pallets all the ammunition that was not going to be issued to the troops before they departed for France. This caused a great flap to get the lumber and make the pallets. Of course, once the pallets were made, forklifts were required to pick up, load, and unload them. Most of the pallets would be offloaded onto the beaches of Normandy or placed in the hedgerows just off the beaches. Clippers to cut the steel straps around the pallets were a critical item for troops who needed the ammo. Johnson said to me, "You're going to have to go over with the combat troops and act as liaison in Normandy. I hope we can work it out with the Germans so that they'll leave us the right kind of equipment that you're going to need to unload those ammunition pallets when y'all get there."

Now that comment sounds facetious, but one of the greatest worries that I have concerning our plans for logistic support in any future war is the fact that we plan to use containerized surface ships with ammunition and other supplies inside standard containers on pallets. The plan is to move these loaded containers practically from the point of production in the United States to the point of consumption in the combat area. That's great! But I hope we have material-handling equipment when they get there to unload these throughput containers and to lift out the pallets inside.

After we got the ammunition on pallets in England, we received classified emergency directions to examine the lot numbers of all artillery ammunition in the theater and to reclassify them into categories A, B, or C. Col. Leslie Simon, from Aberdeen Proving Ground, the father of sampling techniques, determined through tests that certain ammunition lots had so many variances in production that you couldn't afford to fire them over the heads of troops in close support, and still others were unsafe to fire over the heads of troops at all. We had to locate all of the lots in the depots and in the hands of troops and stamp the letters A, B, or C on them, so that we would know which ones could be fired under what conditions and which couldn't. As a result, we lost full control of the lot numbers. In addition, we had to cut the steel bands holding the packages of ammunition on the pallets and then repackage and restrap the pallets. In some cases, we had to replace stuff that was in combat loads aboard combat vehicles because the direct support artillery and divisions needed to have the B and C ammunition replaced with A. While this was a worthwhile effort, the fact of the matter is, I think, we were trying to be too exact in a war that wasn't that exact. We had to struggle to try to accomplish this after we were loaded for Normandy, and it created some lack of confidence among combat units as well. I've never really been able to ascertain the results of this classification. I think there were too many variables. It's quite possible that the codes were ignored once combat started. I know of very few instances in which defective ammunition caused a short round. Most of the time it was human failure. This examining of ammunition might have been good in normal times, but it was very poorly timed and was not as effective as it was intended to be.

One of the most serious difficulties in planning for the Normandy invasion was the absence of any solid agreement between combat forces and logistic support forces on what the requirement really was going to be; for example, was ammunition to be measured as a unit of fire or as a day of supply? In fact, in May 1944, only a month before the invasion, those concerned with ammunition planning in England disagreed on the specific ammunition requirement and whether or not the logistic supply would meet their requirement. Because of this uncertainty, restrictions were placed upon the rounds of ammunition that artillery could plan to fire and eventually restrictions on the rounds that could be fired once the fight for the Continent began.

A similar situation occurred in the war in Korea in 1950 and would recur if a war began today. The details of the problem in Europe in 1944 are well covered in *Logistical Support of the Armies.*\* Reading these pages and similar accounts of later wars should be mandatory for all those responsible for determining support requirements and the methods that we must use to meet requirements.

In England before D-Day and throughout the battle on the continent of Europe, our activities were very badly hampered by the lack of telephone and radio communication. In England that meant lack of access to the use of commercial lines, military lines, and the U.S. military radio. When we crossed the Channel, it became worse. We did not have light aircraft available, except for a few spotting planes for artillery support. Messages were usually carried by a person driving a jeep, although radio communication was available among the actual combat forces. Logistic support was almost entirely dependent upon those commercial phone lines still operating in France or other lines laid hurriedly on the ground. Our signal troops were able to lay long lines along the road as we progressed across the Continent, but with the chaos and confusion that exist in combat zones, these lines across roads and in trees were subject to all kinds of interference.

Another persistent problem that occurred while getting ready for the Normandy invasion, as well as later all the way through to the end of combat in Germany, was the lack of transportation. This included not only lack of vehicles, but enough command and control to make best use of the inadequate transportation facilities. Vehicles became lost too, even in England, where the British had removed all the road signs to foil any Nazi invasion.

The following episode highlights the combined transportation-communication problems that existed during preparations for D-Day. (It was only some thirty years later that coincidence revealed my unknown helper in this case.) I spent most of my nights in England trying to arrange transportation to meet the requirement for movement of ammunition from depots to port areas in preparation for the Normandy invasion. One night in particular I was having a very

---

\*Roland G. Ruppenthal, *Logistical Support of the Armies, Volume 1: May 1941–September 1944*, U.S. Army in World War II (Washington, D.C.: Government Printing Office, 1953), pp. 537–39.

difficult time finding transportation for ammunition from the depot down to the port in the Southampton area. Although I was one of the few Americans who knew the codes required to use the British military telephone line, the British operator could tell that I was having an unusually hard time locating the fifty 2½-ton trucks I needed. The operator finally told me she knew where the British got their transport when they were faced with a particularly difficult situation, so under the circumstances she thought it would be all right to plug me into that line. A man answered the phone, and after I explained to him my difficulty and my need for fifty 2½-ton trucks, he surprised me by readily offering to help. He could supply me with their equivalent in 1½-ton British lorries. Needless to say, I grabbed at his offer. After I told him when and where, I called my old acquaintance Colonel Meeks, the depot commander, and reported that while I could not be sure, British lorries might be arriving at 0400. At just about that hour Meeks called me to report that 200 British lorries were coming through the fog. The ammunition arrived in Southampton on schedule.

I never knew who sent them or where the ammunition trucks came from. It was like a miracle, so I never questioned it. And when the war was over I still didn't know. But in 1977 on a return flight to NATO headquarters, I sat next to a Britisher who began reminiscing with me about World War II experiences. He explained that he and his brother had operated a transport organization that supported the British war effort. He began to tell me about a call he received early one morning from someone who needed trucks to haul ammunition from Savernake Forest, near North Tidworth, to Southampton. The more he talked, the greater my amazement. It turned out that he was the very person who had provided the British lorries that made that emergency shipment possible.

I would like to include one more example of problems with transportation. Just before D-Day (actually we were not sure when D-Day was going to be), I was told by my boss to pick up several crates of signals, just arrived in England and needed immediately by combat outfits stationed on the other side of Plymouth. These units would need these colored smoke grenades as soon as they hit the Normandy beaches. I set off in a jeep followed by six 2½-ton trucks carrying the signals. Although I had received my orders in the late afternoon, days are considerably longer in England at that time of year. We were approaching the river on the east side of Plymouth that we had to either cross or go around. British rules required that river ferries stop running at 1800 hours (6:00 P.M.), and we missed the last sailing. No one was willing to arrange an

PREPARATION IN ENGLAND                                               37

extra ferry for our little convoy, no matter how important. Our only alternative was to head inland from the seacoast, go around the river, come down on the opposite side, all in the blackout, and look for the units awaiting the signals. Thus began quite an adventure.

First, we found that we were bucking the traffic tide because all the roads were clogged with units headed toward the seacoast carrying loads of men and supplies for the invasion. Our seven vehicles had to buck that traffic on the narrow British roads or try to use farm roads as detours. We couldn't win. We had innumerable delays waiting in narrow parts of the road for combat units to go by. We also encountered delays on the farm roads, including stopping to chase cows off the right-of-way. It actually took us six hours for a trip that should have taken less than a half hour. We did get the signals to the units late that night, but this episode stands out in my memory because here was a high-priority ordnance task that depended entirely on our ingenuity to accomplish a transport mission.

When those of us in the Southern Base Section had just about completed our task and D-Day was very close, Colonel Dillon gave each of us authority to seek assignments that we would prefer from D-Day forward. I jumped at the opportunity, because several weeks earlier I had been offered the chance to become a part of the division ammunition office of the 1st Infantry Division. So when Dillon gave us the go-ahead, I immediately contacted the division ordnance officer who promised to start the transfer immediately.

The next morning when I reported to Dillon that I had made this informal arrangement, he told me, "Joe, that didn't refer to you. I've got plans for you. You call them and tell them to stop any action under way because it will not be approved." My change in career would have given me the experience in an outstanding division that landed on OMAHA Beach on D-Day. I was very sorry to have missed out. However, one never can foresee the future. Once again, I carried out unwelcome orders! But who knows?

I did not realize that I would be able to do far more good where I was. During the invasion, one of my tasks was rounding up enough artillery and basic loads of ammunition to reequip an entire battalion of the 1st Division. It had lost all of its artillery pieces and its basic ammo load during the initial assault. So, working with Col. Frank Napper, a fine officer from First Army Ordnance, I was able to get the equipment and ammunition assembled in England and over to the beach promptly to reequip the battalion. Later, on many occasions, I was able to provide the critical ammunition support required by the division as well as other units in their movement across France and into Germany. I have always been proud to have been able to support the men of the 1st Division, not only in Europe, but also in Vietnam.*

During this period, I also got to know the ammunition officer of Ninth Army, who was preparing ammunition support for that army. Maj. Charles Ostrom later became commandant of the U.S. Army Ordnance School and is rightly a member of the Ordnance Hall of Fame. He is a highly qualified ordnance officer and has been a great influence on me and many others. He might not win a popularity contest, but when it comes to "putting your chips on a man's capabilities," Charlie Ostrom is such a man.

---

*My son Joel is rightly proud of his voluntary service as a company commander in the 1st Division in Vietnam during 1966–67.

# CHAPTER 3

# War in Europe

Large, knowledgeable staffs spent several years determining the transport, both sea and land, that would be required for the invasion of Europe and for the operations across France and Germany that would win the war. Unfortunately, many unexpected things occurred. If combat were necessary today, the availability of transportation and the capability to move the necessary supplies effectively could become problems just as they were in 1944. The invasion of Europe required improvisation by those in charge using whatever flexibility was available to make up for unplanned occurrences that impeded the operation as it went on. For example, the enemy's proven capability to slow our progress aside, the storm that occurred in the first two weeks after D-Day created havoc with all the plans for the approach, unloading, and movement of men and supplies over the Normandy beaches.

For four days in mid-June the storm disabled a lot of the supply ships as well as equipment for unloading the men and materiel from ships and landing craft. Again, reading *Logistical Support of the Armies* gives a valuable picture of the unexpected problems that can occur when embarking on a combat operation, even one that had been very thoroughly planned. I recommend reading this volume to get a better idea of just what can happen to logistic support, especially transportation, in a short but very critical time period.* In fact, in Table 7 in that volume it can be seen that at D plus 15 we had achieved only 61 percent of the planned buildup of supplies on the beaches in Normandy. Other data show that we had achieved troop buildup of over 80 percent. The storm and other unforeseen problems impaired transportation and supply support all the way across France into the area of the Siegfried Line, at which point Lt. Gen. George S. Patton, Jr.'s Third Army had to stop to wait for fuel and ammunition to be brought forward.

---

*Ruppenthal, *Logistical Support of the Armies, Volume 1: May 1941–September 1944*, see especially, pp. 389–426.

But data on the buildup of supplies on the beaches can be misleading. In the confusion of the landing, all the care put into landing the ammunition by separate types could be undone by nearby combat. In some areas trucks and jeeps sent to pick up ammunition for the fighting units drove up to the ammo areas to find the materiel still sitting in the landing nets. Crane operators had to pick up the nets, drop the contents in a pile, and pull the nets out from under the ammunition. This created a huge mass twenty feet high of a dangerous mixture of small arms ammunition, high explosives, blasting caps, chemical shells, and propellant charges. The ordnance men had to set up a roller conveyor and dig through the pile, sometimes under enemy fire. It was slow, dangerous work.

As a result of the storm during the early phases of Normandy and the disruptions to our support plans at OMAHA Beach, a number of high-priority supply items, especially ammunition, required emergency expediting. We had to improvise an unplanned emergency airlift using aircraft that could carry only about two tons of ammunition at a time. This was the first critical-item supply by air in Europe. This same airlift was also used for air-evac of wounded from the battle area.

There were other equally valuable experiences gained during the invasion. Much of the ammunition we sent into Normandy was 90-mm. antiaircraft ammunition. Fortunately, we did not have to use much of it, and as a result, orders went out not to move the 90-mm. ammunition forward across France. That relieved some of the load that had to be moved. Later, however, when V-rockets started hitting troops and facilities in the Belgian and Dutch ports, there was a great cry for 90-mm. antiaircraft ammunition. Where was it? It was back in Normandy, and in many cases the weight of the ammo, which had been on firm ground in June and July, had caused it to sink in the winter mud behind the hedgerows. We had to act quickly. We moved troops back to Normandy to dig out the ammunition, using roller conveyors hundreds of feet in length to get it out of the middle of the Normandy fields to roads accessible by truck. Because of conditions, we had to use caterpillar tractors. At one point I was about to complain to a commander because I could not see the caterpillar we had taken such great pains to get for him. He said, "Look out in the middle of that field." There in the field, about 200 yards away, I could see what appeared to be the head of a man. It turned out that it was the tractor driver. His tractor was completely immersed in the mud. He was working at getting 90-mm. ammunition out of the mudhole onto a roller conveyor and then out to the road where we were standing.

Although I would continue to be assigned to the United Kingdom Base Section well into 1945, I was on continuous TDY on the Continent, serving as a traveling expediter in the effort to unsnarl some of the logistics problems at the Normandy ports and railheads throughout France and to institute a flexible system of ammunition supply. Often my firsthand knowledge of field problems helped my superiors make appropriate decisions.

After the first few days of Normandy our troops were subjected to little air attack, so we could allow ammunition supplies to accumulate, sometimes at truck pools and on railcars at railheads. That gave us the flexibility to move supplies quickly without unloading them, keeping track of them, picking them back up, reloading them onto railcars or trucks, and moving them forward to the combat unit requiring them. Ammunition was also stacked along roads for maybe 200 miles. Generally, the local people didn't bother it. They knew it was put there to defeat the Nazis, and to tamper with it would be considered treasonous. We have been spoiled in past wars by the luxury of allowing such accumulations with few problems. However, it is well to be reminded of one incident.

We tried to use the French railroads as soon as possible, and as soon as we had freed French territory from German occupation, we turned their operation over to the French civilians. At this point transportation–movement control problems erupted. I remember that during the Battle of the Bulge we had moved 1,500 carloads of ammunition into the large railhead at Soissons, close to our major depot. We planned to retain the ammunition in the cars so that we could dispatch these cars as a rolling inventory to wherever they were needed to eliminate local transportation and double handling of the ammunition loads. This was fine until a German aviator, who had been circling the railhead for three nights running, came back to drop incendiary bombs in the middle of these cars. In the ensuing havoc we not only had to salvage the ammunition, we also had to evacuate a base hospital that had been established right next to the railhead. We could not get the French railroad engineers to keep their boilers hot to move the trains out. So until we got some tanks at the railhead, we had to use our soldiers to push a carload at a time away from the burning trains to prevent the loss of the entire railhead. We strung hose lines from the nearest river—2 miles away—in an effort to get water to fight the fires. We spent two whole days trying to get water to that railhead because the water in the hoses froze before it reached the fire. We spent a lot of time replacing hose that split because of the ice. Ammunition troops unloading chemical shells by hand from immobile railcars were repeatedly interrupted by exploding shells but doggedly returned to the cars and finished the job. We finally got most of it under control within seventy-two hours. Through brave action by many troops we were able to save about two-thirds of the 1,500 cars of loaded ammunition.

This ammunition was badly needed in the fight to stop the Germans from reaching Liege and Antwerp. The fire left us with only one single-track line to transport the ammo. But even that didn't last long. While firing at the German planes on the night after the fire, British antiaircraft gunners accidentally knocked down one of their own loaded bombers which landed right in the middle of the single-line track. This caused us to have to improvise our ammunition shipments.

During peacetime we generally do not expect to fight ammunition fires. Instead, we try to move people and property away from them. In combat there are times when it is essential that we know how to fight ammunition fires. When ammunition is in short supply and there is no way to replace it, it can't be left to burn. In my own personal experience on eleven specific occasions it was essential to attempt to move critically needed ammunition out of a fire. No one wants to enter an area where ammunition is on fire, exploding, and blowing around, but when necessary, we must know the best way to do it and how to save the most ammunition we can. "Quantity-distance tables" specify ammunition placement in combat zones, but the safe areas these create are usually limited and greater risks must be accepted. In late 1944, at the time of the Battle of the Bulge, I was dispatched from Headquarters, COMZ (Communications Zone), in Paris, to the port of Le Havre where ships were standing both in the harbor and at sea waiting to be unloaded. Among the problems were inadequate docking space and no receiving area at the port. I was sent to Le Havre because an ammunition company aboard one of the ships was desperately needed to replace the companies that had been disabled by the German attack during the Battle of the Bulge. I took off in my jeep for Le Havre.

In the meantime, the bad weather had spread to the west of France where ice and snow had disabled the communications net very badly. It became almost impossible for normal traffic to be transmitted by voice, wire, or radio to headquarters in Paris, so when I arrived at Le Havre I was "on my own." I immediately told the port commander that I needed to get an ammunition company off a ship in the harbor. He said that he couldn't do it. Knowing full well that the downed lines would prevent his ever checking, I used my boss's rank to get action. I told him that I represented General

Eisenhower and that getting the ammunition company off that ship as a replacement for one that had been overrun in the Battle of the Bulge was a high priority. While the port commander was certainly not very happy to do it, he finally agreed to bring in the troopship, which also was carrying the large part of an infantry division, to disembark the ammunition company.

While I was on the dock waiting to receive the ammunition company and help them get started toward Belgium, down the gangplank first came the major general who commanded the infantry division. He saw me and said, "Lieutenant, you seem to know what's going on around here. How can I get in touch with Eisenhower's headquarters?" I said, "Sir, communication nets are practically all down. My only mission is to get an ammunition company off this ship." He then proceeded to the port commander's office where he got the same unhappy news.

In the meantime, the ammunition troops I needed had disembarked and boarded freight cars, the only transport I could get. I arranged for them to be shuttled out to what was the beginning of Camp Lucky Strike. (This camp would function well in later months as a reception area for incoming troops and supplies and after V–E Day for troops passing through on their way home.) I arranged with the Class I officer there to provide rations. I found out when I arrived that the rations consisted of large containers of corn flakes and one-gallon cans of stewed tomatoes. I managed to get together some combat rations and spread them around, but there weren't enough for everyone. I arranged for the delivery of more combat rations farther up the line, but I'm sure that to this day members of that company will remember that lieutenant who shipped them off with corn flakes and stewed tomatoes in freezing boxcars.

The company was in freight cars in the middle of winter, a very difficult winter, with no heat except for the heat of their bodies. I did trace the train so that I knew that at one point it had to be switched off the main line to another stop because its original destination had been lost to the Germans. If care had not been taken on the movement of this train, to add to its problems the company might have ended up in enemy territory. It turned out all right, and the men became a very valuable asset in ammunition supply.

This is an example of what is actually considered normal for rear-area support in combat. The commander of the COMZ and his subordinate echelons have very little control over what may happen and thus must be prepared, by knowing the capabilities available, to improvise to meet the objectives as effectively as possible. In the COMZ transportation is especially important because it must provide the flexibility needed in a crisis. Equally important were regulating stations that controlled specific choke points on railways and highways. These control points were essential in fluid situations. They do not exist in today's force structure.

We need to recall that many of the logistic difficulties of November–December 1944 were created by the fast forward advances that had been made during the previous summer. The delay in opening ports and the limited capacity of available ports in handling cargoes had a severe effect. As we have learned many times, the United States can ship supplies and materiel to an objective area much more effectively and efficiently than the objective area can unload and distribute these supplies. This was certainly true in the fall of 1944 on the continent of Europe, as well as later in Korea and Vietnam. The port situation was so bad that many ships were actually returned from the ETO only partially unloaded. In fact, in mid-November some 36,000 tons of supplies were scheduled for return to the United States, yet we had shortages of numerous types of supplies and materiel.

During the European campaign U.S. field armies, especially the First and Third, were continuously competing with one another to get more logistic support. There are instances of one army's stealing the supplies of another, or those intended for another, if it felt it should be getting the supplies. Thus there had to be close coordination, command, and control between what went to Third Army versus First Army versus Ninth Army (and later Seventh Army as well). General Omar N. Bradley called a meeting at his army group headquarters with representatives of First, Third, and Ninth Armies to find a way out of the shortage-induced crisis. And, to quote from the history, Bradley later remembered with some amusement that when Patton, accompanied by his chief of staff and G-4, arrived and saw Colonel Medaris, the First Army ordnance officer, he immediately sent for his own ordnance officer, Colonel Nixon. He warned Nixon to be on his guard against Medaris and Wilson, the First Army G-4. "I know them both; they once worked for me," he said, remembering his days in II Corps. He wanted Nixon there to make sure that Medaris wasn't able to run away with things just because Patton didn't have competent experts at the meeting to tell him what to insist on.

While I must say that the Third Army under General Patton was as aggressive as any outfit, I should also indicate that discipline was tight within Patton's army, especially during the time when he waited for supplies and services to catch up with him after his dash across France. While impatiently waiting to attack the Germans at the Siegfried Line, his army established a reputation for soldier discipline, which is the reason, in the last analysis, why General Patton is buried in Luxembourg today rather than in the United States. He was beloved and is beloved in Luxembourg largely because of the way in which his Third Army troops controlled themselves during that very difficult time awaiting support to advance into Germany.

This might be the place to repeat an anecdote that demonstrates this point. The city of Metz, in the area just west of the Siegfried Line, was under German artillery fire for some part of the time that Patton was waiting. One morning he observed a crossroads that Third Army vehicles were using despite the high probability that the German 88s would knock them out at the intersection. Patton angrily ordered that there be no further use of that crossroad. When he returned to the area a month later, the Germans had been routed out of their positions, and the road crossing was no longer under German fire. As he approached the crossroad, a guard stopped the jeep and said, "You can't go across this intersection, sir." Patton replied, "You see the stars on this vehicle. You see my stars. We're going across." The soldier said, "Sir, my orders are that no one goes across." Patton said, "I gave that order a month ago; the situation has changed, and this is stupid. I'm going across." The soldier on guard answered, "Sir, I have my orders. No one goes across. If you're going across, would you please tell me who do I shoot first, you or the driver?" Patton promptly turned around and went another way. In the meantime word quickly got around that that crossroad was to be opened. The next day that MP was promoted to corporal on orders of General Patton. I believe this is a story that could well have been used in the picture *Patton* because it showed a side of the general that most people might not expect.

All types of men made up the command of the U.S. forces in Europe. Almost everyone has heard of Patton, but Bradley contributed just as much, although you had to seek him out. My wife and I were at a White House reception shortly after the film *Patton* had been released and noticed Bradley seated alone at a small table in a hallway. We went over to talk with him and brought up the movie. I said that, in spite of the antiwar feeling generated by Vietnam, everyone that I had heard, young or old, who had seen *Patton* thought it was great. But I told him, "General Bradley, the one adverse comment I have heard was that the part of Bradley was underplayed." Bradley, who was technical adviser for the film, quickly remarked, "But Joe, you've got to recognize that the name of the picture is *Patton*." I remember that because it was so characteristic of him. I'm sure, although I have no way of knowing, that many times during the war in Europe, Bradley must have said somewhat the same thing to himself during Patton's breakout across France: that the name of the game is Patton, not Bradley. He had the wisdom to remain relatively invisible and yet recognize that he had to pick up the pieces as the war went across France and into Germany.

The "Red Ball" operation that supported Patton's advance across the continent of Europe in World War II is described, as it should be, in glowing terms in most histories of the war. It is considered a great logistic effort to support the requirements of combat troops. Ammunition and fuel were particularly essential in the Third and other U.S. armies. The rapid movement of supplies across France had exhausted supplies forward of the ports. Many provisional truck battalions and truck companies were formed, even from infantry regiments. All were essential for the rapid forward transport of supplies. Command, control, and communications became critical. In truth the operation of the Red Ball Express was a success because of the actual volume of movement, and while not entirely documented, it is important to recognize that several factors reduced its potential effectiveness.

First, command and control was not as effective as it should have been. Regional control, as initially attempted, was discovered to be unmanageable. The control of roads, partially because of a lack of discipline and partially because of a shortage of MPs, was also very poor. In fact, the discipline of some drivers of the Red Ball trucks was nothing we could be especially proud of. Because we did not have adequate control of the trucks, we did not have adequate control of the stocks. This lack of control quickly led to wide-scale black market activity. One of the most notorious of these black markets operated at the base of the Eiffel Tower. Word quickly got around that civilians were ready to buy anything the GIs could deliver. The Eiffel Tower, which could be seen from miles away, was a logical site for a black market. It required no knowledge of Paris and its suburbs for an American to point his truck at the tower in the far distance. Unfortunately, this robbery continued for a long time. Paris was really an open city, and in such a fast-moving war enough MPs and civilian authorities were not yet available to control black markets.

In some cases drivers who had the nerve actually became hijackers, taking by force trucks and supplies that were not intended for their units. This may sound melodramatic to the uninformed, but I can assure you that in combat if one's outfit needs something and the lives of those men are at stake, unless there is adequate control and discipline, those who can will appropriate whatever they think necessary for their men. They usually do not recognize a priority higher than their own unit. It is most probable that, in the future, circumstances like those that occurred on the Continent in World War II will recur, at least to some degree. This is very important for us to understand; it is why command and control and discipline in logistic operations are essential. That is one of the reasons why hoarding of inoperable equipment and critical items in the combat zone is a very difficult command management problem.

Likewise, I know of many instances during World War II, and later in Korea and Vietnam, when a senior officer insisted that he be issued more of a critical item than we were capable of issuing in accordance with the priorities laid down. At such a time one has to use good judgment and seek the guidance of higher echelons to determine if the officer's demands reflect the appropriate priorities. Of course, officers who insist on supplies are doing their jobs as they see them; they have a responsibility to support their men. But the logistics commander, likewise, has the responsibility to be sure that, especially on critical items in short supply, proper allocation is carried out.

At one point in Brittany before the mission of his Third Army was widely known, Patton stormed into an ordnance depot and told the commander that he wanted two-thirds of all of the stock in the depot. It was in the early days of the depot organization, and there wasn't a great deal of stock. Patton did not have authority to do this, but because he had a combat mission to perform and he needed supplies during the early days of his drive across France, he used his rank to demand supplies through improper channels. The depot commander used good judgment. After Patton left, he called for instructions. When Patton's trucks came into the depot area, he was prepared to give them what he had been told he could give them. Whether this was close to two-thirds of depot's stock was another matter.

There were instances, especially during the crisis of the Battle of the Bulge, when entire ammunition trains headed for one army found themselves in another army area, having been commandeered by officers from that other army. This is not so surprising when one realizes that we are dealing with officers and men who are dedicated to supporting their own units and who take advantage of any situation they can. Thus, command and control becomes very essential, but command and control depends upon the discipline that exists within the units. We must maintain command discipline.

Perhaps the problem that concerns me most—it certainly caused me more trouble than ammunition fires or transportation or communications problems in all my combat experiences throughout my career—is the ability to embark troops and supplies in CONUS and disembark them at port areas or on beaches in the objective area. First of all, in the continental United States we have proved again and again that we can outload troops and material faster than they can be handled at the landing zone, whether in a developed country or an undeveloped area. We devised the best scheduling possible in England while preparing for the invasion in Normandy, but inevitably because of circumstances beyond human control, the schedules seldom worked as planned. This is not criticism, it is simply recitation of fact. Because there are so many things that can go wrong, the probability that many of them will occur is very high. As a result, we run into the same problems again and again.

D-Day logistics is a case in point. When the bad weather forced General Eisenhower to make a last-minute postponement of D-Day from the fifth to the sixth of June, some of the ship convoys were practically within sight of the beaches. They were ordered back to the English ports they had left just hours before only to find them crowded with ships loading for the second wave. Despite all the excellent planning, the fact is that we overcrowded the port areas and marshaling areas in England because embarkation did not flow as planned. The follow-on troops and supplies continued to arrive. In the resulting confusion the wrong units boarded the wrong ships, and some units were actually lost track of by the command-and-control system. One corps commander personally returned to England during the landings to track down one of his regiments. The confusion was so great that he had actually lost a whole regiment.

The same problems continued on the beaches and beyond. It could be expected at OMAHA Beach, where the enemy was stronger and where the Channel currents were more difficult for smaller craft operation. But confusion occurred not only under the pressures of establishing beachheads at Normandy; it also occurred in the ports of Cherbourg, Le Havre, Antwerp, and Rotterdam. It happened again under similar conditions in Korea and in Vietnam.

I quickly concluded from these experiences that flexibility is the single most important element in wartime command and control. It is absolutely mandatory that those in command have the flexibility to improvise in order to cope with confusion. Flexibility must be built into the troop support structure so that at least some American-trained troops are available to the logistics and combat commanders to get the job done in spite of the problems that they know will occur and recur in combat. I believe it is especially important that choke points, bottlenecks, and other predictable problems be examined closely and simulated in exercises to provide the necessary experience in determining possible alternatives.

WAR IN EUROPE 49

Further, U.S. troops must know how to deal with and direct support that comes from other sources.

During World War II we used what was actually a forerunner of today's concept of host nation support. Once in late 1944 I was ordered to Belgium with a Polish-speaking sergeant to pick up a trainload of Poles displaced from German prison camps. We scrounged food, tents, and mess gear for hundreds of these men—a tough job in wartime Belgium—and formed them into one of the first labor service companies organized during the war. These troops served in the COMZ until the end of the war, and their fine work was one of our greatest success stories. We kept them in France because of the generally sympathetic attitude of the French toward the Poles. In fact, the soldiers never returned to Poland after the war. Many eventually earned French citizenship, but they and their sons continued to serve in their own national units with U.S. forces in NATO. In 1967 some of these units moved to West Germany with the COMZ.

In Italy we took into the U.S. Army Italian ammunition companies which had surrendered to our forces. They did a great job for the rest of the war. We also used German and Italian prisoners to service ammunition supplies. Once I came upon small stacks of ammunition piled along a road in southern Alsace. When I asked why it had not been loaded as ordered on trucks for transport to the front, I was told that our very conscientious German laborers had weeded out these rusted shells because they probably would not fire properly. Our base section in Normandy, established later in the war to support port activities, was manned to a significant degree by German prisoners under their German officers.

Such support was valuable as a supplement to U.S. troops, and what we now call host nation support continues to be valuable. But it won't work well unless it is built around a cadre of U.S. logistics general support units to provide command and control and flexibility to host nation support. Yet today the critical need for such troops is not being given the proper emphasis.

Another problem that needs to be stressed is the return and recovery of men and equipment from forward areas. In every war in which I have served, we paid considerably more attention to forward movement of men and supplies than we did to the retrograde of men and supplies. In some cases it seemed that no thought at all was given to the need for retrograde. Yet it is an absolutely essential part of any operation. This retrograde movement of men, including dead and wounded, is normally regarded as outside the sphere of logistics. This is wrong; it is an essential part of logistics.

It requires movement to the rear using the same logistics movement facilities necessary for forward movement. It requires troop replacement. In addition, in World War II, as in Korea and in Vietnam, the refugees and noncombatants posed very difficult problems that interfered with the best planning and execution. If there is no appropriate planning for return from the front and for a refugee civilian population, then, needless to say, they become even worse problems.

From the time we hit the beach in Normandy, we were firing artillery ammunition that had been packed in brass and steel shell cases. As we moved from Normandy across France, we left artillery shell cases all over the place. This was a serious problem because the metal had to be recycled. We had captured a German ammunition depot at Chartres that we used as a depot for the shell cases and other reusable residue. Later we scheduled the return of brass from this depot to the United States for reuse in artillery ammunition production. No plans had been made for such a function or for such a depot. Nor were there troops trained to operate it. A solution had to be improvised on the spot. We organized recovery companies that were equipped and trained to do nothing but recover equipment. We also had ammunition renovation companies whose only job was to inspect, repair, and repackage returned ammunition for reuse in the forward areas. Both of these types of specialist units have disappeared from our troop lists, and almost all the necessary skills have disappeared too. Yet it has been my experience that such skills are still very important for support of intense combat.

Ammunition renovation is an important matter in the combat zone. Unpackaged ammunition may be defective, and as we quickly learned in World War II no combat soldier wants to trust it if he can avoid it. This wastes a great deal of ammunition in forward areas because when missions are curtailed or changed, the ammunition that had been planned for use has already been unpackaged. Later such ammunition either gets dumped, buried, or returned as retrograde. Ammunition shortages are usually critical in forward areas, even though there might be a good supply of ammunition in the rear, because in combat not all ammunition gets moved all the way to the forward areas. Local distribution problems usually occur. We never have enough to allow us to waste ammunition and say we won't worry about it. It has to be returned, inspected, renovated, repackaged, and put back into the support pipeline. The more combat becomes based upon mobility and maneuverability, the more this type of support for ammunition and equipment will be needed.

The increased reliance on reusable containers that is being planned for the modern Army makes the problem of supply returns even more essential for command and control. In every combat situation we have had containers—ammunition brass and so forth—that needed to be returned, yet we have had difficulty in enforcing the discipline required to return the material. Furthermore, when the material was returned, we had difficulty in properly handling the retrograde. Communications capabilities are always limited.

I would like to underscore another major logistics problem—inventory accuracy—that persisted from World War II to Korea and into Vietnam. In reality it's an extension of a peacetime problem into the combat zone. However, it is far more important to solve this problem in combat because inventory accuracy can exact a high price during wartime when it affects success in battle and lives of men. As we in logistics, whether commercial, industrial, or military, know, inventory accuracy is very difficult to achieve. In fact, recent reviews of inventory accuracy by the General Accounting Office indicate that the government's knowledge of what it has, where it is, and its condition is subject to considerable question. First, a determination needs to be made of the degree of accuracy that is required and how many resources should be devoted to accuracy in order to meet the requirement. A happy medium must be reached.

In the combat zone, however, the status of such supplies as ammunition and petroleum products is more important than in peacetime. And yet because of the pressures encountered in battle, it is extremely difficult to maintain an accurate account of what you ship, have in transit, receive, and consume, and what you still have in stock, including its condition and location. In the case of ammunition, and to some degree fuel, you have to maintain the identity of the particular item that you have in inventory. In the case of ammunition, for example, inventory must be maintained by type and lot number so that you can determine what ammunition is where.

The difficulty begins with shipment. Procedures call for advance detailed notice of what is being shipped, where it is being placed in any shipment, what is in transit, and when it should arrive. In many cases this advance information does not arrive in time. In some cases the advance information itself is inaccurate. Add to this the fact that in a combat zone, the weather, the enemy, and human error can upset schedules at the receiving end. If accurate and timely advance information is not available to plan for the receipt of shipments, then it can be expected that combat support groups will have a hard time determining inventory with accuracy.

In the case of the invasion of Europe in 1944, inventory accuracy became an extremely complex and difficult problem. From the time boatloads of Class V supplies (ammunition) began arriving on the beaches of Normandy, it was almost impossible to keep track of them. Some had been destroyed, some consumed in fire, some lost in the hedgerows just off the beaches, some carried forward by attacking units to make sure that they had enough ammunition with them, and some left behind by moving units that couldn't carry it all. These things occur and recur during combat. Logistics has to be prepared to cope with these combat facts. There is little excuse to allow logistics procedures in rear areas to become as chaotic as those in forward areas where the situation is truly much more difficult to control. The necessary ingredient is command and control discipline.

In the relatively calm environment of planning for combat, the logistics records certainly should be as close to perfect as practicable, especially for combat-essential items. Combat decisions often rest on logistics facts, that is to say, upon the accuracy of the ammunition and fuel inventories. As the combat operation begins, this accuracy will surely decline. The discipline of following procedures as carefully as possible will ensure as effective a supply count as can be made. The probability is great that some critical items will be in short supply, which means combat commanders will have to curtail consumption.

I have seen regimental and battalion commanders pleading with tears in their eyes for an increased allocation of certain types of critical ammunition. For example, in the early days in Normandy there was a great need for more 81-mm. mortar ammunition to get at the Germans who were firing at our advancing troops from behind the hedgerows. Despite a shortage of this ammunition, it was essential to protect the combat troops. Inventory accuracy was extremely important. We certainly did not want to issue ammunition based upon a falsely high inventory and later leave troops unprotected. On the other hand, we did not want to refuse to provide the required ammunition to the combat troops based on an inaccurately low inventory. The problem occurred in battle both because the enemy interfered with our logistic operations and because we failed to maintain the discipline we needed to record the ammunition under its proper name and location and in the correct amounts. Many times we had records that indicated that certain quantities of ammunition types were available in a storage area. However, when we could not find those amounts, then we had to be sure of what we knew we could actually lay our hands on and, as soon as we could, bring our records up to date.

It is essential to provide for inventory teams that maintain constant surveillance over the location and count of supplies in the field under combat conditions, in depots in the continental United States, and in the communications zone. It is especially important that accurate inventory counts be maintained in the combat zone so that lives are not lost because of inaccurate inventories. Commanders need to keep in mind that if the local supply of ammunition is inadequate, strong defensive positions can easily be overrun. Weak commanders will never in their judgment have enough logistical support, but strong commanders still need to keep the levels of ammunition in mind at all times.

My primary emphasis has been on location and count. I did not mention another essential element—condition. But in fact, to report as serviceable ammunition that needs renovation before it can be issued is just as bad as to issue an inaccurate count. Equipment condition is such a serious factor in combat that logistics commanders have been relieved of command because of failure to report accurately the condition of the material on hand.

My final point to make about logistics in the European theater is the need for movement control. A review of the problems with the resupply of troops during the first 90 to 120 days, starting at the Normandy beachhead to the Siegfried Line in Germany, underscores the importance of control in depth. SHAEF plans called for Brest and smaller Brittany ports as well as Cherbourg to be available to support our troops, relieving the burden of unloading supplies across beaches. This was expected to occur sometime in August 1944 with some shipping being received and unloaded in the larger ports beginning as early as July. As it was, Cherbourg did not really begin unloading cargo to relieve the beaches until September 1944. Nor were Brest and the Brittany peninsula captured until September. The beaches and the very small ports in the Normandy area had to make up the difference. Fortunately, these facilities did very well in spite of considerable bad weather.

When the flow of supplies through the ports became reasonably proficient, it was limited by the lack of rail and trucks, and so port discharge could not reach expected targets. Once this problem was at least temporarily solved, the choke point shifted to the limitations of the line of communications. We did not have enough transport and storage space available to empty out the ports. When we finally got this functioning fairly well, we discovered that we needed far more material-handling equipment and dock transport at the ports. The choke point later shifted to line haul from the ports. We had to turn combat units into Red Ball truck companies to move the supplies once the limitation on discharge and storage space had been solved at the major port areas.

When we began using rail lines in late summer, we created another problem by using too many railcars for supply storage. We tied up the rails so badly that in December we actually had to stop using rail in Belgium because the tracks were clogged with loaded railcars and there were no storage depots available to put the supplies into. At this point storage in forward depots was stuck. We had a traffic jam all over the area north and east of Paris. The inland waterways provided very limited relief. With winter setting in, the barge canals were damaged, flooded, and frozen.

Much of this deterioration of logistic support was the result of a lack of command and control to integrate capability and potential to provide the greatest effectiveness under the circumstances. By October 1944 SHAEF had come to realize that central control of transportation was essential. A Motor Transport Service was organized to provide command and control over all throughput motor transport. Gradually, facilities, marshaling yards, communications, and maintenance were established with effective control so that the entire operation of logistic support from ports to forward areas was greatly improved. But it took over six months to do it. Before then, the lack of command and control of maintenance of transport equipment caused the original 2 percent replacement factor for vehicles to be raised to 8 for 2½-ton trucks and to 6 percent for the 10-ton semitrailer combinations.

Transport operations, both by highway and rail, showed it was essential to control the movement of supplies to support combat. But combat requirements proved to be subject to volatile changes. Movements needed to be rescheduled quickly to meet these changes. All of these unforeseen problems created a very serious reduction in the logistic support rendered to the armies by COMZ. The combat forces claimed never to have had enough supplies where they were needed. This led to considerable animosity at all levels directed toward those responsible for support that lasted right up to the end of the war in mid-1945.

Back at Fort Myer shortly after the war, I found that by chance I had seated myself next to Chief of Staff and Mrs. George C. Marshall at the base movie house. Since I was "batching it" at the time and had no pressing projects, I continued to attend the movies night after night. In fact, we all three did, and we generally sat in the same reserved seats. Eventually we struck up informal conversations, with the result that I was invited to their home for dinner. By now I considered logistics central to our victory and assumed that everyone else was as anxious to discuss it as I was. As I recall, however, General Marshall and I never got around to discussing logistics problems.

CHAPTER 4

# War in Korea

Sug and I had no intention of making a career of the Army. In fact, while stationed at the Pentagon after the war I arranged on three occasions to take my final physical the next morning so that I could accept three different jobs. Once I was going to become the park and recreation director of Lynchburg, Virginia; another time I was going to become athletic director of the Washington Boys' Club; a third offer was regional manager of the Cape Cod, Massachusetts, artificial gas region, owned by a sergeant who had worked with me during the war. I was within twenty-four hours of returning to civilian life three times, and each time either Colonel Dillon or some other superior said, "Look, we'll guarantee you a job after the Army making that much money somewhere if you'll stay on." So we stayed on. Finally, on 31 December 1946, the deadline for applying for integration into the Regular Army, my wife and I drove down to Washington's main post office and handed my application in to the clerk at the window to be sure it was postmarked before midnight. That's just how close we came to passing up a career in the Regular Army.

While serving in the Pentagon during this period as an executive officer in a division within the Office of the Chief of Ordnance, I was promoted to the rank of major. It was the kind of staff job that required my almost continuous presence in the Pentagon to provide the stability and continuity needed in the front office of that type organization. But I wasn't always chained to a desk. On one occasion I was sent with Maj. James P. Hammell to the small town of Huntsville, Alabama, to decide if the site of two surplus Army plants would serve as a missile training and research and production center. We agreed that the plants should be reclaimed for this purpose, thus starting what would become one of the largest permanent boomtowns in America.

Another executive officer duty in those days was that of the War Department's Disaster Officer. This responsibility kept me close to the department's Staff Duty Officer, who had to be alert to my whereabouts at all times. It was a job that increased my knowledge of explosions. This was particularly true during the destruction brought about in Texas City, Texas, in 1947 when a French ship loading ammonium nitrate—for fertilizer—produced by an Army ammunition plant caught fire and blew up in the harbor. This led to fear around the country wherever ammonium nitrate and similar chemicals were being loaded and transported. I found myself putting rumors to rest in many places, including Baltimore harbor which was closed one night because of fears that a ship loading ammonium nitrate was heating up and about to blow.

This sometimes exciting and always time-consuming assignment was complicated by the fact that, at the request of the commanding general of the Military District of Washington, the Chief of Ordnance had also assigned me the special duty of playing on MDW's baseball team in all its scheduled games against other military teams. While I loved to play ball, it did make it difficult to meet the requirements of my Pentagon job and play errorless baseball at the same time. It worked out okay, thanks to the patience of all with whom I had to deal.

Except for OCS in 1943, I did not attend an Army school until my assignment to the Command and General Staff College at Fort Leavenworth, Kansas, in 1949. At that time I was advised that attendance at an industrial course would be much better for an ordnance officer. Even the Chief of Ordnance told me he was not sure he was glad I was going to Fort Leavenworth.

I feel strongly that the idea that a logistician should not attend the Command and General Staff College is absolutely wrong. In my own case I learned many new things even though I had served through World War II in a combat zone. I learned things that I would never have otherwise known about how the Army is supposed to operate. In addition, I made friends with officers from the combat branches whom I never would have met in such a casual way. By exchanging experiences we learned from each other.

On my last weekend at Fort Leavenworth, in June 1950, the post baseball team was scheduled to play against the naval air station team at Olathe, Kansas. Because the regular first baseman could not make the trip, I was asked to fill in. The team had allowed me to get some exercise practicing with them from time to time, so they knew I could play the game. I was lucky. I got five doubles, helping to beat the Navy. That game in Kansas was the last game of hardball I ever played. While we were returning to the fort, the radio program was interrupted by a special report announcing that the North Koreans had invaded South Korea. All of us in the car were interested in this news flash, but we certainly did not realize what effect the news would soon have on us.

At the Command and General Staff College graduation ceremony we were told that some students would not get a signed diploma because they had not completed the course satisfactorily. I received mine, tied appropriately with a blue ribbon, but it still sits in the "secret" drawer of my wife's cedar chest. I have never untied the ribbon because I couldn't be sure the diploma was signed. I believe in leaving well enough alone.

After graduation my family and I left Fort Leavenworth on my first leave since the end of World War II. The family now included a third child, our second daughter, Joan, who was born at Walter Reed Hospital on Christmas Day, 1946. We drove to San Francisco to visit Leo Dillon, then stationed at Sixth Army headquarters, before setting out for Mexico to see what that country was like. Before leaving I gave Dillon our scheduled itinerary.

As we passed the Marine base at Camp Pendleton, California, a convoy of trucks loaded with marines pulled out of the main entrance. Farther down the road, our kids saw some of the trucks at a hamburger stand, so we stopped so the family could talk to the marines. They were headed for San Diego to board ships for South Korea where they were to take part in the "police action" there. Realizing that they were headed for combat in a far-distant country, we began to feel a real concern for them.

In San Diego that evening we went on down to the waterfront to watch those same marines load onto troopships to the sound of band music. The bands played melodies like "Auld Lang Syne" and "God Bless America" that really stirred us. We caught the ferry to Coronado Island and went out to the beach to watch the troopships sail toward the Far East. We watched until the last lights on the ships disappeared, feeling sorry that those marines were leaving for a strange place called Korea.

## Logistics in the Pusan Perimeter

At 0500 the next morning I received a phone call from Military Personnel telling me to report to San Francisco by midnight for duty in the Pacific. Again an important chapter in my career began by chance, this time because Colonel Dillon knew where to find me. The order left me in need of many things, including a place for my family to stay. The Navy gave us splendid support, finding a home for Sug and the children at the Coronado Naval Station for the duration of my assignment to Korea.

That night I boarded a plane loaded with senior Army officers—I was the only one below the rank of full colonel—apparently considered essential for immediate duty in response to the North Korean invasion. We flew to Japan by way of the Aleutians where we crash-landed at fog-shrouded Adak thanks to an inexperienced control tower crew. (Adak was in the process of closing because of the need to reduce military spending.) We were almost over a cliff when the plane came to a halt.

On our way into Camp Drake in Japan, we were treated to coffee and doughnuts by a group of American wives, including the wife of Maj. Gen. Hobart R. Gay, who commanded the 1st Cavalry Division. The 1st Cav had been suddenly ordered to Korea, and the wives, with no word from their husbands, feared the worst because of the radio and newspaper reports on the difficult situation being faced by the division.

While I was in the process of finding a bunk for the night, the loudspeaker called for Major Heiser. When I reported, I was told, "Don't worry about a bunk, draw your field gear, because you're going right out to Korea." I was issued a .45-caliber pistol, but I asked them instead to find me a Thompson submachine gun somewhere because I knew what a Tommy gun could do and I had very little confidence in my ability to use a .45. With my Tommy gun slung across my shoulder, I went back through the line of 1st Cav ladies again. They recognized me from my earlier trip, and when I told them that I was going to Korea, they all dug out letters and asked me to deliver them to their husbands. That was my first logistics job in support of combat troops in Korea—a much-needed mailman.

I boarded the Maru Line ship that left Japan each night from Sasebo and arrived in Pusan early the next morning. One of my assignments would be to make sure that the Marine brigade which was about to land in Pusan had its basic load of ammunition. When those marines that my family and I had been feeling so sorry for in San Diego arrived at Pier 1 in Pusan, I was waiting to work out their ammunition requirements. I have told many marines since then that I will never again feel sorry for them before I know whether I should feel sorrier for myself.

We were confident that they would fight well, and they did. Lt. Gen. Walton H. Walker, the U.S. commander in Korea, used them for all they were worth. Every time the enemy seemed about to break through a weak spot in the perimeter, he would use the marines to push the enemy back. As soon as they succeeded, he withdrew them into a central reserve position. This was repeated many times in the first few weeks of the war. I am sure the North Koreans must have thought that we had ten times the actual number of marines. Of course, it was only a brigade. They were used repeatedly and eventually wore out.

We tried to supply the marines with adequate ammunition when they left Pusan to join the 1st Marine Division in September for the Inch'on invasion. Unfortunately, we lacked enough 60-mm. mortar ammunition to give them more than six rounds per tube, which was certainly not enough. I promised their commander that if he would delay a ship, I would try to find some shells that we thought were in the mass of cars at the railhead at Pusangin in the center of Pusan. The commander agreed to leave one ship behind for a few hours. After looking most of the night, we did discover two cars of 60-mm. ammo in the middle of Pusangin. We then had to find a way to move the cars to a siding where we could unload the ammunition and haul it to the ship. Through the cooperation of the marines and Army ordnance and transportation units, we got the ammunition to the ship on time.

In the three wars I've been in, we have had to adapt to be able to provide ammunition support. For example, in the early days of Korea there were three divisions in combat with no ammunition companies to support them and no ammunition supervision except one major, me. At one point a tall, pale officer walked into the building where we had our ordnance office. He looked like he was lost, so I asked him where he was trying to go. He said, "I'm looking for the ordnance personnel officer." I asked, "Are you assigned here?" He said, "No, I was in a hospital in Japan. I had ulcers, and I was just wasting time in the hospital, not doing any good for myself or anybody else, so I decided to come to Korea to see if somebody could use me." I said, "You mean you don't have an assignment?" He told me, "No, I'm AWOL from the hospital." When I asked his specialty, he told me that he was a maintenance officer. I got him our only copy of FM 9–6, the ammunition supply manual, and said, "When you read that, you're no longer a maintenance officer, you're an ammunition officer." Capt. Donald Leeper served with me for many weeks before we finally got ammunition officers and ammunition units. Later on, he got a maintenance job, but he was one of the best things that ever happened to me. He even saved my life in one of those close calls we had in the early days around Pusan.

We had some very close calls in those early days. Many days and nights were spent under enemy fire trying unsuccessfully to find ammunition to put on waiting trucks for delivery to the combat divisions. A large part of the needed ammunition was listed in our inventory, but in the absence of trained ammunition personnel, boxes of ammunition had been unloaded and piled on the docks, not always together, and incorrect estimates had been made of the number of rounds received. Our records were worth little or nothing, merely telling us we had ammunition that we could not find. We worked round the clock trying to find ammunition in railcars in Pusangin or in the holds of ships, hoping to fill the requirements of the combat divisions.

This same lack of stock control had occurred many times in World War II, even with trained ammunition troops on the job. Just as at the ports in Normandy six years earlier, we had to establish a sorting area just outside the railhead. Here we sorted the mixed ammunition by type and lot number so that we could then ship it forward properly to the troops that needed it. I know of ammunition commanders who were actually relieved of duty because incorrect ammunition status reports were forwarded to combat commanders, both in World War II and in Korea. Inflated figures could influence command decisions and cause the loss of lives and battles. I believe the status of stocks of fuel and ammunition (Class III and V) are so important in combat support that there is no margin for error.

Because POL (petroleum, oil, and lubricants) and ammunition are vulnerable to the environment, they can be destroyed readily if not stored properly. Those in charge of storage must know their commodity and know how to handle it. If fuel or ammo starts to explode or catches fire in the combat zone, it often cannot be allowed to burn out. The correct command decision must be made to save the supplies or to clear out. Most of the time stocks are so critical that any supplies that are not actually exploding or burning should be retrieved. Sometimes risks must be taken, even though saving the stock requires a greater risk than one would normally take in peacetime or in rear areas where the location of the materiel is not so critical. Experience has proved that prompt action by courageous troops can save the day. In many cases, such action has made it possible for our forces to win the battle. But we must be trained to do it right. In fact, only recently I learned that the Munitions and Missiles School was not teaching how to fight ammunition fires; instead it was recommending that troops just clear out and let the stuff blow. I explained to the school the absolute necessity for fighting ammunition fires in the combat zone, and as a result such instruction is now under way.

In early September 1950 cargo ships of the Maru Line arrived daily at Pusan. Each carried about fifty to one hundred troops and transported limited but badly needed types of supplies, including ammunition. The ships would tie up at the land end of Pier 1 for unloading and then return to Japan the next day. One afternoon, while Korean dockhands were unloading the daily ship, a British troopship pulled in astern of it and tied up. The troopship was bringing a British brigade to join the United Nations forces in Korea. They were scheduled to disembark the next day.

That night around 2100 hours, a noise attracted my attention while I was in my ammunition section about one block away. From the window I saw what looked like fireworks exploding over Pier 1. A gondola being loaded with ammunition on a rail siding on the pier was burning. Korean stevedores had been unloading boxes of grenades and grenade fuzes. Unfortunately, they were nailing the boards used to brace the load directly to the wooden boxes of ammunition. This unsafe practice caused an explosion when a nail hit one box of the fuzes. The explosion started a fire in the wooden boxes; the entire five tons of ammunition carried in the gondola should have exploded.

The fire-fighting platoon arrived in its one fire engine about the time I did. The outfit had just reported to Pusan the day before. They looked at me to see what to do. I knew that the fire would reach the rest of the ammo at any moment, but if we could get the fire out first, we might still save the dock area. At that time the port of Pusan was probably the most important single area of the entire Korean peninsula. It was the terminus for all supplies from Japan. Together we climbed up onto the gondola and started moving boxes of grenades away from the fire so that we could get to it. We succeeded without another explosion, but there were boxes of fuzes and grenades spread all over that part of Pier 1. I wanted to get it cleared up before the British troops started to come off their ship at daybreak. I happened to spot two American civilians standing nearby. Introducing themselves simply as Mytinger and Seese, they explained that they were inspectors from the depot in Japan where the ammunition came from. I promptly "drafted" them to help clear up the mess.

When the sun came up, I discovered that, although the explosion had killed or wounded a dozen men, our fire fighting had prevented a major disaster. Checking the warehouse that ran down the center of Pier 1 approximately 20 feet from the explosion, I discovered that chemical shells containing phosgene and mustard gases had been placed inside. I later learned that these chemical gases had been sent over from Japan in response to orders to ship all ammunition to Korea. If the explosions and fire had spread to the warehouse, we probably would have blanketed downtown Pusan with mustard gas and phosgene. In addition, because the enemy was pressing on our flanks at that time, the Pusan piers were the only place to unload supplies for our forces in the Pusan Perimeter. With no place else to put it, we had stocked ammunition all along the waterfront close to the pier. We thus had the makings of the destruction of the vital center of the port of Pusan. The courage of the fire fighters, helped by some Korean longshoremen, prevented catastrophic destruction. The loss of life and injuries that would have resulted is hard to estimate.

I talked Mytinger and Seese into staying in Korea to help us in organizing an ammunition distribution system, including a storage depot, a landing area, and the rest. They remained "AWOL" from their own depot in Japan for over a year to assist us both in the perimeter and in other areas of Korea after the breakout. The truth was we lacked trained personnel needed to staff an ammunition headquarters or ammunition companies. We had to convert an ordnance recovery company into an ammunition company to establish our first ammunition supply point. Because of safety concerns, we decided to unload ammunition out in the harbor away from the docks. We fortunately had another company to operate DUKW amphibian trucks and unloaded the ammunition ships arriving from Japan and the United States in a bay just north of Pusan called Haeundae. We stored the ammunition in a valley off the bay that we hoped to turn into an ammunition depot. One night after we had stored our total depot stocks—several hundred tons—I got a report that the Air Force was going to turn the valley into a fighter base and that we had to get the ammo out by morning. This was necessary because we had lost use of an air strip at Taegu as a result of heavy enemy artillery fire. The next morning, bulldozers began building the temporary airfield, and within eighteen hours fighter planes were using the airstrip.

This development really upset our immediate plans because we had run out of storage space on the beach and had to find somewhere else to stack the ammunition. All the level rice fields in Korea at that season were under water. About 3 miles north, along the dirt road that passed through Haeundae, there was some elevated ground where the road passed through some steep hills. We got some engineering equipment and dug out the sides of the road near the surrounding mountains and stored our ammunition in the excavations. This was the beginning of the first sizable ammunition storage area that we created in Korea. Later, after the rice had been harvested and the winter weather had dried and hardened the ground, we used the fields for ammunition storage as well.

While constructing this ammunition depot, I had another one of those encounters that can happen to a young officer during a war. One afternoon I met a distinguished Korean gentleman accompanied by a tall, graceful European woman. They turned out to be the President of Korea, Syngman Rhee, and his English wife, who were out walking while visiting nearby. We chatted, and in the end I had tea with the first family of the republic. This was quite a social occasion for a busy ammunition officer about 10 miles from the enemy lines.

In the summer and early fall of 1950 ammunition was scarce, and our stock control was so poor that our records showed us holding ammunition that we did not have. I told my superior that we really did not have as much ammunition as our stock records showed and that I was going to correct the inventory to match what we really knew we had (for example, as few as 2,500 rounds of 105-mm. artillery ammo). He agreed, but when the corrected report went up to higher headquarters in Japan, he was criticized because the revised inventory showed a significantly decreased ammunition supply. He called me into his office and told me to report what had been on the record, whether we knew where it was or not. At this point I told him, "Sir, I could not sign a report that indicated we have ammunition that we cannot find." He said, "I'll sign it." I said, "Sir, that is your right, but this can be misleading." He said, "From now on, on those receipts that we get, report half of them as increases to our stockage and subtract half of them from the known deficit until we match up with what we actually have."

Fortunately for me, I was transferred before this was initiated. Unfortunately, the records of ammunition inventory being shipped, received, and on hand were so poor that no one recognized what was happening during the time it took to make up that deficit. These are records that were maintained outside the combat zone in Japan. A reader might wonder how this can happen. However, if you imagine yourself in combat under enemy artillery fire or under the pressure of unloading where space and labor and trained men are scarce, there are times when amounts are estimated with the honest intention of making an accurate count in calmer moments. Before a calm moment arrives, another crisis occurs and the recount never takes place.

During the early months of the war we were hard-pressed to meet the daily requirements of the combat divisions. The shortage of Class V ammunition was especially severe. We tried to keep the divisions on the line supplied whenever they demanded specific amounts and types of ammunition. It meant that at times we searched the holds of the ships in the bay for the kind of ammunition they wanted. Unfortunately, the cargo lists were not very reliable, causing us to spend many hours searching for ammo listed on one ship that might well be somewhere else. That's the way we supported the combat units in the first few months of the war.

This same uncertainty existed in the Pusangin railhead. Ammunition unloaded from the ships was put into railcars, which sat in the railhead until shipped to wherever necessary. We had no control of the cars being shunted within the yard, which was operated by the South Korean Railroad, and we had to scout the cars twenty-four hours a day to keep track of what was happening. The environment in Pusangin was very bad. In addition to our lack of control over the ammunition, we were surrounded by occasional firefights within the city during the night. Searching for ammunition reported to be somewhere in Pusangin was not always safe, especially during the hours of darkness.

As an ordnance officer, I suspect that the greatest lesson I learned about transportation of ordnance occurred in these early days of Korea during the Pusan Perimeter fighting. General Walker, who commanded the forces in Korea at the time, was so concerned about the shortage of ammunition that often he helped count the rounds of 105-mm. artillery in order to know what he could expect to be distributed to the two divisions then in contact with the enemy. I literally found myself, as a major, walking along counting the 105-mm. rounds with General Walker. One day the general called to tell me that he wanted certain ammunition distributed immediately to the 24th Division, which was about 20 miles away on our left flank and in contact with the enemy. We managed to find the ammunition and turned it over to the transportation officer at the Pusan railhead.

I got a call from General Walker's assistant asking if the ammunition had been distributed to the 24th Division. I said, "Sir, we turned it over to the transportation officer at the railhead at 1000 hours." Then Walker got on the phone and said, "Major, I didn't ask you who you turned it over to at the railhead. I asked you did the ammunition get to the 24th Division?" I said, "Sir, I don't know. I'll have to check it out." He said, "I told you to get it to the 24th Division. Now do it." I must say that I will never forget that conversation.

It turns out that the ammo had moved on a railcar out of the railhead, but it had not arrived at the 24th Division. No one seemed to know where it was. So, a transportation officer and I requisitioned a railroad handcar. We left Pusan heading west, pumping the handcar, looking for that ammunition car which we found on a siding about halfway to the 24th Division.

I can assure you we made certain that car got to the 24th as quickly as possible, and then we called General Walker to tell him that it was in the hands of the division. The lesson I learned then was when someone gives an order, don't count on somebody else to carry it out. Your job includes follow-up to be sure that the order has been carried out. That lesson also made clear to me that an ordnance officer not only needs to know ordnance, but he needs to know how the current systems of transportation and communications work to make sure that a job has really been done.

Much of the planning at Eighth Army for the breakout from the Pusan Perimeter, which was to coincide with the X Corps landing at Inch'on in September 1950, centered on ensuring that there was enough artillery ammunition on hand to support the attack. At one of the final staff meetings, the Eighth Army G–4 asked if all the plans were ready for execution. I felt it necessary to point out that there was a gap in the planning. We were expecting a shipload of combat-ready 105-mm. artillery ammunition, but I had learned from examining the manifest that the ammunition was unfuzed. We had time fuzes to place in each round, but the projectiles had been hollowed out to allow room for a longer, proximity fuze. Without a proximity fuze, a supplemental charge had to be added before inserting the time fuze. But we lacked those supplemental charges. There were bewildered looks on everyone's face except the Eighth Army ordnance officers. They had decided that this subject would not be raised at the meeting. But I had raised it. Coming from a lower echelon, the Pusan Base Command, I faced a room full of people who wished I was not there.

As a result of my statement, supplemental charges were flown in from the United States under the highest priority. They arrived in time to set up production lines in a field outside Pusan to insert both the supplemental charges and the time fuzes. I am sure that at that particular time my action certainly was not helping my career. In all fairness I must say that those other ordnance officers who were aware of the problem had convinced themselves that, theoretically, the supplemental charge was not necessary and that the round would operate just as well without it. If my stand was incorrect, that fact was not brought to the attention of the G–4. Although I did not know the technical answer, I reasoned that the projectile would not have been designed to accept a supplemental charge if it could be fired effectively without it.

It is true that one must follow orders in the military. This does not mean, however, that one must carry out every order right or wrong. In the first place, part of the integrity of a military officer is to make sure that the officer giving the orders understands whether they are based upon factual information and whether they can be carried out. We have an obligation to ensure that those above us, no matter the rank, know everything necessary to make a correct decision. If it appears that a decision is being made based upon poor information or lack of knowledge, the officer or enlisted man has a responsibility to clarify this for the superior making the decision.

I have been in this position a few times in my career in the Army. In each case I had to explain tactfully what I considered to be the facts. If my boss decided not to follow my advice, that was his decision. If I thought it important enough not to carry it out, it was then my responsibility to say so, tactfully, and be relieved of the responsibility. As indicated earlier, this happened once when I could not sign an ammunition status report that I knew was false. I was transferred after I had done what I could.

## Service in the 7th Division

After the September offensive in 1950 I was no longer one of a few ordnance officers in the Pusan area (now designated the 2d Logistical Command under Eighth Army). We had, if anything, too many officers in this no longer critical sector. I had just been promoted to lieutenant colonel (a battlefield promotion), and I pointed out that perhaps I could be used to better advantage elsewhere. I might well have regretted this suggestion in the months that followed when the rapid retreat of UN forces in the face of the surprise attack by Chinese units caused General Walker to initiate planning for the evacuation of the Eighth Army through the port of Pusan. I was hard at work preparing for this eventuality when Col. Charles Ostrom, an old friend, showed up without notice from Eighth Army headquarters to see how things were going. The following day I received orders to report to Headquarters, X Corps, for further assignment to the 7th Infantry Division. I flew up to meet the X Corps' ordnance officer, Col. John D. Billingsley (later professor of ordnance at West Point for twenty years), who gave me some wise and badly needed advice as he drove me by jeep through the bitter weather to 7th Division headquarters.

The 7th Division was in pretty bad shape. It had been used as an unofficial replacement depot in Japan in the early days of the war. While some of its training had been excellent (its artillery instructors had been brought in from the Artillery School and were the best), its fighting ability was questionable because of the presence of so many inexperienced Korean soldiers, who had been integrated as fillers when many of the division's own men had been sent to Korea as badly needed replacements in units already in battle. By the time the division arrived at Inch'on, it was over one-third Korean. Despite this problem the division participated in the X Corps advance to the Chinese border on the east coast of Korea. It suffered severely during the subsequent withdrawal and fierce fighting under appalling conditions around the Chosin Reservoir. When I joined the unit it was nearly surrounded by enemy forces in the mountain area to the northeast of the Pusan region. Lt. Gen. Edward M. Almond, the X Corps commander, had convinced General of the Army Douglas MacArthur, the Far East commander, that the division needed a complete shakeup. Its commander was about to leave, along with two of its regimental commanders and logistics officer. It had just gotten a new assistant division commander, Col. (later Lt. Gen.) Robert Sink. Billingsley gave me a lot to think about on that drive, but his information was most useful and let me know what to expect and what I would have to do.

The division's logistic support was especially poor. Combat commanders had told Almond that "for all the good it did, ordnance could have stayed in Japan." Accordingly, when I met with Almond he told me, "Heiser, you're a young Regular Army officer, just promoted to lieutenant colonel. Your future career is at stake—you improve support to the 7th Division or your future is nil."

Needless to say, I was distressed as I took the rough jeep drive over the mountains to the division headquarters. I knew the division was in poor condition, and I was afraid I would be unable to do the job. When I reported in to the division commander, Maj. Gen. David G. Barr, he said, "Heiser, it's good to have you, but we didn't need a new ordnance officer. The corps commander ordered me to accept a new ordnance officer, and you're it, but what we really need is a new ordnance unit." Now here I was in 7th Division headquarters, in a valley almost completely surrounded by the enemy, being shelled by mortars and artillery, scared that I couldn't do the job anyhow because all I knew was how to read what it said on the outside of an ammunition box, and the commanding general tells me he doesn't need me; he needs a new ordnance unit. Well, I walked out of that headquarters probably as down as I trust I'll ever be.

Walking down the road without really knowing where I was going, I saw a sign that said "DIVARTY" (Division Artillery). Deciding that I might as well introduce myself, I walked in, and the first guy I ran into, the executive officer, was Lt. Col. (later Maj. Gen.) William McGregor Lynn, Jr., from my class at Leavenworth. I found out quickly that DIVARTY had the best communications in the division. Lynn got on their net and talked with all battalion commanders in the division, not just artillery, but infantry too. It turned out that three-quarters of all the battalion commanders of the 7th Division were my classmates from Leavenworth. So the word spread, "Joe Heiser is here, and ordnance is straightened up." A lot of them didn't know me from Adam except that I was in their class, but it was that kind of relationship. Before I got there, they had literally refused food to ordnance soldiers because they weren't getting any ordnance support. It was a very serious situation, which explains why they ordered me to relieve the ordnance officer overnight.

It turned out the commanding general was completely wrong. There was nothing basically wrong with the ordnance unit; it was the ordnance officer who was lousy. I got a good reputation because anything I did was an improvement. My predecessor had restricted and restrained his unit—then the largest company in the Army, over five hundred men. He refused to send out contact teams. He even refused to give up his so-called safety level of 105-mm. guns that he held in the ordnance outfit 180 miles to the rear even though the division's artillery units did not have all the guns they were authorized.

When I got down to the ordnance unit from division headquarters that first night, I immediately called the division G–4 back at headquarters and said, "I need 200 trucks." He said, "When it's daylight, look out from wherever you're standing, and you'll find 200 trucks." Thirty percent of all the trucks in the 7th Division were unserviceable and parked with the ordnance unit, a 36-hour round trip by jeep from division headquarters along a dangerous one-way mountain road.

A scene I witnessed on that first night in the unit typified the unit's problems. I came upon a frustrated soldier, who had just arrived after the eighteen-hour drive down from one of the division's combat units. He had come to get some badly needed antifreeze, only to be told by an implacable supply sergeant that his requisition form was improperly filled out and that he had "to go back to your unit and get the paper work filled out right." The stupidity of it all infuriated me. "Do you know what you're doing?" I asked the clerk. "From now on the rules in this unit can be boiled down to one: we are in business to support the soldier; supporting the units of the 7th Division is our only business." The soldier got his antifreeze immediately, and from then on we got serious about supporting the division.

With morning approaching, I had not set up my bed yet, so I decided to check security around the perimeter. We were completely isolated in an area open to enemy fire. After almost an hour, I came upon a noisy and lighted set of tents where the cooks were preparing breakfast. I decided to pay a visit and bum a cup of coffee.

I often say that I became a general officer because I was a good KP. After I finished my cup of coffee and the men started to line up for breakfast, I noticed they were one KP short; the soldier who handed out hotcakes was missing. I got behind the big container and began handing out hotcakes as the line started through. The look on the faces of those men when they saw their new commander doing KP was startling but so gratifying that I decided to keep it up for the rest of the breakfast. I really believe that their initial impression of their new CO amazed the men so much that they gave me the benefit of the doubt and figured I was a great guy. As a result they never let me down. Whatever I asked them to do, they did, and it showed in their work and in their support of the combat soldier. It showed in the number of combat decorations that they received based on recommendations from combat commanders, who really appreciated the support they gave, most of it forward within the regimental and battalion areas of operation.

Before the morning was over the men had a chance to show their stuff. When I realized that our unit was almost 180 miles from the 7th Division's fighting units that we were supposed to support, I knew we had to move. I issued orders to pack up at once and form convoys to move the supplies north over the mountains to the 7th Division command post (CP). The men performed this herculean task with speed and in good spirits. Each NCO and officer had to decide what to take along because we could only haul less than half of what we had. The rest we turned over in place to a nearby and somewhat startled depot company.

I sent an NCO with a lieutenant forward to select a site ahead of the division CP. We arrived at our new location around noon the next day. Maj. Gen. Claude B. Ferenbaugh, the new division commander, had arrived at his CP that same day and called a meeting of his commanders and principal staff for 1800 hours. He promptly began the meeting by announcing that the 7th Division was going on the offensive. He said, "I want all of you to move out, combat commanders and support." He turned to the chief of staff and G–4 and asked, "Has the new ordnance officer reported in?"

WAR IN KOREA                                                              71

They answered, "Yes. Heiser." I stood up in the rear of the room. Ferenbaugh said, "Heiser, I know that you're 180 miles to the rear, and I want you to get your outfit up here where they can give support to the fighting soldiers of this division." I said, "Sir, the ordnance unit is now five miles ahead of your CP." He reacted with, "That's what we need here. If all of you move out like Heiser has, we'll make a name for this division."

I must tell you that particular moment began a great time for the 707th Ordnance. With the full commitment of the men, we provided probably the best ordnance support that was ever given to a combat unit. We had competent men who knew what to do. All I had to do was let them do it and provide the occasional guidance necessary to get the job done. From that moment on, the division commander, General Ferenbaugh, and General Sink never questioned what ordnance was doing. In fact, my efficiency report covering my service in the 7th Division carried a statement which said, "Heiser should be promoted to general officer just as fast as possible."

We devised many initiatives to provide better support to the combat troops. For one, we established direct exchange for component repair parts and other supplies. We'd deliver serviceable items to the forward units, place a shoe tag on the unserviceable ones, and issue the replacements without further paperwork. We also attached logistical contact teams to each forward combat unit. These teams maintained equipment and arranged for the distribution of supplies to the combat unit, relieving the fighters of the time-consuming chore of going back to the rear for supplies and support. When Col. (later Maj. Gen.) Nelson M. Lynde, Jr., representing the commanding general of Army Field Forces, came over from the United States to see how ordnance service was being performed, he said, "Heiser, I don't want to talk to you; I'm going forward and talk to the units." Three days later he came back and said to me, "Heiser, you've got these people hypnotized. They said if I wanted to know what's going on in ordnance, I'd better go see Heiser. 'We don't see any problems.' What are you using to hypnotize these people?" I told him that I learned from the engineer battalion that if you put your support units with the combat units and tell them to provide the support required, the combat guys will love you. They'll feed you; they'll protect you; they'll do anything you ask them to do. By establishing forward contact teams with all the combat units, we were supporting them. And one way or another we solved their problems. I told him, "We have great men in support. All we have to do is let them do it."

I then explained to Lynde that we should revise the TO&E so that I wouldn't have to disregard it by setting up contact teams that didn't conform to current doctrine. Lynde returned to the Army Field Forces and recommended a reorganization that was the basis for the maintenance battalion now found in all divisions, with forward support companies and a base company to back them up.

In the 7th Division we did almost all of our repair work forward, thereby avoiding many return trips on the bad roads which would have tied up transport. The division had only about half its authorized equipment, so we fixed damaged items on the spot if we could, eliminating considerable retrograde. That kept more equipment moving, shooting, and communicating.

I not only gained experience as the ordnance officer, but unexpectedly learned some of the broader aspects of command as well. One morning about 0300 hours I received a call from General Ferenbaugh saying, "Heiser, you're now the division rear-area commander. You need to have a defense plan for the rear area and, further, you need to explain this plan at 0800 hours to the new Eighth Army commander, General James Van Fleet. Have you got a plan?" I said, "Sir, we don't have a plan, but we will by 0800." I promptly got the S–3s of the tank battalion and the engineer battalion along with the commanding officer of the reconnaissance company to meet me at my CP where we spent the rest of the night drawing up the first 7th Division rear-area defense plan and operation order. Complicating the work was the fact that we had no infantry or artillery units available in reserve. All the battalions and regiments were fully committed at the front.

At 0800 hours I reported to the division CP. It wasn't long before Ferenbaugh was questioned by Van Fleet about the division's rear-area defense plan. Ferenbaugh said, "Colonel Heiser is prepared to present the plan if you wish." I was on the spot. The fact is we had a good but untried plan, and I was afraid that Van Fleet would ask, "How has it worked?" But he didn't. He was so taken by the fact that it was a good operation plan, according to the Leavenworth format, that he said, "That's great, best in the Eighth Army," and he went no further into it. Afterwards, Ferenbaugh called his G–3, Col. James Lynch, a classmate of mine at Leavenworth, and told him, "You get with Joe Heiser. I want to see operation plans for this division modeled after what Joe presented to General Van Fleet this morning." By the way, our rear-area operation plan worked well under later enemy attacks.

One morning about 0900 hours, I received a call from General Sink who said, "Heiser, we have lost three infantry battalion commanders. Have you got a man who can take over the ordnance outfit for you?" I said, "Yes, sir." He said, "Well, be prepared. If we don't get three acceptable replacements from Eighth Army before 1400 this afternoon, you're going to be assigned as a battalion commander in the 17th Infantry. Do you think you can do it?" I said, "Sir, you know I'll try, but I must say I will have much to learn." He said, "You'll do it." Fortunately for the men in the 17th Infantry, the replacements from Eighth Army did arrive, and I remained the division's ordnance officer. This experience, like the division rear-area command episode, emphasizes that no logistician can forget that he's a soldier first. He can't do only one part of the soldier's job. He's got to be prepared to do some of both, simultaneously, in any assignment that might be handed to him.

Even though I never commanded an infantry regiment in Korea, I kept myself well informed about the tactical situation. I believe I should recount here a tactical situation in the early days of Korea that had, in my opinion, a very disastrous result. I recite this from my viewpoint, that of a field grade officer, who because of his position as ammunition officer was able to feel the direct impact of the conflict that existed between Far East Command headquarters in Japan and the senior commanders in Korea. I do so in the hope that such situations will be avoided in the future.

When the war in Korea broke out, General Walker was sent to Korea in command of Eighth Army. In the very early days of the war most of his headquarters was still in Japan, with only some elements at Pusan. He reported to General MacArthur in Japan, who had his hands full, being in charge of the reorganization and reconstruction of that still-occupied nation. During the Inch'on landings a separate Army organization, the X Corps, entered Korea. The X Corps was commanded by General Almond, who at the same time retained his position as chief of staff in MacArthur's Far East Command back in Japan. This confused command setup immediately caused problems.

In October 1950, when Almond's X Corps was preparing for its drive up the northeast coast of North Korea toward the Yalu River, the Chinese border, it demanded ammunition from those supplies stocked in Korea for the Eighth Army, especially supplies located in the Pusan area. General Walker claimed all of it was Eighth Army ammunition and offered Almond only those items that the Eighth Army did not need. General Almond escalated his request to General MacArthur, who wired the X Corps and Eighth Army that all ammunition available in Korea was to be shared, equally, to meet the requirements of both X Corps and Eighth Army. This reply was countermanded to some extent by an Eighth Army wire which explained that "available to X Corps and Eighth Army" meant that X Corps could only get what the Eighth Army did not require. Thus it fell to me, a young field grade officer, to use my best judgment on what should be issued to X Corps, much of it *not* excess to Eighth Army's needs.

As a field grade officer I was not privy to what really took place between the X Corps and Eighth Army at the time of the Chinese intervention in Korea. I am certain, however, that this rivalry between the commanders contributed significantly to some of the problems that occurred during the Chinese attack in the cold winter of 1950. I do not believe that the history of this unsatisfactory relationship has been recorded or understood by many. It presents a lesson to be learned. Even though MacArthur did a great job in Japan, I am not sure that he fully understood what was going on within the Army in Korea. I don't believe that the problem was really solved until X Corps became part of Eighth Army under General Matthew B. Ridgway.

General Ridgway caused many changes in Korea, including winning the Army's permission to abolish segregated units by mixing black and white soldiers throughout the units of his command. Actually, this historic action did not officially take place until later in 1951, but well before that time racial integration had been occurring in some parts of the Far East Command. Integration was not allowed within Almond's X Corps, but as the 7th Division's rear-area commander, I commanded an all-black Ranger company. These black troops were good for my rear-area responsibilities; however, their segregated status was not best for the 7th Infantry Division. I convinced General Ferenbaugh and General Sink that as soon as the division was transferred out of X Corps, we should immediately break up the black Ranger company, composed of over five hundred black soldiers, and integrate them into the division as a whole. Shortly thereafter, the 7th Division was assigned to the IX Corps, and we took immediate action to integrate the soldiers of the division. Questions of racial justice aside, our action achieved a positive result, both for the individuals involved and for the effectiveness and efficiency of the U.S. Army.

During the worst days of the Korean War in the winter of 1950–51, the 7th Division was having difficulty getting the ammunition it needed and moving it close enough to make resupply less difficult. We had convinced Charlie Ostrom at Eighth Army headquarters to move the ammunition up to a mobile ammunition supply point on the edge of the division's rear at a railhead at

Chech'on. Charlie was right to be hesitant about placing ammunition stocks too far forward, because Eighth Army had lost too much ammunition to enemy action. Sometimes it was our own fault.

We once almost lost all the resupply ammunition stored near the 7th Division area because of a fire that resulted when some Korean troops were unloading Japanese ammunition at Chech'on. This railhead was being used as the ammunition supply point for the 7th Division, which at the time was in a tight battle and needed the ammunition. Actually, an Eighth Army ammunition company had scattered and left the area as soon as the first explosion took place. When we discovered the fire, no one was doing anything about it. We had to try to save the ammunition that was not exploding or burning by moving it away from the fire. In addition to that, the POL supply point for the division was on the edge of the railhead. We had to act promptly, or we would lose both the division's entire ammunition and POL resupplies. Replacements were over 100 miles away through mountainous terrain.

I was about 2 miles away from the railhead when I heard the explosion and saw the smoke. Knowing that we had all our ammunition in railcars at the railhead, I could guess what had happened. My driver and I drove to the railhead in our jeep. As we approached the fire, we stopped at the empty office of the railhead transportation officer to use the phone. I tried to reach someone at the phone in a railcar up at the railhead, but no one answered. The entire section of the town surrounding the office I was calling from had been abandoned and some of the fragments from the explosions had torn into the building.

I was not really looking forward to approaching any closer to the explosion to see what was going on, but my sergeant and I got back in the jeep and drove on for the 200-some yards to the railhead. From that point we could see that the explosions were taking place at the south end of the railhead and that most of the rest of the railhead and the POL across the way were not yet on fire. I told the sergeant to go get some men. I wanted them to use a tank or a tank retriever to pull the undamaged ammunition cars away from danger. In the meantime I was busy running toward the fire, getting as close as I could to the burning and exploding cars and uncoupling the strings of undamaged cars so they could be pulled away.

The ammunition cars were standing on approximately fifteen tracks. Each track had as many as fifteen to twenty salvageable cars. I would unhook the car next to the burning one, and then when the tank retriever drove up, other soldiers pulled those cars to the other end of the yard and out of danger. We repeated this for each string of cars. After about six hours of this dangerous operation, we had saved about two-thirds of the ammunition and all of the POL. This was the same technique that we had used earlier at the Soissons railhead in Europe in 1944.

As you get into an action such as this, worry and fear disappear. In my case I knew that I had stopped to call because I was afraid of what could happen to myself and the driver, but then I got so thoroughly involved in doing what I had to do that I forgot the danger. Once I started running up and down the railroad tracks, my fear was replaced by a knowledge of what had to be done. I was repeatedly knocked down by ammunition blasts. I even found myself leaping over shells that were knocked down the tracks in my direction by low-order detonations. It is difficult to imagine yourself or anyone else leaping over 155-mm. projectiles and other flying explosives coming your way as you head into them. But that's what you do.

Early in this salvage operation I turned around to discover a soldier following me. I tried to run him off, but he wouldn't go; he just kept doing what he had been doing, that is, following me. He turned out to be a medic who had decided to stick with me in case I got hurt. This kind of behavior really causes you to understand the greatness that exists in people. As it turned out neither of us was hurt, except for some scratches.

We were very, very fortunate to save most of the ammunition. One of the boxcars we moved away from the fire was loaded with frozen dynamite. Frozen dynamite, if jarred, is supposed to explode instantaneously. This car was standing next to a car that was blowing up. We managed to uncouple it and, without knowing what was in it, push it away. Only later, while inventorying the ammunition, did we discover that the dynamite had survived.

The supplies were saved at very little expense of life or limb, although several members of our ammunition crew as well as the division's ammunition officer permanently lost some, if not all, of their hearing from the ammunition blasts. General Sink, who had come down to the railhead to watch the rescue efforts, said later in a briefing that there was so much debris flying about that he returned to the front line where it was safer. Many medals were awarded later to those men who had stood and saved so much of the ammunition and POL so badly needed for our division.

In my experience this was only one of many occasions when I found it impossible not to be afraid of getting hurt; fortunately, I also found that I could overcome this fear by going ahead with what I saw as a duty that had to be performed. I mention this very personal reaction because, while I am not sure what goes on in the minds of other soldiers in combat, I believe that for many at the beginning of an operation, or even before it begins, fear must invade the mind to some degree. What is important is to recognize that this is natural and does not make one a coward. A coward would give in to fear and abandon his duty. Duty includes what one must do both for himself and for his fellow soldier. What is important is that most men overcome their fear by carrying out their duty in spite of obvious danger.

On the other hand, perhaps there are some who never have fear. I am not so sure that this is good in a soldier because, it seems to me, fear is like pain—when your body is ill or hurt, it warns you to be careful. My World War II friend Norm Bennett summarized the effect of fear in three phases: fear of hurt, dutiful action when fear is supplanted by the need to act, and the aftershock when you realize what has happened. It does not take long to pray. I think prayer can help bolster the courage necessary to challenge the danger.

Unfortunately, many in the Army feel that ammunition support is just a case of putting some strong backs to the task of moving ammunition to the combat troops. This is wrong. First of all, credible stock control is absolutely essential, and ammunition troops need strong discipline to maintain accurate records of ammunition lot numbers and type as well as condition. It has been my experience that too many decisions have been made based on incorrect ammunition stock records. Further, ammunition troops need knowledge of field storage of ammunition in accordance with safety regulations. Any resourceful enemy will attempt to destroy ammunition, both to deny it to our forces and to create the damage that exploding ammunition causes. When stored ammunition explodes during combat, that which was stored unsafely in the field causes greater losses than that which was stored properly. In short, ammunition troops need far more than strong backs. They need a thorough knowledge of ammunition supply, policies, and procedures.

In the staff position of division ordnance officer, I quickly learned that keeping my bosses informed was the best policy. We were in the mountains, flanked on both sides by Republic of Korea divisions, a critical position that lasted most of my tour. I attended both morning and night war-room sessions, held mostly in tents or wrecked buildings, reviewing what had happened tactically that day and what was planned for the next day and the longer-range future. As the ordnance officer responsible for support of firepower, communications, and mobility, I considered it essential to be well informed so I could plan to support the required action. Once General Ferenbaugh complained there were too many people at these briefings. His chief of staff told us that the morning briefing would be restricted to the senior general staff. I explained that while I understood what General Ferenbaugh meant, I thought he might want me to continue to attend because of the effect of my ordnance information on the success of his tactical plans. The chief of staff said he was just carrying out the direction of the commanding general and, if I wanted to raise the question, I should do it directly with the general. I entered the commanding general's tent and said, "Sir, I can't do my job properly if I don't know what takes place in your morning and night briefings." He quickly said to me, "Joe, I know you are supporting us up front; I also understand why you have come to me. You tell the chief I didn't mean this ban to apply to you. You are the only staff officer not on my general staff who will be at the morning briefing." I thanked him and went about my business. I had pursued the point because I felt my direct contact with the commanding general and his deputy in this case was absolutely necessary to do my job.

In his testimony before the Iran-Contra Committee Secretary of State George Schultz made the same point. He concluded that you can't just leave it up to staff-level communications, you've got to make a point of talking directly to the boss on significant, important issues. I believe this is especially so when there are critical decisions to be made. I can't stress enough my conviction that you must have clear channels of communication with your superiors and that at all times you must provide the most accurate and truthful information possible. I learned this lesson well in 1947 or 1948, when as a young major I was assigned to the Office of the Chief of Ordnance. I accompanied the Chief, Maj. Gen. Everett S. Hughes, when he defended Ordnance requirements before a House committee. Congressman Hamilton Fish of New York was particularly hard on Hughes in his questioning. In answering one question, Hughes admitted that he had made a mistake. As I remember the exchange, Fish then promptly said, "General, if you make mistakes, how can we depend upon your being right?" Hughes answered, "I make many decisions every day. In our national pastime, the game of baseball, the hitter is considered outstanding if he can hit between .300 and .350 percent, which means a hit one out of every three times at bat. I consider that I do make mistakes, but I don't repeat them if I can avoid it, and I am positive that my batting average is at the highest level. But when I make a mistake, I admit it so that I can be sure that I prevent its recurrence." The congressman promptly replied, "General Hughes, you have been honest with me, and I understand what you say. If you say you need it, I support it. I have no further questions, Mr. Chairman." Hughes won the day by leveling with the committee about his mistake. I have never forgotten that day, and in making presentations I have always tried to adhere to my conviction that you must know the facts and tell the truth in order to instill others' confidence in your position.

When American replacements became available in early 1951, our ammunition outfit picked up about 400 to 500 of those Korean soldiers previously assigned to our combat units. We used these men for security, allowing our skilled ordnance personnel to get some rest and perform their specialties. This expedient worked very well. A couple of times, however, we discovered that the Koreans had located some sake wine and, as a result, a large number became inebriated. Once I "bawled out" their commander, a young Korean captain, and demanded that he take immediate disciplinary action. In making the rounds shortly thereafter, in snow about a foot deep, I discovered just how different discipline could be in another military culture. All the men who had violated orders were stripped naked and doing pushups in the snow. If they stopped, there were noncoms ready to strap them with belts.

Their captain had been studying for the ministry in the United States when the war broke out and had immediately been recalled and put on active duty. A few months after he joined our unit, the war was pretty well under control, and I received a letter from Headquarters, Korean Army, asking my permission to discharge the captain from the Korean Army so that he might resume his studies in the United States. According to the letter, this could not occur without my approval. I quickly agreed, with the provision that his replacement be of equal caliber. The captain was a fine leader, and his knowledge of English had helped us overcome the language problem. We really missed him after he left, even though we did receive a good replacement. So the first man to rotate from our outfit when the war situation eased turned out to be not a weary lieutenant colonel, but a Korean divinity student returning to his classes in the United States. I finally rotated out of my command in the 7th Division in September 1951 and sailed for home.

St. Charles Preparatory School baseball team, 1931. First baseman Heiser, standing, second from left.

Basic training, Camp Sutton, North Carolina, 1942.

Sergeant and Mrs. Heiser and their children Annette and Joel, 1942.

First Sergeant Heiser calling the roll at Camp Sutton, North Carolina, 1942; *below,* Red Ball Express trucks moving through a regulating point.

A break from D-Day preparations. Lieutenant Heiser at SHAEF headquarters, London 1944.

General Eisenhower at Cherbourg talking to an ammunition handler during a routine inspection.

Brig. Gen. Benjamin O. Davis

Using roller conveyor and other equipment to collect supplies stored behind the hedgerows, Normandy, 1944.

Piers 1 and 2 at Pusan, where most American supplies were landed, August 1950; *below*, the 7th Infantry Division ordnance support base, Korea, January 1951.

The port of Pusan, with a view of the Pusangin railhead and the major port facilities beyond.

Loading wounded onto a C–54 transport at Landing Strip K–9 (Dogpatch) in Korea; *below*, rekindling the Eternal Flame at the Arc de Triomphe. Brig. Gen. and Mrs. Heiser with General Lyman Lemnitzer, Supreme Allied Commander, Europe, Paris, 4 July 1965.

PART II

# Transition to High Command

## CHAPTER 5

# Teacher and Student

Among the many deficiencies we experienced in the early days of the war in Korea was the absence of effective preventive maintenance on equipment. This only compounded the problem of severe shortages that struck the Eighth Army when it was thrust suddenly into battle. Lacking the ability to maintain and repair, we tended to throw away things that didn't work, in some cases only because of minor problems. I've seen vehicles, including scarce tanks abandoned on the side of the road, used for target practice by U.S. units. In some cases the only thing wrong with the equipment was a lack of fuel.

As a result of this serious problem, Secretary of the Army Frank Pace in 1951 ordered all general officers of the Army, especially those returning from duty in Korea and all those scheduled for duty in Korea thereafter, to attend a specially organized course in preventive maintenance. The project was given highest priority by Secretary Pace and General Mark W. Clark, commander of Army Field Forces and later General Ridgway's replacement in the Far East, with classes to start in January 1952 at Aberdeen Proving Ground. The instructors were quickly assembled from among colonels and lieutenant colonels of each of the technical services who had just returned from duty in the divisions in Korea. Harvard University, under contract to the Army, gave these instructors a quick course in creating case studies (covering unidentified but actual U.S. units in Korea) as well as the instructional know-how required to use the case-study method.

During the Christmas weekend of 1951 I received orders to report to Aberdeen to teach the Senior Field Force Commanders Preventive Maintenance Course. I had just settled in with my family at the Indiana Arsenal on my return from Korean duty. We were enjoying the best quarters of our career, a spacious home overlooking the Ohio River. After some difficulty, we found a small apartment in Towson, Maryland, a suburb of Baltimore. This turned out to be a blessing because the children could attend a fine school, and they were most fortunate to make a lifelong friend of Father Martin Schwalenburg, who has been a tremendous practical influence for good on our entire family. My interest in athletics once again was an important link, because Father Schwalenburg was the school coach as well as the parish priest.

The classes at Aberdeen actually contained between thirty and forty general officers and a dozen or so colonels. The course was taught for three years, then stopped because of a general Army rule that curtailed all short courses. (When it was revived three years later at Fort Knox, Kentucky, with somewhat the same curriculum, I was invited down to assist in its reactivation.) This maintenance course for senior officers was most valuable because it gave these leaders a practical view of the importance of logistic support requirements and how best to ensure readiness of their people and equipment. It is still being given, but now the students are field grade officers about to take command of battalions and larger units.

While I was teaching at Aberdeen, Maj. Gen. Guy S. Meloy, Sr., the commander of the Infantry School at Fort Benning, Georgia, came to give the keynote speech at one of the senior preventive maintenance courses. He came for the day but stayed for the full course of week-long instruction. On the last day he asked me if I would accept assignment to the faculty at Fort Benning. It was a high compliment, and I jumped at the offer. Unfortunately, Meloy failed to win Washington's approval for my transfer. I mention this incident because I think the Army has failed to get across to combat officers the capabilities and limitations of logistics, a problem that could be solved if it assigned some top-level logisticians to the faculties of the combat arms schools to teach the fundamentals of the science and art of logistics. Combat students do not get a basic understanding of the correlation between combat arms capabilities and logistics responsibilities. They will not get it later at the Command and General Staff College at Leavenworth nor at the senior war colleges. Such instruction at branch schools would, in my opinion, provide a sound basis for understanding logistics and its importance to the combat arms mission.

As the course at Aberdeen stabilized, I had time for other things in addition to the twenty-eight hours weekly in the classroom, so I became the executive officer of the Ordnance School under Brig. Gen. Willis Slaughter, who had also been my first commander when I enlisted in 1942. These assignments lasted until 1954 when my teaching days ended and I once again became a student.

In the early 1950s the Chief of Ordnance each year selected five leading ordnance officers of the rank of lieutenant colonel for a postgraduate executive training program in business management at the Business School at Harvard University. This program, requiring a two-year tour of duty in Boston, had been in existence for several years. In 1953 one of the students, Col. (later Maj. Gen.) John Zierdt came to Washington to see the Chief of Ordnance. He reported he had left Boston because he was frustrated with what was happening at Harvard. Almost all of the students in the courses with these ordnance officers were young men and women who had just completed their undergraduate degrees. Most of them had been in school all their lives and had little or no practical experience. In addition, the ordnance officers, who already possessed considerable management experience, were for the most part in classes discussing the ABCs of management. Zierdt concluded that sending officers to this course was wasteful and recommended that it be discontinued. His recommendations led to the program's cancellation.

Thomas Shaughnessy, the educational adviser to the Chief of Ordnance, was given the task of finding an appropriate replacement for the Harvard program. He recommended that a postgraduate course combined with practical experience in business be set up. He first worked out an agreement with five large business corporations in the Chicago area to provide five lieutenant colonels each year with an intensive, practical course in business leadership along with each corporation's own high-potential young executives. At the same time Shaughnessy arranged with the Business School of the University of Chicago for five ordnance officers with degrees to be accepted as candidates for a master's degree in business administration through attending the Executive Program of the University of Chicago. This course required classes two nights a week, with the other nights and weekends set aside for homework. These officers would be detailed to the Chicago Ordnance District, which would assign them tasks in procurement during breaks in the program.

The Chief of Ordnance approved the concept, and I was among the first five selected for the thirty-month course in 1954. The five student-officers in the program spent some time at the home offices and plants of Inland Steel, Borg-Warner, International Harvester, Sears Roebuck, and Motorola. We were individually trained, sometimes teamed with one or two of a corporation's own young executives. I worked with Brooks McCormick of International Harvester. During our time in the program we worked as assistants to the vice president in charge of manufacturing. (Later, Brooks became president and chairman of the board of International Harvester.) At Motorola Col. William N. Sloan, Jr., and I worked alongside Bob Galvin, the son of the president and chairman as well as founder of Motorola. Together, we prepared a proposed reorganization of Motorola to match the expanded work of the corporation. (Bob Galvin is currently chairman of the board of Motorola.)

The five companies did not charge the government for this practical approach to executive leadership training. They gave us first-class attention and provided us with every opportunity to learn those things that appeared most pertinent to our future objectives. Without exception, we were given the run of the corporation, and, in fact, many of us had the opportunity individually and in small groups to participate in actual discussions that led to significant policy and operational decisions.

One of the striking lessons I learned in this program was the need for communication between blue-collar and white-collar employees and top executives. There were strong unions in some of these industries. Most of them had been organized under strong management opposition, especially at Inland Steel. It was important for us to observe and understand the game plan of industry management in negotiations with labor for new contracts and to learn from individual problems which emerged later. We had the opportunity as individuals to sit in on negotiation meetings and to see what made both sides tick. We learned the value of what is now known as "participatory management."

At Borg-Warner we learned that an overhead staff of some two hundred people operated about forty different individual corporations of which Borg-Warner was the holding company. Control of these subordinate corporations was primarily based upon a simple organization in which the comptroller at Borg-Warner was directly responsible for the comptrollers at each of the subordinate corporations. This official had the network which tracked all forty bottom-line operations. With the exception of the comptroller's organization, most of the Borg-Warner headquarters was made up of legal personnel, especially those qualified in patents and copyrights. It was an interesting approach to business operation and management.

At International Harvester we observed a problem resulting from diversification that affects other corporations as well. International Harvester was a worldwide leader in the manufacture of farm implements. Its founder was Cyrus McCormick, inventor of the reaper. The company had established its reputation with deeply engineered farm machines that could operate in all kinds of terrain, weather, and storage conditions. Then, during World War II, it diversified into appliances such as refrigerators and freezers (the white goods business), weapons, trucks, and heavy industrial equipment.

Diversification into the automotive industry caused the Harvester work force to become affiliated with the United Auto Workers. The high wages negotiated by the Auto Workers caused problems for the company because many of its product lines lacked profit margins that could absorb these wage levels. Because the margin of profit in the white goods industry was very small, the higher wages demanded by the union caused Harvester eventually to get out of that business. While we were at Harvester, we recommended that they take a hard look at product engineering in the truck division and in the white goods division. We raised the idea that they were overengineering trucks and other products so that they were not competitive. We questioned whether the same problem wasn't affecting other divisions as well. Since that time, International Harvester has had considerable financial difficulty and has reorganized more than once. (It is now called Navistar International.)

While we were at Sears Roebuck, we were asked to participate in an interview with a reporter from *Business Week*. We objected because we feared we might unintentionally divulge some private corporate information in an interview. We asked our supervisors in the Pentagon not to approve the interview. They told us, however, to proceed with it. As senior officer of our training group, I asked the Sears vice president who was supervising our individual training programs if Sears approved of the interview and, if so, would like to send a representative. He saw no problem and told us to go ahead without Sears. That was a bad decision. Although we tried to be honest and to go lightly on negative aspects of the corporations, the reporter was more interested in hearing about the problems we had seen than in the good things we were learning. His article suggested that Army colonels were finding mismanagement in Chicago businesses, especially in Sears Roebuck. The article created quite a stir in New York that quickly reverberated back to the Sears headquarters in Chicago. The chairman of the board and the president called us together to find out what it was all about. They did not blame us, but rather those whose poor judgment had allowed the interview to take place. One of the criticisms we made during the interview was that "the right hand didn't know what the left hand was doing." This was enlarged to indicate that industry—not just Sears, but large corporations in general—had the same problem as government and the Army in communicating with one another so that they could make an integrated effort. This comment made by one of us was blown up to charge that Sears had a very poor management communication system. This unfairly hurt the credibility of the Sears organization.

At Motorola we discovered a unique situation. Motorola was not unionized. In my opinion this was primarily due to the early initiation of a profit-sharing plan participated in by all Motorola employees, both management and labor. The plan was managed in such a way that every Motorola employee felt he was personally contributing to the success of Motorola and, therefore, to the profits in which he shared. When we were at Motorola in 1956, there was a great push by labor to organize all electronics manufacturers. But the Motorola employees turned the organizers away. A recent *Washington Post* article states that unions have not been able to organize a single plant in the 58-year history of Motorola.

While the profit-sharing plan installed by Paul Galvin and his people early in the history of Motorola was probably the primary reason for this labor-management relationship, I believe that there are some other related leadership practices that contributed. For example, Galvin would not allow management to wear coats inside a plant or a plant office. Further, he barred executive dining rooms. Management ate in the same cafeterias with the people who were producing equipment on assembly lines. In one case a production worker came in while I happened to be in Galvin's office. Mr. Galvin explained to him who I was and asked if the worker wanted me to leave. He said no, so I was able to observe the relationship firsthand. This ten-year employee of Motorola needed $10,000 because his wife was being operated on for cancer. Galvin wrote out a personal check for $10,000. The worker said, "I don't know how or when I can repay this." I quote Galvin's answer: "I know you, and I have known you for ten years. I don't have any worry about your returning the money. I know it will be repaid as soon as you can do it." That ended the conversation. I don't know whether the money was repaid, but certainly that man and his family and associates would always be loyal to Galvin and the company.

Although this may have been an unusual occurrence, the friendly relationship that existed between management and the people working on the line really made one feel good to be a part of the organization. For example, Motorola had a "no defect" program to eliminate quality defects. When mistakes were made, notices of the defects were posted along the production line, indicating when and where the mistake was made, what it was, and so forth. But I observed, personally, that management and supervisors avoided chastising the individual. Instead, they tried to help the employee solve the problem.

Galvin was explaining to some of us eating lunch with him that Motorola was going to expand, at least triple, in the next three years and that planning was required to accomplish this effectively and efficiently. I asked him, "Sir, how can you plan on tripling your business in three years when your competitors are having a difficult time maintaining their current level of business?" Galvin's reply was, "Joe, my competitors make decisions by committee. Here at Motorola I make the decisions." I believe my experience at Motorola and elsewhere has indicated that if you allow committees to take over decision making, with the innumerable reviews and delays that happen while attempting to get a unanimous decision, many decisions can be delayed far too long. Galvin was not saying that he didn't listen to the recommendations of others, including those on committees. He was simply saying that when he thought the time for a decision had come, he didn't hesitate. He made the decision while his competitors were probably still reviewing the data. I have thought of his advice many, many times while observing the decision-making process in regard to major recommendations within the Army, the Office of the Secretary of Defense, and elsewhere.

Early on, Motorola became a producer of Sears automobile radios. The Galvins were one of the first to work out an efficient and effective method to place radios in automobiles using the automobile battery. However, Paul Galvin made an early determination that he would allow no buyer to buy more than 49 percent of any one product. This was to prevent that buyer's becoming so strong that it could control Motorola. This policy saved Motorola from much trouble with large buyers such as Sears.

While we were at Motorola, the company was having trouble maintaining its shortwave radios used by state police. To support the state police, Motorola had established depots in each of the forty-eight states, but it was still having trouble keeping more than 50 percent of the radios working. It just could not keep the necessary parts on hand locally. I participated in a group at Motorola that agreed we should test a plan that would centralize parts at a Chicago depot and, using fast communications and transportation, provide the required parts from there to several state police departments. The test proved so successful that it was expanded so that all the state police systems were supported not by what might be called retail depots in each state, but by a centrally managed depot using improved communications and fast transport. This proved very successful and, in fact, in a few months the number of radios on the air increased by 30 percent.

This experience gave me an appreciation of the approach that we initiated later in Vietnam called "inventory in motion." This approach was a better way of supporting an Army weapon system. Instead of flooding the distribution net with so many parts that no one part could be found when the system became inoperable, we went to what is called "direct support" in 1969. This system, like the one at Motorola, has proved that you can obtain greater operability of weapon systems by using fast transport, automation, and communication that are controlled centrally. The "just in time" inventory management concept was not originated recently in Japan as the media would have us believe.

The Executive Program at the University of Chicago in which we were also enrolled was designed to train industrial executives, seventy-five at a time. The results of this program have been exceptional, and admissions have been very competitive. It continues today. Unfortunately, the U.S. Army Ordnance program that combined industry training with the university training ceased about 1960 or 1961.

The university made an exception in my case. I lacked a bachelor's degree, having left college at the end of my second year, but because of my experience I was accepted, although I would be ineligible for the master's degree and would receive a certificate of attendance instead. In the end, the university's Faculty Board decided that my grades and performance were good enough for consideration beyond the certificate of attendance. On their own initiative, toward the end of the course they agreed to consider me as a candidate for a master's degree on a very special selection basis. I would be granted the degree if I passed comprehensive examinations in five major areas. I was the only nonbaccalaureate to receive a master's degree in business administration on our graduation day. This time spent with industry and the University of Chicago proved to be a great step forward in my education and training.

I returned from Chicago to assignment as executive officer to the Chief of Field Services in the Office, Chief of Ordnance. I worked for two old friends and mentors, Generals Hansen and Lynde. I enjoyed the job and worked hard. I think I did all right because when I left to go back to school General Lynde remarked, "Now that Joe's gone, I guess I'll get to run my division."

My assignment as a student at the National War College in 1960 was another major step in my education and a great assignment for me, especially as an ordnance officer. Not many ordnance officers have the opportunity to attend that top military institution. Few logisticians in general get the chance, not because they are considered second class citizens, but because most are assigned to the Industrial College of the Armed Forces instead. Of potential senior officers, more combat officers go to the National War College;

more logistics officers go to the Industrial College. The percentage of officers who attend the National War College and who make the general officer list in the next year or two is especially high.

Once again I discovered that my ability to play ball gave me an advantage in getting along with classmates, even at that age and rank. The National War College always tried to field the best athletic teams practicable to compete with the Industrial College of the Armed Forces, which had a much larger enrollment and somewhat younger students. I was surprised by the rivalry that existed between the two schools. If one school found it had an officer or civilian student who excelled in athletics, he immediately won respect faster, especially since competition between the colleges was more intense at the start of the course. I was fortunate to be able to represent the National War College in baseball, basketball, tennis, and volleyball. Because of sports, I got to know other students more quickly. It was also easier to work with them because of the feeling that we had been friends for some time. This would not have been the same if I had not participated in the athletic competition.

At the National War College I met senior officers of all the armed services as well as top civilians from State, Commerce, and the CIA. The curriculum separated the students into various committees. In participating in the committee work, I also discovered that my knowledge of budgeting, including the Planning, Programming, and Budgeting System (PPBS) recently installed in the Defense Department by Secretary Robert S. McNamara, came in very handy. In fact, I became the budget expert in every committee on which I served, and, frankly, I enjoyed that because it gave me a chance to be of value to others who weren't as well acquainted with the subject. Most combat arms officers were not anxious to accept budget responsibilities.

The education I received at the National War College was very valuable for my future assignments, but the contacts and friendships I made were also extremely useful. I might have had a difficult time establishing the same rapport and understanding with many officers and civilians if we had not been classmates. An example was the friendship that developed between me and Jack McGuire from the State Department. Later, when I was assigned as the senior Army officer dealing with the U.S. embassy in Paris and the French government, the friendship established with McGuire at the National War College made us a team working together for our mutual benefit and for the United States. Normally it would have taken time and care to establish such a relationship between an Army officer and a high-level representative of the embassy. To some degree, the jobs we were doing could have just as easily caused difficulties rather than mutual understanding. There were no difficulties in my dealings with McGuire and later, through him, with Ambassador Charles "Chip" Bohlen.

I want to stress how important attendance at these senior schools is for logisticians. A continuing problem has been the lack of opportunity in the Army for logistics people to study with officers from the combat arms, a problem that goes right through the Army school system all the way up to what's now called the National Defense University. Such classroom integration is important for logisticians because they get to know tomorrow's top combat leaders and to understand their needs and problems. It's also important for combat officers to gain the respect and understanding of logisticians on whom they might someday depend in a combat situation.

CHAPTER 6

# Reorganization of Logistics, 1962

In 1962 Secretary of Defense McNamara instituted a far-reaching reorganization of the services' logistics systems. Although I was not personally involved in the discussions that led to this momentous event, I was intimately involved in its consequences. Before offering my analysis of the reorganization, I believe it appropriate to review briefly the logistics structure within the services as it existed before 1947, when the Defense Department was created by merging the War and Navy Departments and a separate Air Force under a Secretary of Defense.

As an enlisted man and junior officer I served under the Chief of Ordnance, part of the organization of the Chiefs of Technical Services. There was no question in those days about who was responsible for firepower and mobility, including research and development, procurement, production, and field support in the U.S. Army. This responsibility remained, almost exclusively, the mission of the Chief of Ordnance. He commanded his own arsenals, procurement districts, and depots; he did his own contracting with industry; and he trained and managed his own Army ordnance people. He was supervised by the Deputy Chief of Staff for Logistics (the G–4 of the Army), but he alone was responsible for making certain that trained professionals, whose careers he closely managed, adequately supported ordnance weaponry.

The Chief of Ordnance's organization was based on a commodity-related (ammunition, combat vehicles, weapons, etc.) system with a functional breakout within each commodity, such as research and development, acquisition, and field support. After World War II, General Hughes, a former Chief of Ordnance, told a congressional committee that was looking into Army reorganization that "you can draw an organization chart, and you can indicate that you want functionalism at the top, but at each level you need commodity expertise right below it." Hughes went on to explain that when you can have the general function of maintenance, right below it you also need the specific function of maintenance that deals with the particular commodity. With functionalization at the top, then you will see ranged below it commodity/functionalization, commodity/functionalization right down through the structure. As Hughes said, "It's just a matter of who makes the decision as to which way you look at the chart. We have proved to ourselves in the Ordnance Department that first we must know our commodity and from the commodity we derive the functions that pertain to it."

It was not difficult in those days to determine the levels of responsibility required to manage the various logistics commodities and functions, even though each of the seven technical services in the Army had its own system.

During World War II, as can be readily discovered by a review of the Army's official account—the so-called Green Books—the services had many systems for logistic support. The Army had seven technical services, and the Navy had various bureaus. Each one of these logistics services had its own peculiar system of support. Whether their logistics organization was the most effective and efficient possible is another question. However, one of the arguments against a postwar reorganization of the logistics structure was simply that logistics support had worked—victory had been achieved.

When the Defense Department was created in 1947 and the Army Air Forces was split apart from the Army, the Air Force introduced yet another logistics organization. Its Air Force Logistics System did not adopt a structure based upon the Army model, but rather went to an early form of the functional approach with concentration on weapons management. Its primary structure was based upon specific types of aircraft, with functional support activities provided for each aircraft type including major subordinate commands which at the time were called Aircraft Management Activities.

The separate Army, Navy, and Air Force logistics systems continued into the early 1960s, when Secretary McNamara decided in the name of economy and efficiency to impose a standard logistics structure. The reorganization of the services' logistics systems that followed represented his attempt to reshape support activities in the armed forces. He exerted continuous pressure on his own staff and on each of the services to standardize their procedures for logistic support as well as to standardize organizations to implement such support. In the case of the Army the Chiefs of Technical Services were abolished. Responsibility for logistic support was vested in the Deputy Chief of Staff for Logistics for overall supervision and in the Army Materiel Command for the wholesale responsibilities having to do with weapons, research and development, procurement, production, wholesale inventory management, maintenance, and distribution. A similar type of organization was formed within the Navy Department; however, unlike the Army, the Navy retained certain logistics functions in specialty services.

Immediately, the Office of the Secretary of Defense (OSD) and its newly formed Defense Supply Agency, which had taken over most of those common functions formerly under the Quartermaster General of the Army and his counterparts in the other services, came under great pressure to issue standard policies and procedures covering such things as shipment of supplies. OSD caused the first military standard systems to be issued, which established DOD standards that all the services had to meet. Earlier in the 1960s it had implemented a standard Planning, Programming, and Budgeting System (PPBS), which tied in with the military standard systems being promulgated. In the case of the Army, the field organizations were also simultaneously reorganized. Army combat service support units, in the past organized by technical services, were now reorganized upon a functional base. This reorganization was called COSTAR (Combat Support of the Army). It took place throughout the Army, both in management and field activities. It took place not only in the United States and Europe, where I became closely involved, but also in Vietnam, which was just beginning to emerge as a very important part of the Army mission.

The 1962 reorganization solved some of the problems and set the stage for future progress, but it also created some new problems. It overemphasized functional support at the expense of commodity expertise. As a result, we produced a bunch of generalists who had never had grease under their fingernails or knew how to support specific commodities. In peacetime this is no problem because, with time available, skills and expertise can be found. But in wartime we need without delay trained professionals—officers, warrant officers, enlisted troops, and civilians—who know how to support the specific ordnance hardware used by the combat troops. Functional knowledge is not enough. It is not sufficient to have a staff of noncommissioned officers and junior officers who are only generalists, who know only functions; we must begin with personnel trained in specific commodities and then broaden their knowledge to include functional support. When I became the ordnance officer of the 7th Division, I could have had problems because my knowledge was limited to general ammunition supply procedures. I knew how to read the markings on the box and tell how many rounds were in a package. My lack of specific technical knowledge of ammunition and other commodities made me very uncomfortable. I thank God and the Chief of Ordnance to this day that we had efficient and commodity-trained enlisted men and officers. General guidance and support were all that was required of me; those men knew their jobs and did them. Most were not Regular Army men. At one point there were only three Regular officers in all divisions forward of Eighth Army headquarters. Others were almost all experienced reservists who had remained on active duty after World War II and were available for duty in Korea. They were specialists in particular commodities. Most retired after twenty years, and very few of these men, experienced in two wars, were available in Vietnam.

In 1962 we also lost the very important emphasis on commodity career paths for enlisted men and officers. Today, the consensus is that to be successful one must know function. This is very dangerous. If we first train our personnel to know the commodities, they will understand the functional aspects as a natural progression.

One of the major errors made during this reorganization was the decision to eliminate the tech service manuals and catalogs, which had been perfected over the years to provide policies, procedures, and parts catalogs for the logistic support and service of various hardware components and weapon systems. After reorganization new directives, manuals, and the rest had to be drawn up as soon as possible. As a result a great gap was created, which had to be filled quickly when increasing combat activity in Vietnam began to require professional combat service support. This transition from one type of organization, the tech services, to another, functional systems, within the services was one of the basic reasons why the Army, from the early Vietnam period up to 1968, had logistic difficulties beyond those caused by the enemy. Some of the problems, such as cataloging, still continue to exist.

There naturally was strong opposition to both the reorganization and the increased standardization of the services within the Defense Department. Some of this was the initial resistance to be expected in any reorganization, especially when all concerned had not been fully informed of the objectives involved. But beyond this, some serious opposition arose among experienced technical services personnel. They were concerned about what they considered somewhat arbitrary actions taken by McNamara and his immediate staff to achieve the reorganization. They mistakenly believed that the Secretary of Defense would rescind some actions if they could make a persuasive enough case.

Even to this day, serious opposition to the new logistics alignment rears its head on occasion. For example, Richard P. Godwin recently resigned his new job as Under Secretary for Acquisition because he could not get the authority and responsibility he felt he needed across the Defense Department to achieve the objectives established for his position. This is not new. David Packard, in my opinion one of the best Deputy Secretaries we have ever had, did his best to gain service cooperation to standardize logistic support. He stated publicly that one of his reasons for leaving the department was that he could not obtain the cooperation he felt necessary—this in spite of the fact he had earlier indicated publicly that although he had been running into service opposition on some things that needed doing, he could force them to take appropriate action. It turns out that the services merely waited out his determined action.

I was a firsthand witness to some of this opposition. My immediate boss in Europe, where I was stationed during the time of reorganization, was Maj. Gen. Webster Anderson, an outstanding logistician who had been the last Quartermaster General of the Army. He told me that he was going to leave it up to me as his deputy to do the reorganizing of the tech service functions within the COMZ. At the same time, Lt. Gen. William C. Baker, Jr., an engineer who was at that time the Chief of Staff of U.S. Army, Europe, and thus supervised Anderson, strongly opposed the reorganization of the tech services. He told me in no uncertain terms that reorganization was going to "stop at the water's edge," and we were not going to extend it to the European theater.

It was under these opposing directives that we had to reorganize the field units as well as the supply control agencies, which had been maintained by each tech service within the COMZ to manage materiel in Europe for each of their branches. Ironically, although I had earlier fought to retain the ordnance system, I was now the one ordered to reorganize logistics in the COMZ to prove that this reorganization could work in peacetime in Europe. I faced a similar assignment later on in Vietnam, where the reorganization of logistics was still in its transition stage in the field army.

I want to emphasize that, probably as much as anyone in the Army, I recognize the problems that existed in the tech services before 1962. After all, I am one of the few remaining officers who not only was part of the problem—the old tech services—but worked in later years to find a solution. I believe that we have made much progress since 1962 in creating a standard logistics organization throughout the U.S. Army, and I am not fighting the McNamara reorganization. At the same time I am convinced that, if any real meaning exists in the old cliche "lessons learned," we need to avoid repeating the mistakes of the past, including those of 1962.

The McNamara reorganization, at least temporarily, left a very significant mark on Army logistics, particularly in Europe. Unfortunately, immediate action was dictated from the Secretary of Defense level, which caused many actions to be taken without thoughtful consideration. If some of these actions had not been taken, problems could have been avoided. Because most of the Chiefs of Technical Services opposed McNamara on reorganization, McNamara demanded immediate response. Many of the useful policies and procedures that existed throughout each of the tech services were cast aside, thrown out, including the technical manuals and field manuals. It is true that reorganization required some changes, but much of what was in these manuals was still applicable to current materiel. The reorganization had to be based on this same hardware, even though the tech service control of this hardware was being changed.

It is important to note that the existing ordnance organization had been based upon commodity commands as the centers of knowledge, management, and operations for each piece of ordnance hardware. These commands were the key elements that allowed the reorganization to take place. As long as each commodity command could continue to manage its area, the Army could be supported. That is what got us through this very tenuous time. At the same time the new Defense Supply Agency took over most of what had previously been Quartermaster Department functions. The DOD objective was to manage common supply items with a single agency, now called the Defense Logistics Agency (DLA). But the outcome was quite different. The takeover meant a review of each supply item to determine which were common to more than one service, followed by a transfer of those common items to DLA control with the attendant support problems such as budgeting and procurement that have remained constant problems to this day. There is still considerable opposition to the DLA and its functions; many in logistics feel that a number of functions given to the DLA should have been retained by the commodity commands and other agencies.

The effect of COSTAR in its reorganization of the field units became particularly significant when the buildup of the Army in Vietnam began to take place. In Europe and in CONUS we could more easily and with less damage to the system work out the reorganization of tech service units into COSTAR functional-type units. However, during the Army buildup in Vietnam we were placing units that had just been reorganized or had not completed reorganization into the combat zone to support combat units. This made reorganization very difficult and caused some of the logistics problems in the early days of Vietnam. Logistics did not settle down in Vietnam until about the middle of 1968.

In regard to the 1962 reorganization of the tech services, I must pay tribute to two very important people. One is Lt. Gen. John H. Hinrichs, who was the Chief of Ordnance in 1962. When Secretary McNamara called the final meeting on reorganization, he asked if anyone still objected to it. Hinrichs, who it had been rumored was to be the first head of the Army Materiel Command (AMC), felt it necessary to express his continuing opposition. His stand at that meeting probably led to the choice of Maj. Gen. (later General) Frank S. Besson as the first head of AMC. Besson, who was the Chief of Transportation, did not object to the reorganization probably because the Transportation Corps was less affected than the other tech services. Hinrichs, offered a subordinate position, promptly retired. Edgar W. Lancaster, the civilian executive in the Ordnance Corps, whose planning and wise guidance had led to the organization of the corps' commodity commands, also opposed the reorganization. As a consequence, he was relegated to a rather low subordinate position in AMC and, along with many other senior ordnance experts, chose early retirement.

The experiences of General Hinrichs and Mr. Lancaster reflect the fact that the atmosphere at the time of reorganization was not good. The Ordnance Corps and the other tech services were really low on the totem pole. Those who were supporting Secretary McNamara moved out quickly to achieve his objectives. In doing so the Army accomplished much, but we could have achieved even more by using the good parts of the tech services and not throwing out the baby with the bath water. Many very fine people were hurt, and their ability to assist the Army in the future either ceased or was greatly hampered.

On one visit home from Europe in early 1962 I was asked to address the advanced classes at the Ordnance Center and School at Aberdeen Proving Ground. This was immediately after reorganization, and I was to be one of the first senior officers to talk to these young officers. Their entire horizon had been changed by the reorganization just directed by the Secretary of Defense. I met with a dozen or so ordnance general officers to find out what they thought I should talk about in the classes. The consensus was that I should tell the young men that this reorganization would not work and that they could expect further changes so that once again the Ordnance Corps and the other tech services could support the Army the way it should be supported.

I decided not to say that this reorganization would have to be rescinded. In fact, I decided that I would say that we had to make the reorganization work; otherwise, the logistics system and its effectiveness within the Army would be a disaster. I am glad I took this approach because, as the future would show, reorganization was the best thing for the Army. Before the reorganization the Army had seven or eight different logistics systems, each based on a tech service that performed logistic support in its own way. This overall system had worked in the past, but the fact of the matter was that with improvements in transportation, automation, and communication, we had to standardize for the good of all concerned. The tech services were fighting this attempt to standardize because they really believed that since their commodities were different, the structure, policies, and procedures of each tech service needed to be different. In the last analysis the McNamara reorganization had to happen, either in 1962 or some year very soon thereafter.

I want to reiterate that the only lasting problem of the 1962 reorganization is the fact that we threw away a lot of good that the tech services represented. In fact, today we are trying to recall and redo and reinvent many of the policies, practices, and procedures that had already been put into operation by the various tech services. For example, under the former Chiefs of Technical Services, technical intelligence was a high priority. Specialists were trained and organized to take advantage of everything we could learn on the battlefield. The worth of this program was proved when the ordnance technical intelligence units captured German rocket specialists such as Werner von Braun and other outstanding scientists. Many other types of technical intelligence were gathered and promptly put into a system of research and reverse engineering.

In addition, we were always prepared to use enemy equipment when it was captured to supplement troop requirements in the combat zone. Enemy equipment became a source of supply and in many cases provided our own troops with improved capabilities. Many considered the AK-47 Russian assault rifle captured in Vietnam a superior weapon and used it at times when they could get their hands on it. In my own case, as I've already mentioned, my favorite weapon was the Thompson submachine gun. I carried it all during World War II and Korea, although by the time I got to Korea the weapon was no longer standard issue. The same thing happened in Vietnam where I had to use one captured from the enemy. Having that Tommy gun available proved personally valuable in all three wars.

## REORGANIZATION OF LOGISTICS, 1962

The 1962 reorganization also affected logistic services in the Army. Many of us tend to think of logistic support as those functions concerned with supply, transportation, and maintenance. While it is true that these are important functions of logistics, there is another function just as important—logistic services. Before the reorganization, many of the logistic services were under the Quartermaster General; afterward they became the responsibility of the Deputy Chief of Staff for Logistics.

Many changes have occurred since then, including the establishment of the Troop Support Command at Fort Lee, Virginia, but I believe a critical need remains for close attention and supervision of services required by the combat troops. For example, the graves registration and mortuary services do not receive much attention in peacetime, but they are supremely important in wartime. I believe our experience in Vietnam was an excellent illustration of the problems that can be avoided if we are only able to do the job properly. I suspect that there is a lack of understanding of just how fine a job was done by the graves registration and mortuary services. Once the war was over, the attention paid to some of these services lapsed. As a result their capabilities have declined considerably. Recent disasters in peacetime such as the mass suicide of the Jonestown religious cult have required the entire civilian staff of the mortuary and graves registration services to handle them. Major tasks were performed under contract with civilian resources.

There is a requirement to mobilize such specialists immediately upon outbreak of a combat crisis. When working with General Alexander Haig in NATO in later years, I reported that we lacked the capability to bury our dead. Haig, on a visit to the Pentagon a few days later, reported this to the Secretary of Defense, who replied, "That's scandalous." However, he didn't indicate any action would be taken, and I am not sure any action has yet been taken to correct this very significant deficiency. It is a part of the declining capability of combat service support. This same inattention to service has allowed us to become deficient in such materiel as bakery, laundry, and bath equipment. (I understand some of these deficiencies have been provided for in recent modernization programs.)

Other types of combat support services not too often regarded at higher levels in peacetime are refrigeration and air conditioning, bomb disposal, field ranges, laundry and bath, messes, and clothing (including shoes and socks). In combat, especially in winter, these can be very serious service requirements and, like antifreeze, tend to be neglected until all of a sudden they are required. Our experience in Korea indicated the kinds of problems that can occur when we neglect these services in peacetime.

Of course, in looking at these logistic services, we also need to recognize that various items of materiel, even such things as ranges for cooking and clothing for the troops, create a maintenance requirement. We need the capability for shoe repair, for example, and stove maintenance. Now that computers are being used so widely, there is a significant requirement for computer repair all the way down to the forward echelons.

In later decades DOD reorganizations would contain specific objectives for further standardization of logistic support. They would include the continuing troublesome objective of common supply and service support to the extent determined to be effective and efficient. This requirement has been on the books since the days of Secretary McNamara, but its application has been very limited, even during the war in Vietnam. Today there are no specific plans for common supply and service support should we be involved in another crisis. If we were to achieve such commonality in some future contingency, it would likely be on an ad hoc basis—as in Saudi Arabia in 1990 when the Army was appointed executive agent for water supply in the desert—rather than as part of a well-planned operation.

Again, while I believe that reorganization made it possible to improve logistic support to the Army and its soldiers, I definitely believe that some regression has occurred, especially in areas having to do with the management and organization of logistics units, including ordnance. Reorganization has had a bad effect on the officers and enlisted men, who are the backbone of the logistics units involved. I believe that since 1962 we have seen a lessening of that professionalism in technical commodities which is necessary for readiness and sustainability of logistic support in time of emergency. I believe this professionalism to be an absolutely essential part of the deterrence capability necessary to ensure the maintenance of peace.

I have already emphasized the need for commodity know-how. This know-how has decreased day by day in the Army (and possibly in other services) since 1962 because of the shift in emphasis from commodities to function. This lack of basic logistics commodity knowledge is exemplified perhaps best in one very important and costly problem: the failure of all defense logistics activities to ensure that the number of repair parts for weapon system support are only what is needed—no more, no less—to the practical extent possible.

Under the arsenal system that existed during World War II and before, the ordnance arsenals produced trained civilian and military personnel who knew the entire commodity areas of their responsibility, covering primarily firepower, mobility, and communications. This knowledge at the arsenals provided the base for the expansion required during mobilization preparations before Pearl Harbor and the actual mobilization of the armed forces and industry during World War II. Included in this arsenal know-how was a broad experience in maintenance engineering. Trained military and civilian personnel who knew their commodity areas and the maintenance required were readily available. These experts helped to determine the technical procedures and policies for support of weapon systems being developed and produced for field use. They used testing facilities called mop shops (maintenance operating procedures), where newly developed systems were disassembled to determine where the wear and tear would occur in the field. Based on this testing, parts provisioning was established. The determination of repair parts requirements and the proper distribution of repair parts, along with the test equipment and tools required for field maintenance, are the more difficult logistics tasks. Requirements determination policies and procedures were established based on the engineering know-how of the maintenance experts and then followed up with analysis of demand data and consumption data to achieve an efficient and economic field support system.

Before 1962 the various tech services had their own separate catalog for each commodity area. The catalogs contained extremely useful information that helped in deciding spare parts inventories. The Ordnance Corps, for example, had a serviceable, five-volume set of standard nomenclature lists (SNL) covering all ordnance materiel. These manuals, along with manuals for training, operation, supply, and repair, were thrown out when the priority shifted from commodity management to functional management.

Very few weapon systems are totally new; between 40 and 80 percent of the components of each new weapon system are already used in the field. Previous experience with those components makes the job of repair part support much easier because of familiarity. By more effectively using parts already in the system and providing incentives to enlist contractors' support, the cost of repair parts could be reduced 30 to 50 percent. Even more important, we would be better prepared for combat with a realistic parts inventory covered in adequate catalogs. Further, the proponents of reducing combat service support could base their support needs on this reduced inventory. Fewer duplicated spares combined with increased efficiency resulting from the use of better automation, cataloging, transportation, and communications would enable us to improve vastly our readiness capabilities with far less equipment.

Current catalogs, however, are unsatisfactory because of lack of proper description, end item identification, and cross references for substitutability and interoperability.

An official Army history of combat support in Korea summarized the basic supply problems in the combat zone: an oversupply of repair parts and a shortage of critical items.* We had up to 30,000 lines in the authorized stockage list of the 707th Ordnance in the 7th Infantry Division. Ten percent was actually required. By reducing the supply to the 3,000 needed parts, we were able to support the combat troops of the 7th Division more effectively than when we had ten times as much. While we were trying to reform the system in Korea in 1950, the experts at Aberdeen Proving Ground were designing and organizing their "Project 170," which sought to attack the problem on an Army-wide basis.

I would make a 1970 congressional report, *Military Supply Systems: Lessons from the Vietnam Experience,* mandatory reading for everyone who participates in weapon systems acquisition.** It describes the principles and practice of repair parts support as it existed in 1940, 1960, and 1970. I was asked recently by Senator Pete Wilson of the Senate Armed Services Committee if it was true that I had said this House of Representatives report was still valid today and that if the date were changed from 1970 to 1987 it would still be completely applicable. My reply was, "Sir, it is exactly right."

---

*John G. Westover, *Combat Support in Korea* (Washington, D.C.: Government Printing Office, 1987).

**U.S. Congress, House, *Military Supply Systems: Lessons from the Vietnam Experience,* 91st Cong., 2d sess., Oct 70, H. Rpt. 91–1586.

CHAPTER 7

# Europe in the 1960s

After I had finished the National War College course in 1961, I was assigned to the 4th Logistical Command in Verdun, France. I had been informed that I would report to newly promoted Brig. Gen. Ferdinand J. Chesarek, who had himself assumed command of the 4th Log only a couple of weeks earlier. I had never heard of General Chesarek, so I had no idea of what kind of commander he was. I reported in at the beginning of the Berlin crisis. Soviet actions in the early 1960s had led to the crisis, requiring that the theater be reinforced immediately to ensure that U.S. forces in Europe could withstand the pressures coming from the Eastern Bloc.

One of the measures taken in this crisis was to extend the tours of all colonels in Europe. Therefore, when I reported in to become the new Chief of Staff of the 4th Logistical Command, I found that the positions of the Chief of Staff, the Deputy Commander, and the G–4 were all still filled. I immediately in effect became a supernumerary. After some manipulation, the G–4 position was opened for me, and the other colonels were moved into the front office with the Commanding General. The result was that even though I was assigned to the G–4 position, I had three colonels, including my predecessor, supervising G–4 operations. As holder of what was normally the prime logistics job, I was reporting to the commander through three levels below him. I also discovered that General Chesarek, a very dynamic, active commander, more often than not assigned jobs individually to members of the G–4 staff, ordering the results to be reported directly to him. Chesarek would write *C* (for Chesarek) notes giving specific direction for specific actions. I discovered that most of the target dates for these C notes had passed by the time the action was given to the commander.

During my entry discussion with the commander, I found that he perceived me as "somewhat of a prima donna of the Ordnance Corps." He told me rather directly that his command did not need a star, but expected a team player who would cooperate and coordinate with the rest of the command. I later found out that this prima donna idea occurred because the Chief of Ordnance had refused to allow me to come to Europe unless I was guaranteed a top job like the one I had been promised. When the colonels' rotation home was disrupted and the chief heard that I was to be given a secondary task, he refused to allow my orders to be cut for Europe. He told the Army Chief of Staff he had more important assignments for me in the Ordnance Corps, such as at the Automotive Command in Detroit. Completely unknown to me, at one point my orders for Europe were rescinded because I was going to Detroit. (This underscores the power of the Chief of Ordnance in those days.) I only discovered the change in assignment on the day of my departure from Washington when the Ordnance Corps personnel officer told me that my orders for Detroit had been canceled and I was to go to Europe. I never knew that I was not going or that an agreement had been made between the Chief of Ordnance and the Deputy Chief of Staff, Army, that I would get a primary-colonel position in Europe regardless of the Berlin crisis. I assume this is why the nominal staff changes were made upon my arrival.

At any rate I reported to General Chesarek, and after hearing that he did not need a star, I was able to tell him that I had played ball on teams all my life and that I didn't know where the idea came from that I was a prima donna. In fact, I added, I considered myself very fortunate to have been able to attend the National War College and now to have a good assignment in the 4th Logistical Command. After all, I had been placed in the G–4 job, which for the first time moved me from a purely ordnance-oriented assignment to one with responsibilities for logistics across the board.

In this first discussion I suggested to Chesarek that because all the C note items were late and overdue, I would concentrate on getting these tasks carried out on time in the future. If he would assign the tasks directly to me, I would coordinate them within G–4 and the other organizations. If, as chief logistician in a logistics command, I could meet with him at 0800 each day, I added, he could then give me his instructions and guidance. I could report to him on progress that had taken place earlier, and then I could go about getting the logistics job done in and by his logistics organization. (There had been a definite increase in the work load and responsibilities of the 4th Log Command because of the reinforcement of supplies, equipment, and units as a result of the buildup associated with the Berlin crisis.) Chesarek reacted sharply: "I go to the john at 8 o'clock. You can meet with me at 8:30." That ended our first discussion.

On the social side Sug and I had another not-too-happy lesson to learn. At the first reception held after we joined the command, we had our initial opportunity to meet the Chesareks informally. Our first impression—and I emphasize first impression—was not good. We are rather simple people who tend to be quiet and unobtrusive, and the Chesareks tend to be the life of the party. We wound up in a corner of the reception hall so we wouldn't get into people's hair.

We usually pride ourselves on making a quick study of people we meet, but in this case our first impression, fortunately, was completely wrong. We learned quickly that while the Chesareks really enjoyed themselves and vocally and visibly portrayed that enjoyment, they were solid people. It appears, as they later stated, that during our first few weeks and months together, they decided that I was destined for higher rank. They thus tactfully caused us to train ourselves to be ready to provide the social as well as the professional leadership required at the higher rank. They included us in their personal planning for community endeavors, which gave us both some insight into the kinds of problems and objectives that were common in peacetime for leaders in an American overseas community, especially one somewhat isolated from the local communities. They also emphasized that one of our principal objectives would be to try to get the American, French, and German community leaders and people together to lessen the isolation of the Americans. By the time the Chesareks left about nine months later, they had succeeded in opening our eyes to many things that we later found we needed to know.

Even though the Chesareks had told me I was going to be a general, I didn't believe it. Despite the assignment to the National War College, I really had no expectation that I would ever make general officer. On the evening the news came, my wife and I were alone at home doing the supper dishes together. The Chief of Staff of COMZ, Maj. Gen. Charles F. Tank, called and asked, "Is this General Heiser?" I said, "This is Colonel Heiser." He said, "You're wrong, it's General Heiser," and he proceeded to tell me then that I was on the promotable list. I didn't even know there had been a board. I didn't have the slightest inkling. My wife and I literally cried like babies. That's how shocked we were with the news.

The promotion followed swiftly on the heels of a racial incident that, if it had turned out differently, would have certainly knocked me out of all consideration for a flag position. At that time athletic competition between the major commands in Europe was at its height. Senior commanders were going all out to get outstanding athletes assigned to their commands so they could field winning teams. The COMZ was not able to draw many outstanding athletes and was not doing very well in football in the fall of 1961. Nevertheless a football game between the COMZ team and a division from Germany attracted a considerable number of American spectators to the football field at Verdun. COMZ did not put up a good game and was skunked by the opposition. As the COMZ team walked off the field after the game, some fans, unhappy with the their poor performance, began to berate the players as they walked by. A fight started between spectators and players. It soon appeared that the fight was taking on racial overtones because most of the spectators directly involved were blacks and the team was mostly white. One small black fellow seemed to be the ringleader in what was turning into a race riot.

As the senior colonel at the game I was responsible for restoring order, but I was new and not in uniform so that very few people recognized me as the senior officer present. While trying to stop the fighting, I became entangled with people trying to put me out of the fight. Maj. (later Lt. Gen.) Julian W. Becton, Jr., and Sgt. Isaiah Gray came to my rescue. Gray, who was an all-Army player in almost every sport from football to volleyball, literally picked up the ringleader and carried him away from the crowd into the middle of the field. Becton, who was well known, got into the crowd and not only kept me from being hit over the head from behind, but helped me stop the fighting. Their quick action contained an incident that could have escalated into something serious. I am indebted to them, for I would have borne a large share of the responsibility if this incident had exploded into a true race riot. I served with Gray and Becton in Vietnam, among other places, later in my career. I cherish their friendship very much.*

After two months on the job I was moved by General Chesarek to the combined assignments of Deputy Commander and Chief of Staff. The other three colonels had been finally released for duty in the United States. At that time Chesarek, still a brigadier, told me he was going to be transferred to Washington and be promoted. He said he appreciated our teamwork not only in making logistics progress in the COMZ, but in strengthening logistic support across the entire Army as a result of our recommendations to higher echelons. He predicted that he was going to end up in a

---

*Becton has just completed a tour as the director of the Federal Emergency Management Agency (FEMA), having been appointed by President Ronald Reagan when FEMA needed a strong leader. He is now president of Prairie View University in Texas.

four-star position, which he would retain for a year and a half before going into commerce to make a million dollars. Because of what he considered our great teamwork, he promised that as he advanced in grade, he would ensure that I became his deputy every step of the way. When he retired from the four-star billet, it would then be mine to assume.

I listened to this with great interest, but I must say I had no idea how he could be at all sure of what he was talking about. History proved that he knew what it would take to achieve his promotion objectives, and he achieved them. In fact, they were all accomplished between 1962 and 1969, and he did arrange for me to follow him as he moved forward. He never recommended that I go to Vietnam, and in January 1969 he wanted me to leave Vietnam to become his Deputy Commander at AMC. I succeeded in convincing him that I should not be his deputy in this new four-star billet, but that he should get Maj. Gen. Henry Miley in order to strengthen his research and development and procurement areas, those areas in which I did not have as much experience as Miley. It all worked out accordingly. Miley eventually succeeded General Chesarek as the four-star commander in AMC while I became the DCSLOG of the Army.

Chesarek was succeeded by Brig. Gen. Donald G. Grothous as 4th Log commander while I, now on the brigadier general promotion list, was assigned as Chief of Staff and Deputy Commander of COMZ. Despite opposition from U.S. Army, Europe, General Webster Anderson, the COMZ commander, directed that I reorganize the tech service functions within COMZ. We established a supply and maintenance activity at COMZ headquarters in Orleans, France, placing within it the divisions that had previously managed materiel for each of the tech services at supply management activities spread across France and Germany. At the same time we were installing computer programs to handle all commodities and all facets of materiel management while simultaneously reorganizing the field units as USAREUR's part of Project COSTAR, so that we didn't have separate logistic signal, ordnance, engineer, chemical, quartermaster technical service, and transportation units (except those whose task was actual transport), but rather support units that managed all types of materiel. The same type of organization applied to all other functional areas.

In 1963 Secretary McNamara decided that the surface line of communications across France should be at least partially closed down. This was a result of a conversation in which General Curtis LeMay, a top Air Force strategic commander and later Chief of Staff, supposedly told McNamara that "the Air Force has supported itself by air since the beginning of Air Force independence. Why can't the Army do the same?" Of course, no one apparently had informed LeMay or McNamara that while the Air Force moved most of its aircraft repair parts by high-priority air, most of the other support the Air Force needed was moved on the ground through Army lines of communications. This support included food, clothing, construction materials, fuel, munitions, ground equipment, vehicles, and just about everything else. Based upon this false perception, McNamara began a series of actions which minimized surface lines of communications. (Later, in 1966, he ordered the Okinawa support installation, which was in effect the major element of the COMZ for Vietnam, closed. This did not in fact happen, but only because the dynamics of war prevented its closure until 1974.)

Evidently Secretary McNamara had told the President that he could reduce the 1963 Defense Department budget by $10 billion (approximately 15 percent of the defense budget) without harming readiness. As a consequence, we in Europe were ordered to reduce the COMZ budget by $32 million, a program that required closing most of our line of communications activities throughout southwest France. This included the newly completed facilities at Captieux, the most modern ammunition depot in the Army's inventory. It also meant closing down the Port Area Command under our control and three ammunition depots, as well as other important storage, transportation, medical mobilization, and service installations.

We employed over 30,000 French nationals in these installations. We were ordered not to divulge our plans to the French government, telling them only what was necessary. Naturally, news of the effects of these shutdowns on the local French population soon reached Paris and President Charles de Gaulle, who hit the ceiling. In my presence, along with U.S. Ambassador Chip Bohlen, he accused the United States of dirty pool because we were taking unilateral actions that directly affected the French economy and French plans for those areas around our installations.

Under the Status of Forces Agreement (SOFA), we Americans had command of the installations we operated. This was unlike the situation in other allied countries where the U.S. commander was responsible for the operation of the American functions, while the installation remained the responsibility of the commander appointed by the national government involved. In France a French officer was assigned as liaison to the American commander, but he had no command responsibilities. Because de Gaulle felt that we had not played fairly with him and had not kept him informed of our plans to close the French installations, he directed his Ministry of Defense (MOD) to draw up a list of installations that France would demand be returned to French control. Our relationships with the MOD and Minister Pierre Messmer were excellent, and because of these excellent relations, the ministry asked us to nominate the installations we would return to French control. As I recall, we listed nineteen, some of which we had already reduced or relinquished control of. This list was presented by the MOD to de Gaulle. He knew these installations were of very little importance and deduced that the MOD must have obtained its list from the U.S. Army. He told the ministry to draw up its own list and to include important installations.

In addition to our closure of the installations in southwest France, other American actions, such as violations of agreements on air space, were upsetting the French President. By the mid-1960s de Gaulle had become weary of what he considered our country's dominating presence in Europe and France. Therefore, he wanted a close review of the existing SOFA between France and the United States. He had instructed his deputies, including the Minister of Defense, to reverse this "U.S. domination." Among the things to which the French government objected was the continued presence of U.S. installations in France commanded and operated by American commanders.

In the mid-1960s a series of strains began to appear in the relationships between France and its NATO allies. Major strain centered on the specific missions that the U.S. Army and Air Force were carrying out on French territory. Basic to all that occurred during this period was the fact that de Gaulle wanted to raise French prestige and assert his nation's sovereignty. At the same time the Secretary of Defense was intent on reducing the defense budget and, of course, logistics as usual took a low place on the totem pole of priorities. McNamara's continuing doubt that a surface line of communications across France into Germany was essential to the readiness and sustainability of the American forces facing the Warsaw Pact placed an even lower priority on the expenditure of defense funds for this logistics activity. In the negotiations that took place between French and U.S. authorities, this background played a most important part.

The 1963 closure of American facilities, which had been maintained and recently extended in southwest France, was the first step in dismantling the line of communications in Europe. The fact that the planning for this action was kept secret from the French authorities, to the maximum extent practicable, made this an important part of what occurred in the next few years. It became apparent that de Gaulle was going to exact greater authority and demand more control over what France would agree to in its dealings with its allies in NATO, including especially the United States. Negotiations for the renewal of the SOFA in 1965–67 were very difficult and resulted in withdrawing U.S. operations in the communications zone in France. This meant the complete evacuation of all U.S. Army facilities and personnel. As we moved out of France the French government negotiated other agreements with countries such as West Germany, allowing them to use French facilities, some of which had been formerly used by the United States.

Based upon my observations, I believe de Gaulle was not solely responsible for our being forced out of France; Robert McNamara wanted us to get out in order to reduce budget costs, as promised to President Lyndon B. Johnson. De Gaulle unconsciously helped him to carry out his budget objective. It was clear to us in Paris, for example, that the United States would come closer to achieving a renewed SOFA if we agreed to French command of our installations in France. We would operate within agreements under the French command. This was not unique; we were doing this in other countries, including Greece, Turkey, and Spain. But we could not obtain Washington's approval for this change, even though the U.S. Army and Ambassador Bohlen were willing to accept it. State Department channels indicated the negative reply was based not upon its refusal, but on McNamara's refusal to agree to such a change.

As Deputy Commander of the COMZ in 1964 I wrote a personal letter to the then Vice Chief of Staff, General Creighton W. Abrams, indicating that my boss, General Anderson, was retiring and that with his retirement would go valuable knowledge of Army and Defense logistics management. I suggested that he be retained on active duty in Washington to head up a review of the existing logistics system in light of the improvements in transportation, communications, and automation. Anderson would be the best person to ensure modernization of the logistics system using current and future improved logistics tools. He could help create an integrated logistics system that recognized that oceans and distance and time were now lesser obstacles for an Army-wide integrated logistic system.

I later discovered that Abrams accepted my premise that integrated logistics needed to be considered, and he offered the job as deputy head of the review board to Anderson. In the end the review board was formed under Lt. Gen. Frederic J. Brown, who created a task force to work on this project with Maj. Gen. Horace

Bigelow, who for a very few months had been the last Chief of Ordnance, as his deputy. This task force produced what in my opinion is probably one of the best reviews of logistics—the so-called Brown Board Report—ever made. In fact, it set a pattern that is still operational today, some twenty years later. (For my reaction to some of the Brown Board's findings, see Appendix C.)

Among the objectives that I had in mind in suggesting this review was that those things that fell into the category of wholesale logistics operations should be operated and supervised by the wholesale manager, which for the Army is the AMC. Thus AMC would extend its supervision overseas to those wholesale operations that were necessary and appropriate to be done overseas. That would mean that depots and depot maintenance, wherever they were located, would become part of the AMC. AMC would be prepared to train people to operate such wholesale activities. The problems caused by lack of adequately trained people to supervise wholesale operations in theaters of operations that I observed both in Europe and later in other places, including Vietnam, reinforced my opinion.

I had not met General Abrams until the early 1960s, when he commanded an armored division in Europe and I was a colonel in the COMZ. Abrams was to play a very important part in my future career. My first direct personal contact occurred one night when the COMZ-Verdun basketball team played his division team for the championship of U.S. Army, Europe. At halftime I was invited to have a cup of coffee with Abrams, who commanded the post where the game was being played. In passing, I said, "Sir, we are losing right now, but by the end of the game we will have made up the difference, and we will win." Abrams sternly looked me in the eye and said, "Is that so?" and promptly moved away, dismissing me from any further conversation. I thought I had really put my foot in it. I was left with the clear impression that he did not intend to lose. I quickly learned that he didn't intend to lose any game, or anything else, in which he participated. (By the way, we won the championship.)

As a representative of COMZ, I later had several opportunities to brief Abrams when he became corps commander. I also remember one incident when, as the Boy Scouts of America commissioner in France, I attended a Boy Scouts senior leaders' conference in Garmisch, Germany. General Abrams had the floor, and at lunch, without any warning, he called on me, a brigadier general by this time, to ask the blessing. I concentrated very hard on asking God to bless all of us, especially the Boy Scouts of America in Europe. I concentrated so hard on what I was saying that I neglected something essential. When I finished no one said anything, no one sat down, and there was an embarrassing pause, until Brig. Gen. (later Maj. Gen.) Carl O. Turner, the Provost Marshal of Europe, finally said "Amen" for me. Only then did everyone sit down.

During these years I also had to go about my day-to-day business in COMZ. Among the many incidents that taught me something about leadership, two simple ones stand out. One centered on a pool table. I probably attended one of the few schools that offered an athletic letter in table pool, so I have always seriously accepted the notion that pool was a genuine sport. Although not the best in my school, I was pretty good at it, and I got in a lot of practice later as a ballplayer amusing myself in an era that hadn't yet discovered night baseball. On Christmas Day in 1964, I was visiting a unit in COMZ that rarely got a chance to see the brass up close. Going through the day room, I met some soldiers playing pool. One of them invited me to take a shot. I said, "Sure, rack them up and break, and then I'll try putting a couple in." Good fortune was on my side, and I proceeded to run off all fifteen balls. It was just luck, but the men seemed amazed by my perceived skill. I got out of there as quickly as I could before I destroyed this impression of a somewhat senior officer's invincibility. I tell this story to point out again how some ability at sports and a willingness to get out there and play can help a commander at almost any level of command.

In COMZ I also had my first experience with the problem frequently faced by Army leaders in accepting gifts of value. COMZ had a contract for dairy products with a cooperative dairy in Austria. To my knowledge no senior Army person had ever visited this dairy. It happened that near Thanksgiving in 1964 I had accepted a request to make the keynote speech in Berchtesgaden for the Boy Scouts of America in Europe, and it occurred to me that since I was so close to our Austrian contractor, I might combine the visits in one trip. A further thought caused me to suggest that, together with the veterinary staff, we put on a Thanksgiving dinner for the contractor and the families at the Austrian cooperative dairy location. It seems that the cooperative had a famous cowbell that was placed on the lead cow as the herd came down from the mountains to the valley every fall. The dairy wanted to present me with this bell as a token of esteem for the United States. This presented a problem since the bell—made of bronze covered with silk-embroidered leather—was worth several hundred dollars. I was to be presented this bell at the dinner, and yet accepting it would violate the rule against receiving a valuable item. At the same time I didn't want to offend my guests. I avoided any problem by receiving the bell publicly but privately paying for it.

That Thanksgiving dinner was, as far as anyone knew, the first public, official Thanksgiving dinner ever celebrated in Austria. But if I avoided one problem, I still had an embarrassing surprise. None of the approximately 100 guests ate the sweet potatoes. It turns out that they considered sweet potatoes cattle fodder. Everything else went exceedingly well.

After General Anderson retired in 1964, I became acting COMZ commander in his place. General Andrew O'Meara had just arrived in Europe to become CINCUSAREUR (Commander in Chief, U.S. Army, Europe), and soon after I took over the job, he decided to make a one-week visit to COMZ in company with retired General Williston B. Palmer to ascertain what was right and wrong with the COMZ. Palmer had an intimate knowledge of the COMZ because he had planned the original concept. The visit followed in the wake of complaints from O'Meara's staff that COMZ had been managed unsatisfactorily and needed to be straightened out. (Actually, some senior people at USAREUR headquarters resented the fact that COMZ operated all Army logistics in the theater.)

During his opening briefing, O'Meara gave us quite a beating on our supposed poor performance. I responded with a few straightforward facts, stating that COMZ really deserved credit for doing an outstanding job. O'Meara listened, and at the end of my statement he said, "We'll see." His senior aide, a full colonel who had been with O'Meara for over ten years, told me as we left the briefing room that I should be careful in my responses. He was surprised that O'Meara even listened to my coverage of COMZ performance, since it disputed what his staff had told him. In fact, the colonel's exact words were, "In the over ten years that I have been with General O'Meara, I have never heard anyone respond to him like you just did. You are very fortunate to have gotten away with it." I replied simply that I only did what was right and told the truth and that I would be able to back up my words during his tour of the command.

I must say that the week of O'Meara's review of COMZ and its operation proved to be fair and thorough. After it was over he and Palmer both congratulated us on the work we were doing and the way we were doing it. In fact, he told me that he had agreed that a major general should command COMZ only because he did not know me or the work that was being done under my supervision. If he had known then what he knew now, he said, he would have told Washington he didn't need another major general. All they needed to do was to promote Heiser.

I was a brigadier at the time and had served primarily in the past as an ordnance officer. Because of my Ordnance Corps assignments I was not well known throughout the general officer corps of the Army. When Maj. Gen. Robert C. Kyser assumed command of the COMZ, I was reassigned as special assistant to General O'Meara. O'Meara explained to me that, as soon as some changes were made, he intended to make me the commanding general of the 7th Army Support Command, which carried a three-star grade. He promised that I would get my second star. Shortly thereafter I was in O'Meara's office when General Harold K. Johnson, the Army Chief of Staff, called from Washington to say he wanted to reassign me to DCSLOG (Deputy Chief of Staff for Logistics) as Assistant DCSLOG for Readiness. O'Meara said, "I was going to assign Heiser to a three-star slot as Commanding General, 7th Army Support Command. I will agree to your taking Heiser on the DA staff provided you promise me that he will be promoted to major general at the earliest opportunity." I could not hear Johnson's response, but I gather he agreed that he would try to obtain my promotion. I mention this only because I am sure that many officers, like myself, have difficulty in really explaining the promotions they have been fortunate to gain, especially at the general officer level. I was given a rare opportunity to learn how I moved from brigadier to major general. As it turned out, when I arrived in Washington for duty, I learned that Johnson had directed the next promotion board to include my name on the list recommended for promotion. I do not know this to be the actual truth, but I understand that this is what occurred. If it did, I understand that it was one of the very few times such action has ever been taken by a Chief of Staff.

# PART III

# Senior Logistician

CHAPTER 8

# Transition to Vietnam

In January 1966 I returned from COMZ, Europe, to become the assistant to the Deputy Chief of Staff for Logistics, Lt. Gen. Lawrence J. "Big Abe" Lincoln, Jr. On the day I reported in, I met General Abrams, who was now the Vice Chief of Staff, in a receiving line at the State Department. He said that he had been waiting for me and had plenty of work for me. The work was centered on Vietnam, a country still largely unknown to me, although I had learned about the Army's strong interest in that Southeast Asian country the year before.

In 1965 I had visited Washington to coordinate the commitment of materiel and supplies that we badly needed in U.S. Army, Europe. The meetings with the appropriate authorities were successful, and I was feeling good about what I had achieved for the command. While getting my things together before leaving the Bachelor Officer Quarters at Fort Myer, Virginia, however, I was called back to the Pentagon for further discussions. When I arrived, I was ushered into a meeting where plans and decisions were being made on logistic support for a newly ordered operation in South Vietnam. I soon discovered why I was there. The promised support in materiel and supplies for strengthening the European forces was abruptly canceled. We were to get nothing. The plan for Southeast Asia had changed everything, and I was going home to Europe empty-handed. Needless to say, I was very much upset and wished I had never heard of Vietnam. In Europe I had encountered no immediate interest in the advisory forces that had been sent to Southeast Asia.

Looking back over those busy months of the Vietnam buildup in 1966, I know that I did not take time to question why we were in Vietnam. I understood that we were protecting the freedom of the people of South Vietnam from an invasion by the Communist government in the north. To me this was just one further action in a chain that had started in 1950 when President Truman ordered the services into Korea, knowing that such military action would be difficult and costly, to protect South Korea and resist the spread of communism. This was the so-called Truman Doctrine. As a junior officer I had found myself at Korea's Pusan Perimeter because of the Truman decision. I wasn't sure then why I was there, but I had faith in the Commander in Chief. Later I became convinced that we needed to stop the Communist advance at some point in time, and Korea was probably the best point. In my mind Vietnam was simply an extension of this policy to draw the line on Communist advances against the free world. Nothing I saw later caused me to question our presence in Vietnam. On the contrary, I felt strongly that we were on the right track.

In one of my first jobs as Lincoln's assistant, I represented him in a hurriedly called meeting late one evening in General Abrams' office. I was a brigadier, the junior officer in a group of about ten to twelve three- and four-star generals. Abrams was upset. He explained that General William Westmoreland, the commander in Vietnam, had surprised everyone by wiring a request for support that had not been anticipated. You could see that Abrams was upset because he was unable to satisfy this unplanned request from the combat commander. He quickly said that although he didn't like to do it, we had to answer Westmoreland's wire with an emphatic no. He practically dictated the wire. Then he said, "Who's going to prepare it?" Since most of the requested resources were the responsibility of the DCSLOG and since I was clearly the junior officer in the room, everyone looked at me. Abrams said rather roughly, "Heiser, do you understand what I want?" I said, "Yes, sir." Then I added, "However, if we find out that there are some facts that would change the proposed reply, can we come in and give you that information?" He abruptly said, "Heiser, write the damn wire the way I said."

Early the next morning after several of us had worked at the problem all night (including calling Vietnam for information), we reported back to Abrams. I was carrying a butcher-paper chart with some grease-pencil data on it. When everyone was seated, I placed the butcher paper in front of Abrams' desk. He looked at me and said, "What the hell is that?" I replied, "These are some things that I think you might like to know about before you sign the wire." Abrams brusquely asked, "Where the hell is the wire I told you to prepare?" I handed it to him. He read it, asked several questions, and then looked at me and said, "Okay, what have you got there?" as if to say don't waste time. I went through the chart. He asked several questions; then he looked at me and said, "What

## TRANSITION TO VIETNAM

you're telling me is that I'm wrong." I said, "No, sir, I'm not saying you're wrong. I'm just saying that before you sign that wire you should know what I've just shown you on these charts." He said, "Okay, Heiser, write it your own damned way." I already had the rewritten wire prepared. At that moment I was more afraid than I had been all during the night. I picked it up off the table and handed it to him. The look I received was not very kind. I could see myself leaving the Pentagon rather abruptly.

Abrams read my prepared wire, asked several questions, then signed it. With that, we began filing out of his office. Carrying my homemade chart, I was the last to go. As I approached the door, Abrams called, "Joe, wait a minute." He got up from his desk, came around, put his arm around my shoulders, and said, "Don't you ever quit letting me know what you think the facts are." He said further, "I do get mad. Half the time I get mad because I'm really angry at the problem. The other half of the time I'm really not mad. I really want to see how people react under pressure. You saved me from making a bad mistake; don't you ever stop doing it." There was never again a problem between the two of us—in fact, he treated me like a brother.

Abrams had said earlier that I should go out to the Far East to see "what's going on out there." General Lincoln agreed, and so I promptly prepared for a visit to all of the logistics installations in the Far East. I spent approximately three weeks and traveled some 25,000 miles reviewing the situation as best I could as quickly as I could.

The logistical problems we faced in Vietnam were problems that had occurred repeatedly in the past. It must be understood that the Army can easily overload any combat theater's capacity to absorb support, if that support is not carefully controlled. Since 1965 the support buildup for U.S. combat troops in Vietnam had had top priority throughout the Army. Unfortunately, Vietnam was not ready to handle the tremendous load pushed its way. The resulting backup in shipping around Vietnamese ports prompted Washington authorities to give highest priority in 1966 to unloading supplies, some of which had been awaiting discharge for months. This sudden unloading of ships overwhelmed port facilities, depot facilities that were supposed to back up the ports, and the transportation net that was supposed to move the discharged cargo to the designated storage areas. The logistical nightmare was further complicated by the lack of proper communication between CONUS and Vietnam and between port authorities in Vietnam and the designated storage facilities and the lack of inventory accounting. The notorious Saigon "fish market," with its mountains of supplies piled so high that it was difficult to land a helicopter in the area, was just one of the disastrous results of the failure to control support.

The requirement for improved logistic communications and expertise in transportation movement and control was especially apparent in Vietnam in 1966. We tend to assume such things function smoothly, but during the Vietnam buildup they presented problems. Transportation of supplies from the fish market to destined storage locations, for example, was under very poor control en route, making it extremely difficult to assure proper accountability for all the truckloads of cargo. Some cargo was not arriving at destinations because the drivers, mostly local contract personnel, were selling it on the black market. Nobody in authority knew for sure what was going where and when it should arrive.

I quickly learned on my visit that those in authority in Vietnam did not want to admit that we had very poor troop-support supply records and that we could not identify a large part of what we had in Vietnam. We didn't know how much we had, what condition it was in, and what the real requisition level or support objective ought to be. A review of the situation on my first morning in Vietnam in February 1966 told me that if we assumed the requisitions and the objectives were correct, then we were ordering much more than had been authorized and in many cases ordering what we already had on hand. These indications, supported by some quick counts of specific items I made and then compared to what was on the record cards, led me to the immediate conclusion that some fast action was required. In fact, I relayed this conclusion to the authorities at Military Assistance Command, Vietnam (MACV), and its subordinate command, U.S. Army, Vietnam (USARV), before the morning was over.

As a result of my assessment, I was asked to lunch with General Dwight E. Beach, the commander of U.S. Army, Pacific (USARPAC), just prior to his return to Hawaii. Senior officers at MACV and USARPAC had been attempting to get Beach to ask Washington to recall me because I had reported that they didn't know what was going on. Beach wanted to know what I had found. I recited line and verse of what I had been doing between 0600 and 1100 hours that morning. After hearing my story he turned to the USARV people and indicated that they had better let me continue my assessment and make it their business to be sure that I knew what was really going on before I returned to Washington. It quickly became apparent to those who accompanied me on my inspections that I had been correct in my early assessment. Actually,

## TRANSITION TO VIETNAM

my initial assessment had been an understatement. My experience proved that at times you simply have to go out and "kick boxes" yourself to get accurate information.

Upon my return to Washington I reported in to General Lincoln, who promptly picked up the phone and told General Abrams that I was back. Abrams asked that a debrief be set up immediately. In the debrief I went through the situation as I saw it in the Pacific. In particular I emphasized the fact that we had little knowledge of what was being done in inventory management, requisitioning, and the automation of logistics paperwork such as requisitions, due-ins, due-outs, and the rest. I was in the midst of detailing significant facts that I had observed when Abrams interrupted me and said, "In the light of what you are telling me, what do you think about this plan we just approved for General Besson [the AMC commander] to take over Okinawa and put 180 days of supplies there?" I replied, "Sir, I have not heard of such a plan, but I can tell you that if General Besson is going to put more supplies there, I would say at least temporarily this is the wrong thing to do." Abrams said, "I approved his putting 180 days of supplies in." I answered, "Sir, if he puts 180 days of supply there, they will become lost because they don't know what they've got now. Even if he doesn't put in 180 days of supply, but gives them a due-in for those supplies that cannot be shipped, this will worsen the situation. Over one million computer cards are backlogged now because they can't handle them and don't have a system that can do it." I also said that if they were using the Pacific stockage list to determine what should be sent for 180 days, we would be shipping supplies to the Pacific that had no basis for being there. This supply drain could possibly have a bad effect on AMC stockage for CONUS and Europe and elsewhere.

After hearing my reasons for having said this, Abrams turned to Lincoln and said, "Abe, as soon as we finish here, you call Besson and tell him that my approval is withdrawn and no action is to be taken to implement the plan that we approved yesterday."

The debrief then broke up, and Lincoln called Besson with the news. This upset Besson very much; he wanted to know why Abrams had rescinded his approval. Lincoln said, "Heiser's just come back from the Far East. He debriefed Abrams on the situation, and Abrams as a result said cancel the approval." Besson promptly asked that I be prepared to debrief him and his staff at 0700 the next day.

I debriefed Besson and about fifty of his top military and civilian staff. He listened to what I had to say and then turned to his people and asked, "Do any of you know that what Heiser is telling us is a fact?" There was complete silence in the conference room. Finally, one civilian, somewhere near the back of the room, got up and indicated that he had heard something along these lines at some earlier time. At that point Besson ended the meeting and asked me to come to his office. He said that rescinding the approval of the plan for AMC to take over Okinawa disappointed him very much. He asked me if I would go back to General Abrams and say that I agreed with Besson that Abrams should withhold his disapproval long enough for a small team of experts to go out to Okinawa immediately to verify my assessment. I agreed. I might add it was the only thing I could do. Besson didn't know me, and Lincoln didn't know me well; in fact, hardly anyone at the general-officer level in the Department of the Army knew me except General Chesarek, who was not involved in this issue.

I returned to Abrams and said that I had agreed with Besson's request for an on-site review. Abrams made a couple of calls and said, "Okay, there's a small team going to USARPAC—on a reorganization of the headquarters—made up of General [Maj. Gen. Oren E.] Hurlbut and a couple of other logistics officers. I'll agree and send them immediately to Okinawa to spend three to five days there to verify the correctness of your assessment. If they verify it, then the disapproval of the plan stands." As it turned out, Hurlbut and his assistants immediately went to Okinawa, confirmed my opinion, and the plan was disapproved permanently.

This plan was not something drawn up on the spur of the moment by General Besson. It was part of his objective of taking over all Army depot stocks both stateside and overseas. Thus, to put it mildly, I had thrown a monkey wrench into his plan only one day after he had attained approval for what was the very first step of a long-term objective. As a matter of fact, in the letter I had written to the Vice Chief of Staff about retaining General Anderson, I had recommended that, in view of the progress on automation, transportation, and communications, depot management throughout the Army should be under the depot operating command—in short, AMC. AMC had the knowledge, resources, and ability to train people to do a job that was not being done effectively and efficiently anywhere else in the Army. So while I could not concur with the Okinawa plan under the circumstances, I was in favor of what Besson wanted to do.

Abe Lincoln had told me that, as his assistant for readiness, which included transportation, supply, maintenance, and the rest, I should take the responsibility, whenever I thought it appropriate, to deal with the "front office," meaning Generals Johnson and Abrams and Secretary of the Army Stanley R. Resor, and just keep him informed of important activities in my areas of responsibility. Almost immediately Abrams called me to his office to tell me that he wanted to send 500 inspectors general (IGs) over to the Pacific to get the situation that I had reported straightened out quickly. I told him, "Sir, sending 500 IGs would only confirm to some degree what we already know." It would take the best men we had to make an IG inspection, and I could not advise that. Abrams said, "Well we've got to get it straightened out." I said, "Sir, what we need is something like 500 people, both military and civilian, from AMC and CONARC. We need to be sure they know how to make an inventory, from unit records as well as those at depot level. Then they can firm up our knowledge of what the logistics requirements are and what we have on hand against those requirements." Abrams approved the plan and told me to proceed immediately. I quote from his memo of 18 April 1966 to DCSLOG:

As the evolution of our current logistic system continues, a major deficiency is apparent. No one at Headquarters, Department of the Army level takes the overview of the total logistic system. . . . Lack of overall logistic supervision at the Department of the Army level prevents the anticipation and identification of problems that develop between the source and the user. . . . The staff supervision of the entire logistic system is a DCSLOG responsibility.

This began what we called Project Count. It required selection of 500 military and civilians, who were specially trained and sent to Vietnam for six months' temporary duty. The 500 personnel spaces were authorized over and above the theater level at that time. Project Count was followed by Project Counts II through VI and continued for three years.

One of the things that particularly irked General Abrams in the months following my 1966 trip was that push shipments were still being made to Vietnam. For some months Abrams and his staff in Washington had tried to persuade the authorities in Vietnam to cancel or at least suspend shipments. At one of our meetings he asked me, "Why don't we stop the push shipments? How long are we going to let them stand?" I told him that I had tried to persuade those in the theater of operations to put at least a limited hold on shipments that could be verified as excess. I also explained that they were unwilling to do this because they were so unsure of their inventory data. So the push shipments, as well as other requisitioned supplies, continued merrily on their way. I could not get authority at the Department of the Army level to stop the shipments because

I didn't know what should be stopped, and there was always a natural reluctance on the part of those in Washington to seem to stop supporting the fighting soldier with what he says he needs.

Nobody would argue that we should give less than our all to support combat forces, but there are tremendous lessons to be learned from our past experiences in the logistics field. First, we must determine what the real requirements are. If we throw in extra items as safety levels, if we throw in items for improvisation and flexibility, we must be honest about it so that we know what is really required. Second, if we push supplies, we must push to meet actual needs and not overload the theater so it doesn't know what it has or has supplies it doesn't need. Third, we must stress that logistics should be included when the Army speaks and teaches economy of force, especially in centers of learning such as at the Command and General Staff College and other senior institutions. At Fort Leavenworth, for example, they teach the primacy of the principle of economy of force, but they are actually limiting this principle to the combat forces. Leavenworth is combat oriented, and its teachers rarely even consider logistics. When they do, they by and large subscribe to the idea of "mass logistics," that is, "we don't know the logistics requirements, so just load the system (create a 'mass') and, inevitably, what we need will be there." The Army must turn this thinking around and stress the economy of logistics force along with the economy of combat force if it is to ensure the highest level of readiness.

Toward the end of 1967 knowledge of the level of excess supplies that were showing up in Vietnam had begun to exert considerable pressure for action both in the Pentagon and in Congress. The troop buildup phase had about reached its height, and people were now looking at other phases of the operation. It was obvious that there was too much materiel on hand and that it was being stored under such chaotic conditions that an accurate inventory of supplies was impossible. Word was leaked to the Pentagon just before Thanksgiving week that Senator William Proxmire was going to give the Army hell on the floor of the Senate immediately after the holiday for the poor logistics work at the depots in Vietnam. Assistant Secretary of Defense for Installations and Logistics Thomas D. Morris ordered me and the chief logisticians of the other services to meet him at Andrews Air Force Base that evening for a flight to Vietnam where we would determine what we could do about the excess supplies and uncertain storage conditions reported in the press.

This small group traveled in the Vice President's plane with two air crews to conserve time. On arrival in Vietnam we immediately checked out the problem areas that had hit the headlines, including the stockage of supplies at the fish market. While we could not ascertain how many of these supplies, though poorly stored, were surplus, there was no question that the accountability and credibility of any inventory was highly questionable. These conclusions agreed with what I had reported the year before to General Abrams after my first trip to Vietnam. As a result of that earlier trip the Army had initiated corrective action, including Project Count, but the jam of equipment in the port areas had prevented short-term corrective action.

After three days of observations the Morris team verified a range of problems, most of which had already been recognized by those of us immediately concerned with logistic support in Vietnam. Although he knew corrective measures were under way, Morris explained that some highly visible action was necessary to offset the certain congressional reaction if Senator Proxmire made his charges that weekend. On the return flight on Air Force 2, we decided to form a joint services agency to handle coordination of excess supplies in the Pacific. All excesses would be reported to a central control group which, in turn, would make the surplus of one service available to the other services. We decided to call the new group Pacific Utilization and Redistribution Agency (PURA), after considering and rejecting Pacific Utilization and Redistribution Executive (PURE) because of what the press could do with the acronym.

The Secretary of Defense was to designate the Secretary of the Army as Executive Agent and appoint an Army general officer to head PURA. I was sitting across from Tom Morris on the plane when he told me, "You are going to be the project coordinator." He was pointing in my direction, but I looked around to see if he didn't mean someone else. Tom said, "Joe, no sense looking around, I'm pointing at you."

I worked with CINCPAC (Commander in Chief, Pacific) and his staff and established PURA on Okinawa around 1 December. PURA was supported by the 2d Logistical Command and started work at once, although it would not be operational on a semiautomated basis until April 1968 and not fully automated until sometime later. This sounds a lot easier to do than it actually was. It was an interservice operation, but each service had its own system of supply and a separate reporting system. First, we needed to find a way to identify excess items, including their condition and location, and to report the data to PURA in a standard format. PURA had to translate the data into surplus reports distributed to all the services so they could order items they needed. We used standard Federal Stock Numbers (FSNs) when they were available, but in many cases the surplus was identified some other way. PURA thus posed a tremendous communication challenge. We had to ensure that we did not compound the confusion because of incorrect reports, inaccurate data, and missing information.

There was an immediate financial accounting problem. It was only after considerable pressure had been applied that the comptrollers of all services and OSD agreed that surplus items would be handled on a nonreimbursable basis at the field level. We had to create an accurate catalog that could be distributed to all potential users so that when a surplus item in the catalog was requisitioned, the item that was delivered could be depended on. We spent many frustrating days early in this crash program, but between April 1968 and January 1972 the military services presented $2.1 billion worth of surplus to PURA for screening. Of this, $306 million was redistributed in the Pacific and other overseas commands, and $710 million worth of supplies was returned to the CONUS wholesale system. Approximately 48 percent (over $1 billion) of the materiel reported to PURA was reused. The rest was reported to the Department of Defense as surplus and returned to the originating services for disposal.

In the final analysis PURA proved to be a very valuable operation out of which a permanent system for redistributing surplus supplies among the services developed. The system is still in operation in Europe.

Looking back, it sometimes seems that many of the major logistics problems during the early Vietnam years required speedy action and always rose suddenly on weekends. Paul Ignatius, then Assistant Secretary of Defense for Installations and Logistics, called me one Saturday morning in early 1967 wanting to know how many AVCO T-53 engines we had produced for the UH-1 helicopter and their location. This really started some wheels turning, much of it in frustration.

The fact that the Secretary of Defense had been told that there were not enough T-53 engines in Vietnam to support the helicopter fleet had prompted the call. The truth of the matter was that we were not sure how many T-53 engines had been produced, where they were, or in what condition. In those days the engines cost $65,000 each. (They cost five times that now.) After several days of scurrying around, checking with everyone who had a part in the T-53 engine procurement, we were finally able to report that approximately 2,000 engines had been produced, and we had located some 1,400 of them. Half of that number were in the overhaul pipeline somewhere between Vietnam and the Corpus Christi depot in Texas. Approximately 30 to 40 percent of that group were being returned for second- and third-echelon maintenance, which should have been performed in Vietnam, not at Corpus Christi. We accidentally located the other 600 engines in a contract storage facility outside Corpus Christi. They had been placed there sometime earlier because the depot's overhaul line, already full, could not take them. In time the engines had simply dropped out of our asset control system.

At that point the engine repair pipeline was costing $1.16 million a day, while the normal thirteen months each engine spent in the pipeline required $452.4 million worth of spare engines. Through intensive management and use of air transport, the pipeline time was reduced to 6½ months. That meant a reduction in the cost of the pipeline to less than half and provided higher helicopter readiness in Vietnam.

The helicopter engine fiasco was an important incident because it vividly underscored for all of us just how little control we had over supplies in Vietnam. Something had to be done, and out of this experience came the decision to apply the Closed Loop system, which in reality was an extended direct exchange system developed for control of tanks and armored personnel carriers in 1966, to the helicopter engines. We established an authorized level for T–53 engines throughout the system, especially a limit for inoperable units in Vietnam. We then set up a control system that required a direct exchange of one serviceable engine for each unserviceable engine. The credits and debits had to remain in balance or we stopped issuing serviceable engines at the point of control. It has always been a problem to get field units to return unserviceable items for repair so that we could plan an effective depot maintenance program. With Closed Loop we could manage much better. As a result of our success we expanded Closed Loop to other weapons systems and major components. By 1972 we actually had over 500 items in the system.

Even though the Closed Loop system worked very well, people in AMC didn't want it expanded because it required extra management attention. They supported a policy that used the Closed Loop system as long as a major item or component was short—critically short—but they took the item off Closed Loop as soon as the shortage disappeared. As the Assistant DCSLOG and, some years later, as DCSLOG, I had trouble enforcing a policy requiring all critical items to be on Closed Loop, whether or not they were in short supply. I included items that were critical for combat, were very expensive, or had other characteristics that needed the extra management attention of the Closed Loop system. The minute I would divert my attention elsewhere, I found commands taking items off Closed Loop. These decisions were being taken by individual commodity commands and sometimes by minor subordinates within these commands. In the end I had to insist on approval by the two-star general commodity commander for taking anything off Closed Loop. The opposition never really let up, and I found myself defending Closed Loop to the end of my active service.

In my opinion Closed Loop should be a permanent part of the logistics structure in peace or war. I believe it is one of the best ways to achieve effectiveness economically. If we were in business using our own money, I am positive that a significant part of our critical assets would be controlled through Closed Loop. For less critical items we established another system, Special Items Management (SIMS), a system that to some degree continues in existence today.

As automation spreads to more levels in the logistics structure, we must devise special management controls to flag items that are critical because the item is essential for combat or because it is temporarily in short supply. In my experience in Vietnam we established special management items, critical items lists, Commanders Critical Items Lists (CCIL), and Closed Loop lists that were given individual, eyeball attention beyond computer tracking.

CCIL was one of the early logistics successes in Vietnam. It especially satisfied the division and lower-unit commanders. The list was used every day, and individual items on the list got daily command attention, which resulted in increased readiness. Commanders had greater confidence in the system that was supporting them. The positive response to CCIL in Vietnam had been preceded by a similar reaction in Korea, where I learned the great value of having a CCIL at infantry division level, especially when we were so severely short of many items. Even though shortages in the early days of Korea were rampant, there were always some items we especially needed more than others. The CCIL gave a commander a method of setting up a proper priority for those items he needed most.

Staff members at various levels will inevitably disagree with special management item procedures and policies. That is because special items require more eyeballing, and the more we automate, the more objections there will be to special management. However, it is essential that allowance for special management, supported by automated information, be made in all personnel authorizations at all levels of logistics. Otherwise, we will find ourselves unable to support commanders adequately in time of war.

Looking back to my work in the Pentagon in the mid-1960s, I have a vivid recollection of the contrasting leadership qualities exhibited by Generals Johnson and Abrams; Secretary Resor; and the two DCSLOGs, Lincoln and Lt. Gen. Jean E. Engler. Lincoln was a fine man, basically an engineer who wanted to be kept informed only about important matters that he should know about. Following Lincoln's retirement I got to work with Jean Engler. Engler had designed the basic logistics structure during the combat troop buildup in Vietnam, and his tutelage really prepared me for my job in Vietnam.

I was in daily contact with Johnson, Abrams, and Resor, who, I believe, was one of the finest Secretaries of the Army we have ever had. These were critical times with many top-level problems. It is remarkable that these three men worked so well together. As one who knew them intimately, I cannot remember a single incident when they failed to exhibit complete understanding and respect for the judgment and decisions of each other. Yet each in his own way had a significantly different style of leadership.

General Johnson, a very religious man, demonstrated considerable patience in dealing with me and everyone else, even though in many cases problems were not always resolved as well as he would have liked. Yet he never raised his voice; he never cursed—I never even heard him say "hell" or "damn." He had a "praying hands" plaque on the wall behind his desk. In my opinion that plaque and its meaning exemplified his conduct and thinking.

General Abrams, on the other hand, was a more dynamic individual. He had been the commander of the battalion that broke through the wall of Germans around Bastogne in World War II. Later in the town square General Patton presented Abrams with a medal and told the audience that "next to me this is the best damn soldier in the Army." Abrams was brusque and could lose his temper rather quickly. He showed impatience with problems, especially if appropriate action had not been taken in accordance with his direction, or if someone showed a lack of initiative. It took a great deal of courage on the part of staff officers, including general officers, to confront Abrams with an action likely to upset him. You could tell when he was about to "blow" because the back of his neck would get red and his voice would rise to a higher pitch. He cussed like a trooper, but as I look back, I'm not sure that this wasn't his way of praying.

In contrast, Stanley Resor was a mild-mannered man who, to some degree, was more stern than General Johnson. He knew what he was about; if you had briefed him earlier on a subject and later changed your base of data, you quickly found that Resor remembered what you had said before. He would refer to a little blue book behind him on a table and point out the significant difference between what he had been told before and what he was being told now. You had better have an explanation prepared. On the other hand, Resor would always give any staff person the opportunity to state his case. He was actually very easy to talk to. You just had to be sure you knew what you were talking about. If he discovered that someone was trying to pull the wool over his eyes, he would not react directly during the discussion, but following the discussion he would inevitably indicate to his secretary that the person should never brief him again.

All three men had a great influence on me, but I was probably closest to Abrams. I was always impressed by Abrams as a speaker. I remember especially when Secretary Robert F. Froehlke, Resor's successor, called an unusual Saturday morning meeting of about 100 of the Army's "top brass," both military and civilian, at the National War College in 1972. General Abrams attended, sitting quietly in a corner in civilian clothes. He had just returned from command of forces in Vietnam and was awaiting congressional confirmation as Army Chief of Staff. When Froehlke finally asked Abrams if he wanted to say anything, he answered, "Yes, only a few words at this time." I can hear General Abrams' voice rise and say to all those senior officers and civilians, "You're not it; the 'it' is out there." He meant that in the Army, the soldier in the field was the "it," and those of us who were supporting that soldier, regardless of rank, needed to recognize that we were just incidental. This was the first time I heard him discuss "it," the soldier, but I heard him use somewhat the same expression several times later. Even today when I get very enthusiastic about trying to convince my audience, I find myself unconsciously imitating him. I use his favorite expressions without intending to, trying to put my ideas across in the same way he did.

# CHAPTER 9

# War in Vietnam

During World War II Admiral Ernest J. King is alleged to have said, "I don't know what the hell this logistics is that Marshall is always talking about, but I want some of it." It's pretty well known that before the war ended, everyone knew in general terms what this logistics was that General George C. Marshall talked about and that Admiral King had plenty of it. But knowing in general terms what logistics means is not enough. The purpose of this chapter is to relate in specific terms what logisticians did and how they did it in supporting combat forces in Vietnam. Not only did they support American soldiers, but at the height of hostilities they also supported the forces of the governments of South Vietnam, the Republic of Korea, Thailand, Australia, New Zealand, the Philippines, and others.

When General Abrams was assigned to replace General Westmoreland in MACV in 1967, he sent for me and asked me to go with him. When I quickly agreed, he said, "Okay, I'll talk with the Secretary and General Johnson about this tonight and let you know in the morning. You go and make your peace with Sug." The following morning about 0700 he called me in and said, "I've talked with the Secretary and the Chief, and they have indicated that they can't let you go with me now. But they promised me that they would release you for my command as early as possible. So don't unpack your bags." As it turned out, several months later in 1968, while I was on a trip to Japan, I received instructions to report back to Washington immediately because I was going to be assigned to Vietnam.

When I reported back to Washington, General Johnson took me in to see Secretary Resor and gave me my orders: "Joe, you're going over to work with General Abrams. You know the logistics problems we have over there better than anyone. We're looking for you to straighten it out. God bless you." Those were my orders, nothing more, nothing less. When I then reported to General Abe in August 1968, he told me, "Joe, logistics over here in Vietnam is in a hell of a mess. You've got to straighten it out. In fact, if you don't get it straightened out, you will probably be the last senior logistics commander in the U.S. Army, so it's up to you. But I count on you to do the job."

Actually, logistic support to combat units in Vietnam was good, but at the cost of a very high level of waste and inefficiency. Many news stories, accompanied by telling photos, reported the tremendous excesses of material on hand. Although much of the worst of it was behind us by then, as late as August the front page of *Parade* magazine featured a picture of an Army depot at the Saigon fish market that showed stacks and stacks of containers piled without rhyme or reason, suggesting a supply system out of control. The accompanying article, written by Jack Anderson and his assistants, described the waste. In fact, the photograph used on the *Parade* cover was taken in 1967, over a year earlier. I sent Anderson a photo of the fish market taken from the same spot in late 1968 showing greatly improved storage conditions, but never received an acknowledgment. Most of the storage chaos in the fish market area had come about as a result of unloading the great backup of supply ships in previous years, with the attendant dire consequences for storage, inventory, and accountability. As the picture taken in late 1968 demonstrated, we had gotten a handle on at least some of our supply problems, but in fact many other areas of concern remained. In late 1968 thousands of gray boxes full of unknown supplies were still being shipped back from Vietnam to Okinawa for opening and identification.

I served as commander of the 1st Logistical Command. This command was charged with the logistic support for all of Vietnam except those areas being supported by the Navy and some smaller agencies. Counting both military and civilians, there were over 100,000 personnel within the 1st Log. These personnel were spread from the ocean inland to the farthest American front line and from the Mekong Delta all the way up to the border with North Vietnam. Illness had hindered my predecessor's performance. That was one of the reasons why the logistics problem existed. However, that was not by any means the whole story.

As commander of 1st Log at Long Binh I served under the immediate supervision of Lt. Gen. Frank T. Mildren, who was the deputy U.S. Army commander under General Abrams (who held the dual-hatted job of commander of the interservice Military Assistance Command, Vietnam, and of the U.S. Army, Vietnam). In our first meeting General Mildren let me know that he had little or no faith in logisticians and that his choice for the job was not Joe Heiser but a combat officer because our logistics mess didn't require logistics know-how but a dynamic Army commander to get the job done. He was frankly fed up with the mass of surplus supplies that seemed everywhere and was determined to get some kind of control. He had a strong visual reminder of the surplus. Every day when he left his headquarters building he faced a forty-foot-high stack of telephone poles stored directly across from the chopper pad. As he flew in and out of his headquarters, his helicopter had to fly directly over this massive and unchanging pile which became in his mind a symbol of the Army's logistics mess.

Almost every day when we met in the senior officer mess he would quiz me about the damn telephone poles. There wasn't much I could do. We didn't need them; we didn't have anyplace to store them; and we didn't have the means to send them back home. It was difficult to get this across to Mildren (and to many others), but he did get to the heart of the problem. One day he said to me, "If you don't stop all this stuff coming in, I'm going to send a regiment of infantry over to San Francisco and place them around the port, and we'll stop any ship from being loaded." I replied, "Sir, all I need is your support, and we will quickly reduce our stock, item by item, to assure you that we are using good judgment on those things we do stock." Brave words and well intended, but boy, did that pile of poles go down slowly.

This was the beginning of a rather difficult relationship between Mildren and myself. In fact, within the week I had lost my temper in a private discussion with him because he continued to criticize the logistics community for the many problems with surplus supplies. I told him that if he did not want to recognize that some problems could not be solved instantly and allow me time to make corrections, then he should replace me immediately. This did not end the unpleasantness, and I owe a great debt to General Mildren's chief of staff, Maj. Gen. George Mabry, who served on many occasions as the peacemaker. Mildren liked to use the gathering of general officers in the mess to needle the logistics community. As a result most of our meals were not restful, and generally I found myself ready with a retort for the snide remarks. When I looked about ready to let go with a crack, George Mabry, who usually sat next to the boss, would back off from the table and wave a white handkerchief at me as if to signal, "Joe, please don't start a fight."

We had our job cut out for us. We began immediately to halt the supplies that were streaming into Vietnam faster than we could document, store, count, or manage, and in many cases, more than we needed to support the war. I remember vividly the moment when the pell-mell rush of supplies to Vietnam actually began to stop. I arrived one night in September 1968 at the small port of Qui Nhon in search of some vital helicopter parts. The dock area of Qui Nhon was small, less than a city block in length, but it contained what could truthfully be described as a mountain of military supplies. That night-long search for helicopter parts in the midst of that chaos was a personal revelation. I marched off to a nearby shack made of empty packing cases and prepared a message that launched what we called Project Stop See, designed to halt the movement to Vietnam of all supplies that were already surplus. Henceforth, Stop See messages told our people in CONUS and elsewhere that listed supplies, identified by Federal Stock Numbers, were either surplus or unneeded in Vietnam and were not to be shipped under any circumstances. At that time our surplus was estimated at over 2 million tons. In time we had 163,000 FSNs on the Stop See list. Throughout the rest of the war only 3,000 of those prohibited FSNs had to be deleted from the Stop See list. My testimony later before the Government Operations Committee on supply support to Vietnam provided partial data indicating that Stop See prevented $305 million of supplies from being shipped from CONUS to Vietnam and reduced requisitions by $200 million.

For example, at one point in 1968 we had 50,000 electronic repair parts in our authorized stockage list. I knew it was far too many, but I was not sure what we really needed. I asked Maj. Gen. William B. Latta, then Commanding General of the Electronics Command at Fort Monmouth, New Jersey, to send over a select group of experts to help me decide what and how many parts we needed. Bill sent a five-man team, who reviewed the 50,000 lines in the light of their background and our experience in Vietnam. The experts concluded that all we needed was 5,000 lines, almost exactly 10 percent. We immediately took action to reduce the amount on the stockage list and to ship out the excess. Our later experience showed that the reductions of up to 90 percent achieved in Vietnam could be applied throughout the Army's inventory overseas, not just in electronic items, but across the board. Many "insurance items," if needed at all, could be retained in U.S. depots or by their producers.

The Sheridan tank provided another graphic example of how excesses were generated. We knew that some of the divisions and regimental tank companies were to receive the lighter Sheridan M551 to replace heavier tanks. Congress was doubtful about the combat worthiness of the Sheridan, and we tried some innovative measures to ensure adequate combat support. I received a message from DA (Department of the Army) asking my assurance that the M551 would not be allowed to fall short because of a lack of logistic support. I contacted General Besson at AMC and got him to order a silhouette of the M551 placed on every box containing M551 repair parts. I devised a control procedure in which every noncom and officer responsible for M551 parts would be called "Mr. Sheridan"; they were to ensure as near to perfect repair part support as possible. We received approximately 3,000 unique parts to support the Sheridan. In over a year and a half, however, we used barely 300 of those repair parts. I sent a message to the DCSLOG saying, "Look, you sent us far too many parts. When you start distributing the M551 to Europe, don't send them all these parts." Later, when I returned home and became DCSLOG, I asked what had been done about our request. I was told, "Oh, we didn't send them the 3,000 parts." I asked how many they did send and was told, "We sent them only 2,800." After almost two years' experience in Europe, even with the addition of the Shillelagh, only 500 spare parts were ever used.

Col. (later Maj. Gen.) George Patton III played a part in the other aspect of support of the Sheridan M551 tank. The 11th Armored Cavalry Regiment with its M551s under Patton was probably the most mobile, maneuverable unit in Vietnam. Patton was a fine combat commander and cooperated fully to help us provide the best combat support possible to his fast-moving unit. The lessons we learned have had a direct application to the tactics now under development within the Army worldwide. Fundamentally, combat support of a fast-moving tactical combat command requires, above all, constant communications between the combat unit and its support and a fully equipped combat support unit that can move as quickly and as flexibly as the combat unit itself. This approach was demonstrated between units of the 1st Log and the 11th Armored Cavalry at the Michelin Plantation, a large rubber plantation previously managed by the French and in 1968–69 a responsibility of Patton's regiment. We knew exactly where and when the support was required and exactly what was required. As a result Patton and his people received the necessary support at all times.

Later Patton was assigned to AMC with responsibility for readiness. Although disappointed with this assignment, he soon discovered that with his experience as a combat commander, he brought a much-needed expertise to combat support operations geared to increasing readiness of combat units. Really competent combat commanders are very useful to command management of the logistics structure. The top leadership of a logistics organization should be a top logistician; however, I believe that top logisticians need the advice of combat commanders in order to ensure optimum combat support. Patton did a bang-up job for AMC and the Army.

Another issue in Vietnam was disposal of surplus or damaged property. On the very day that my appointment to the 1st Log was announced I got a call from a congressman's office. They told me that in my new job I would be responsible for Property Disposal Office (PDO) operations in Vietnam, and they wanted me to give as much consideration as possible to our allies' desires for equipment in the PDO, since furnishing it to them was as good as using it ourselves. That afternoon a taxi pulled up in front of my home, and the liaison representative of an allied embassy, who had already visited me at the Pentagon asking for privileged rights in PDOs in Vietnam, came to the door asking for my wife. He presented her with a string of pearls wrapped in a beautiful container. I explained to the representative, a retired general, that such a gift was inappropriate.

Nonetheless, I was met at every stop on my trip to Vietnam with at least some token, such as flowers, arranged by the same allied government. One of the first people to seek an appointment with me in Vietnam was the same retired general. He was pressing his request for a privileged relationship at the property disposal agencies within Vietnam. I tried to impress on these allies whenever I met them that there was only one way in which they could get any privileged relationships, and that was through a government-to-government agreement. It was not within my authority to give them any privileges. In fact, agreements with the Vietnamese government required that the South Vietnamese should have first choice of any PDO materiel. I kept insisting on this, and I notified the U.S. embassy of the problem. However, they continued to try to influence me in every way possible. Needless to say, they never succeeded.

That kind of competition for PDO materiel existed in our relationship with the Korean, Philippine, Republic of China, and even the Singapore governments. In my absence upcountry expensive gifts would be delivered to my office. I told my staff to turn them in to the appropriate place; I didn't want anything to do with them. The Singaporese representatives were seeking PDO privileges, but they were also offering a location in Singapore where we could stage PDO sales. The offer of a sales location in Singapore, where anyone who was authorized could bid on materiel, sounded like an upright proposition. It was investigated by the Army, and the State Department determined that it was appropriate. We eventually did open a PDO yard in Singapore for sales purposes. As far as I could determine, there were no gifts involved.

The Taiwan Maintenance Activity grew out of PDO salvage operations. When Taiwanese authorities asked that we visit their logistics activities, General Abe told me to take his T–39 and make a weekend

WAR IN VIETNAM                                                                 147

tour. I was taken through various activities, including an automotive rebuild shop in a central part of Taiwan. As we were being led through this tour I noticed a group of jeeps off to one side. Pointing to them, I said, "Aren't they M151 jeeps?" The Taiwanese officers answered, "Yes, sir." I said, "Well, I know you all are getting M38 jeeps in your military aid program, but I didn't know you were getting the new M151s." They told me the jeeps were not coming from the United States. "We have rebuilt these from carcasses that we got out of your property disposal office yards in Vietnam."

We put damaged jeeps and other damaged equipment into our PDO whenever repair was economically impracticable. The guidelines covering disposal were based upon the cost of transportation back to the United States, or wherever the repair or rebuild was to be performed, plus the cost of repair. If this total cost exceeded what had been determined as economically feasible, then the equipment went into property disposal. We had arrangements with allies such as Taiwan and others to alert their representatives to what went into the PDO. If they saw a damaged unit that was on their approved military aid program, they could mark it and then move it by their own transport to their own rebuild facility and use the item as an asset against their aid program. Taiwan used its own LSTs to pick up claimed equipment from our PDO and move it to Taiwan for rebuild. That's how these M151 jeeps ended up at the shop in Taiwan.

They told me it cost $450 to rebuild each jeep. I said, "That's great for you all, but we could both gain from this." Thus began a discussion of what kind of rebuild they could do for the U.S. Army. General Chesarek, then the AMC commander, and I made a visit back to the Far East in 1969 after I became DCSLOG. During discussions en route throughout the theater on a special mission aircraft, we talked about setting up a rebuild facility for U.S. support in Taiwan, an arrangement that was immediately welcomed by the Taiwanese authorities. On our way back to the United States through Hawaii, we agreed that in order to get USARPAC agreement we would have to convince General Ralph E. Haines, the USARPAC commander, and his staff that AMC should be allowed directly to command and supervise this proposed activity in Taiwan. We sent a message to Haines asking that he meet with us on board the aircraft when we landed in Hawaii so that we could propose this agreement with USARPAC. Earlier as Vice Chief of Staff in Washington, Haines had known that USARPAC had difficulty supervising depot operations in the Far East, especially maintenance. Chesarek and I were convinced that if we could get Haines to agree in person first, then we would not get the staff opposition that was otherwise likely to occur at USARPAC. It worked out exactly as we planned.

This maintenance management turned out to be one of the finest logistic actions taken by the Army during the Far East operation. We arranged a multiyear contract with Taiwan under which we supplied supervision and certain repair equipment for the rebuilding of specific items from Vietnam such as jeeps, armored personnel carriers, and tanks. One of the provisions of the contract provided for a direct labor cost of 57 cents an hour. This contrasted with the $12 an hour we had been paying in the United States. These contrasting figures, when combined with the lower transportation cost, make it easy to understand why many items previously consigned to property disposal were now retained for rebuild in Taiwan. This saved us much equipment and many dollars.

As a result of the production coming out of Taiwan we were able to reduce significantly shipment of new equipment from the United States to Vietnam. Instead, we used this new equipment to outfit Reserve units in the United States and to begin building up the readiness of our units in Germany and elsewhere. In fact, a few years later, after the United States began to withdraw from Vietnam, congressional committees immediately said that now we could stop sending new equipment to Vietnam and use it in other places. I had to explain to these committees that in actuality such action had already started in 1969 and therefore the reduction in shipments in 1972 and 1973 would not be nearly as dramatic as they might expect. The Taiwan Maintenance Activity is probably one of the most successful, largely unknown logistics operations that occurred in the Far East. It should remind us of the importance of recognizing capabilities that exist wherever they happen to be.

An argument might be advanced that the 1st Logistical Command in Vietnam had four support commands responsible for each of the four regions of Da Nang, Qui Nhon, Cam Ranh Bay, and Saigon. That was correct, but in reality these support commands, although a part of the 1st Log, were, in a true sense, corps support commands. Each one of them had direct responsibility to support the combat corps in its region. Because of the organization and terrain in Vietnam, each of the four support commands was an "island" in itself and operated independently of each other under the command and control of 1st Log. Any interaction between them was the result of direct intervention by the 1st Log. This organization forced the 1st Log commander to be a traveling commander. I found myself spending 80 percent of my time coordinating operations in one or more of the support commands depending upon what was occurring. I did most of my paperwork at headquarters in the middle of the night. It was essential that I communicate in person with each combat commander and each commander of the support commands because of the logistics management environment in which we existed.

For example, MACV was told in January 1969 that we were "getting out of Vietnam." Therefore, we had to move out all the materiel we could—something over 1 million short tons—that was not absolutely needed to support the combat troops who were fighting at that time, and, as combat troops were withdrawn, the support no longer required also had to be evacuated. To accomplish this task, I had to coordinate timed goals for each of the support commands.

Fortunately for us, we had no particular problems with the enemy before our supplies were on the ground and our facilities were in place in Vietnam. But once supply and maintenance activities were in operation, the whole operation was subject to enemy attack. In future theaters of operations, if the enemy can attack supply depots on land or supply routes by sea, an integrated supply system must be part of an integrated defense against enemy attacks.

In late 1968, partly as a result of its defeat in the Tet offensive, the enemy had shifted a great deal of its offensive to destruction of U.S. and allied logistic support capability to avoid direct contact with our combat forces. This was an appropriate tactic for the enemy leadership because our logistics capability in Vietnam was stretched over a 10,000- to 15,000-mile supply route. As a result logistics troops not only had to provide supplies to the combat forces, but also had to defend stores and facilities. The enemy attacked both static targets, such as ammunition and POL dumps, and moving targets along the entire supply route. The limited roadways in Vietnam were choice enemy targets for ambushes of our convoys. Their attacks increased casualties among logistics personnel. The policy also caused us to divert time to combat preparations rather than full-time concentration on logistic functions. Combat operations in defense of logistic support became a regular part of logistics planning. During this period General Abrams asked me if I could make temporary use of an infantry commander who had been sent to Vietnam to take over a division but could not be so assigned for several months. I quickly accepted because I could see an excellent spot to use this combat commander as the logistics command deputy, concentrating on logistics self-defense. This is how we obtained the most valuable assistance of Maj. Gen. Lloyd Ramsey. After a few months he became commander of the Americal Division and later returned home to become Provost Marshal of the United States Army.

## The Logistics Offensive

I believe that in later testimony before Congress I accurately summarized the logistical difficulties in Vietnam between 1965 and 1968. For more than three years supply support was relatively uncontrolled. The zeal and energy and money that went into the effort to equip and supply U.S. forces in Vietnam generated mountainous new procurements, choked supply lines, overburdened transportation systems, and, for a time, caused complete loss of control at depots in Vietnam. Congress concluded that supply support in Vietnam had been a truly remarkable achievement, but the question had to be asked: Did it entail unnecessary, hence avoidable, costs? My answer was, based on the known facts, yes. As Chairman Chet Holifield and his colleagues on the House Government Operations Committee put it in their report, "Supply support to Vietnam was at once a demonstration of superb performance and appalling waste."*

When I arrived in Vietnam I already knew that the Army and DOD needed to move out quickly to solve the problems that the General Accounting Office and we ourselves had reported to Congress. The mood on Capitol Hill was that if we did not take action, they would. Responding to the challenge, the Army, in cooperation with Congress, the GAO, OSD, and the other services, began in 1968 a program called the Logistics Offensive (so named by General Abrams in Vietnam in early 1969) to optimize combat readiness while reducing the cost of providing logistic support. Some elements of the Logistics Offensive were based on procedures that had been initiated earlier. But by and large it was given its impulse, its motivation, by Generals Abrams and Mildren. Its practical aspects created logistics control. For Abrams, it resembled an Army combat offensive against the enemy. In this case the enemy was not only North Vietnam, but also our own errors and omissions.

I recall a conference I recently had with a very senior logistician in OSD who maintained that we began an era of substituting scientific analysis for vital logistic support when Robert McNamara became Secretary of Defense. He recommended strongly that we get back to what he called mass logistics, especially in wartime. He cited what he called the greatest single principle of logistics—the remark of Confederate General Nathan Bedford Forrest that "the secret of success is to get there firstest with the mostest."

---

*U.S. Congress, House, *Military Supply Systems: Lessons from the Vietnam Experience*, 91st Cong., 2d sess., Oct 1970, p. 3.

I contend that this philosophy created the logistics pileup we found in Vietnam in 1968. Every time I've heard this quote from Forrest it has been applied to logistics, and it has been used to justify many things that we logisticians did in the past. In fact, I read somewhere that "firstest with the mostest" had become a principle of logistics. Well, this angered me because, when I became the 1st Log commander, one of the first things I noticed was that the motto of the 1st Log was, "First with the most." Here I was in the midst of mountains of stuff—almost 2 million tons—of which we could identify only about a third. I said in my first staff meeting, "The guy who uses that motto from now on is going to be court-martialed. The motto is 'First,' period. 'With the most' I want taken off everything that anybody's got it on." For years now I've been concerned about this psychological block to good, efficient logistic support. General Forrest's actual reference was to getting there first with the most men, not supplies.

In my forty-eight years in defense logistics, seven in combat zones in three different wars, I've faced many different, serious logistics problems. In each war, because supplies were low or nonexistent or could not be located, we lost critical time getting the support required by the combat troops. The worst situation is to arrive at combat with an excess of noncritical items and a shortage of critical items. We must accept the fact that even the most carefully conceived logistical contingency plans fail to prepare us for the chaotic environment that can occur in battle. On the beaches of Normandy, for example, the freak weather caused considerable confusion when we often had to unload supplies in deep water under fire. As a result we often didn't know what we had or where it was. Needed critical items were probably on the beaches in front of our eyes. The beaches were loaded with a lot of stuff. I mean "stuff," because we received unidentified items and did not or could not properly inventory them. All across Europe identifying stock on hand in the combat zone was a problem, making it necessary to request rush shipments of supplies that were probably available. We managed to oversupply our troops in Europe in spite of losing 24 million tons of shipping to enemy submarines and even returning still-loaded ships to the United States.

This same oversupply situation prevailed in Vietnam when I was assigned to the 1st Logistical Command in 1968. Oversupply is easy to do, when you consider that we finally achieved an airlift rate from CONUS of 20,000 tons a month. For five years we struggled to determine what we had on shore in Vietnam. By that time too much of it was left for the North Vietnamese. I hope they are still trying to sort it out!

The Logistics Offensive in Vietnam and subsequently in the U.S. Army as a whole was a command management attempt to restore a degree of efficiency and increase combat readiness. We had impressive results, reducing the $20 billion Army budget by $9.3 billion in three years. Most important, the Logistics Offensive also provided greater logistics readiness Army-wide in 1972 than we had in 1968, including the combat zone in Vietnam, with less consumption of all types of resources. Between June 1969 and June 1970 we reduced stockage on lists in the overseas theaters from 1,063,000 items to 510,000 (a reduction of almost 50 percent).

No commander or manager of any kind—military, civilian, commercial, or industrial—can get the job done without some form of management by objectives. I am not talking about the formal theoretical approach as is taught by some universities. In fact, as an adjunct professor at several universities, I taught management by objectives theory and its practical applications. I do not believe that all the formal relationships and reports frequently prescribed are necessary. That type of overly elaborate structure is what has caused some people to object to management by objectives. I believe in a pragmatic approach to the problem of command management. Goals must be established, and resources must be allocated to attain targeted objectives within a specified period of time.

Management by objectives is about very basic, logical elements of getting something done. The Logistics Offensive was an attempt to establish management by objectives—over two hundred—and yet never once was management by objectives mentioned as such. If it had been, it would have caused those working with me to misunderstand and perhaps in some cases fail to cooperate as enthusiastically as they did.

The Logistics Offensive met all the classic requirements of management by objectives. It had a timed goal with allocated resources and with periodic review. The reviews in most cases were made using graphs with lines that indicated what was required versus what was accomplished. This approach made such reviews very simple and easy to assess. I believe that this type of command management must exist in order to determine where we want to go and how well we're getting there.

The project called Inventory in Motion, initiated in 1968–69 in the combat zone and still in use in the Army, became probably one of the most widely effective aspects of the Logistics Offensive. Inventory in Motion, a revitalized supply management program, minimized the requirement for large stock levels at immobile depot activities in the theater of operations. Integrated supply and transportation planning, real control of in-transit stocks, and more intensified management yielded a rapid resupply response with smaller inventories and with reduced static stocks on the ground. Today in industry and commerce this Army concept is hailed as "just-in-time" inventory, a technique that some claim we learned from the Japanese in the 1980s.

Inventory in Motion requires keeping a strictly controlled part of the inventory—items of supply, both serviceable and unserviceable—in transit. During our early days in Vietnam plans called for highly centralized command and control of transportation movements. This was appropriate in theory, but as the war developed, with each corps area becoming both a tactical as well as a logistical island unto itself, it became evident that decentralization to a regional transportation movement system with regional support agencies was best. This decentralization did not come easily because the people at MACV headquarters were still planning, and to some extent had already assumed, a central command and control of transportation. It took some time and goodwill finally to decentralize. The final decentralization of traffic management to the regional areas in support of each of the support commands under the 1st Logistical Command worked out very effectively. Each of the regions had its own problems of transportation movement. For example, movement in and around Saigon was very complex and difficult because of the maze of traffic. At one time we had to forbid military transport's use of the center of Saigon during daylight hours, scheduling such transportation instead for the middle of the night.

These schedules underscored another problem not evident to those not closely involved. South Vietnam was a sovereign nation, jealous of its prerogatives, especially since the United States had so many forces within its borders. To some degree the Vietnamese resented our taking control of their highway system with our increased military traffic. It became a serious problem to negotiate transportation movement plans in each of the regions.

The roads were not very good, although our engineers had done considerable work to improve them. The situation in the delta was different from that in the area around Saigon and the territory toward Cambodia. The area around Cam Ranh Bay had very limited roads to carry the supplies, services, and men required. In fact, Cam Ranh itself was an island which resembled a sandy desert. Qui Nhon was different still from the others because of the likelihood of enemy attack not only in Qui Nhon itself but also on the route through the An Khe Pass toward Pleiku and beyond. The situation in I Corps around Da Nang was even more complicated. There was a large concentration of U.S. Marine Corps, U.S. Navy, ARVN (Army of the Republic of Vietnam), and U.S. Army units, plus other agencies, centered in the area. The Navy was responsible for port operations and for support of the marines and the Navy. The result was considerable duplication and layering of supplies in the I Corps.

In regard to transportation in Vietnam, probably the most important aspect for supply and the rest of the logistics functions was what we called the Logistics Intelligence File (LIF). We devised this file to gather all the information we needed concerning inventory that was in motion. We had to know what it was, where it was, how much there was, what condition it was in, and what its schedule was so that appropriate management plans could be made for each shipment. We listed each item by Federal Stock Number, not in generic tons. I repeat, by FSN, not simply in tons. In order to really manage Inventory in Motion, we needed to know specifically what the inventory was. With the help of the Logistics Control Office, Pacific (LCOP), in San Francisco, we began to gather all the logistic intelligence we could find. We filled the information voids until gradually we created the automated Logistics Intelligence File, which enabled us to manage, for the first time, the supplies that really were in motion. We concentrated on supplies in motion to Vietnam; then we spread out to supplies in the rest of the Pacific. (Today, we have a Logistics Intelligence File that covers Inventory in Motion around the entire Army.)

To be effective, this inventory of supplies in motion required complete integration of supply data and maintenance and logistics transportation data so that we could know everything we needed to make logistics decisions. The greater the crisis, the more this kind of information was required. I believe that the creation of this Logistics Intelligence File was one of the finest achievements of our logistics effort in Vietnam. The LIF could not have functioned without automation. Progress in modern, high-speed transportation and supply management could only be realized across the entire Army when combined with modern, sophisticated automation and communications. (Although we always assumed that available communications in Vietnam would meet logistics needs, there were actually many delays in transmission, especially in a crisis.)

Too often in the past we did not keep descriptive accounts of inventory in transit, even though we came to recognize the great cost attached to supply in the military pipeline. We knew only such things as "general cargo," expressed in cubage or tonnage. But an accurate Logistics Intelligence File, which identified specific items

WAR IN VIETNAM                                                                 155

in the inventory in transit—in supply ships and aircraft—allowed the consignee to anticipate receipt of those supplies as the shipper dropped them from his inventory. In some cases we just don't function in war the way we're trained in peace, particularly in the area of maintenance. In wartime we generally don't repair in the forward zones, we replace—the farther forward and the greater the combat intensity, the more we do this. The burden, therefore, is placed not upon the mechanic, but upon supply and the effectiveness of supply. In Vietnam we maintained the highest level of combat effectiveness that has ever been achieved (96 to 97 percent of all ground weaponry was operationally ready, for example). That wasn't primarily because of maintenance, although maintenance was good. It was more the result of the resupply and replacement program. With improved communications and air transportation and with the elimination of the multiple supply depots that were typical in the past, logistics units could be designed with a degree of mobility comparable to the forces they supported.

By 1969 adoption of simplified supply procedures and greater selectivity for stockage reduced the amount of supplies in the theater. Controlled and standardized authorized stockage lists (ASLs) and prescribed load lists (PLLs) contributed to efficiency. Theater authorized stockage lists (TASLs) were limited to items consumed on a recurring basis. Other items used less frequently were provided through rapid transport from sources outside the combat zone on an expedited basis similar to Red Ball procedures.

Still, some forward maintenance remained necessary, and another major innovation in the Logistics Offensive was the use of mobile maintenance support teams capable of quick reaction to accomplish critical repairs and component replacement. This allowed greater flexibility in the scope of maintenance performed at each level. Inherent in this system was the maximizing of module maintenance, replacing components rather than repairing individual parts at the front lines. Expanded use of Closed Loop and direct exchange procedures provided visibility and control of all intensively managed items that were critical to combat effectiveness and economic use of resources. Standard software and integrated hardware that met command management requirements were used to provide logistics intelligence for proper and timely decisions.

Although overstocks and confused supply conditions were probably unavoidable in earlier conflicts, there was no excuse in Vietnam by 1969. Improved communications, transportation, and computer capability, all controlled by improved command management techniques, provided the logistics intelligence required so that the items in transit could actually be accounted for better than supplies on the ground in the combat zone. For example, instead of placing several hundred thousand tons of ammunition in open storage in Vietnam, where it presented a very attractive target to the enemy, we subtracted the amount flowing through the pipeline from CONUS into the theater from the amount on the ground. When ammunition consumption went up or when the enemy destroyed stocks on the ground, the combat commander could still be supported because the Logistics Intelligence File told the logistics commander how much to ship to the combat commander. This same technique was used to supply petroleum. We never had more than thirty days of fuel supply stored in Vietnam.

We had begun this project in late 1968 by reducing the stockage objective for ammunition. We were maintaining nearly 300,000 tons of ammunition on the ground, and we had seen over 100,000 tons destroyed by the enemy and by unsafe practices within a one-month period. At any given time we also had an average of over thirty ships, each approximately 6,000 to 10,000 tons, transporting ammunition between the continental United States and Vietnam. We previously did not pick up control of any of this ammunition until it had been unloaded and stored in depots in Vietnam. Based on our improved knowledge, through the Logistics Intelligence File, of what these ships were carrying, we decided that we could now rely on the ammunition in transit to lower the amount of ammunition stored on the ground in Vietnam, thus greatly reducing depot storage and security requirements. With General Abrams' approval we cut this stockpile to below 150,000 tons. The cut did not reduce the availability of ammunition supply to the combat forces. In fact, it actually increased combat support effectiveness and combat readiness. It did, however, reduce inventory management problems and the military manpower needed to guard what was now less than half as much ammunition on the ground. In the end we had better control of ammunition because we knew what was on each ship approaching Vietnam, and we could then divert a ship to the port nearest where we needed that particular kind of ammunition. This one action reduced the Class V ammunition pipeline by approximately 60 percent, or over $1 billion in costs.

The question arises: what if the enemy had sea power, such as submarines, or air power that could destroy ships at sea or aircraft in the air? In other words was the war in Vietnam unique so that it would be dangerous to apply these lessons across the board? The answer is an emphatic "No." In the first place, if the enemy has air power, it would be easier to attack immobile logistics inventories on the ground than at sea. Further, several sappers alone can destroy large inventories in open storage in the combat zone.

But Inventory in Motion did not and cannot justify taking a complacent approach to logistics. This system calls for a high degree of sophisticated logistics management. If the enemy has the capability to destroy supplies in transit, this capability must be assessed. Proper action must be taken to compensate for his aggressiveness. That is the purpose of a safety level. Although the stockage objective is determined routinely, a "management level" must also be established that provides for an appropriate amount in static storage based upon the environment. This management level must have upper and lower limits within which the inventory will be maintained. I really do not believe that one can say that the experience gained in the use of Inventory in Motion in Vietnam is unique to that combat environment.

Essential to Inventory in Motion was continuous asset control through the coordination of AMC, particularly that command's Logistics Control Office, Pacific, and the many logistics agencies in U.S. Army, Pacific, including those in Vietnam. (This continuous control in any combat support situation is, and must continue to be, maintained so that the item with its Federal Stock Number and its transportation documentation can be followed from the time it enters the pipeline until it is received by the consignee, particularly at the aerial transfer points or seaports.) The cooperation and coordination of such agencies as the Transportation Command, the Military Airlift Command, the Military Traffic Management and Terminal Service (MTMTS), the Military Sea Transportation Service (MSTS), and the transfer management agencies involved played a very important part. The establishment of the 1st Log's logistical intelligence file at the LCOP in San Francisco provided the keystone for this entire system. The maintenance of this logistics intelligence at every level of control provided the logistics system with the tools vitally necessary to facilitate proper planning and, therefore, to operate the logistics system effectively and efficiently. This kind of agency was essential for wartime control. In World War II the Overseas Supply Division did the job, but it was disestablished in the early 1960s as a budget savings.

For too long we tolerated lack of proper planning for the receipt of supplies through a port into a depot. Too often operators at a depot were surprised by what they found arriving in their receiving yard. With the advent of Inventory in Motion, this was no longer the case. We knew at all times where the supplies were, and their arrival at the depot did not come as a surprise to the depot operator.

This recital should not leave the impression that the Logistics Offensive was trouble free. When the 1st Logistical Command began the operation in 1968, it applied only to those agencies under its control. Other logistics agencies, including those used by the medics, engineers, aviation and signal units, and organizations in other services, took advantage of those elements of the Logistics Offensive when they found them useful. None of them used all the elements of our Logistics Offensive; some, in fact, used the 1st Log for things they couldn't get through their own supply channels. In a way they were double dipping on the resources of the United States.

Throughout the war medical logistics operated independently in the Far East, and it seriously overloaded the depots it shared with the 1st and 2d Logistical Commands in Vietnam, Japan, and Okinawa. On Okinawa, for example, the 2d Logistical Command found it difficult to convince the medics that they had to reduce their supplies, which were overwhelming the shared facilities and interrupting traffic patterns in the Okinawa depots. In my view the separate medical logistics system should have been integrated with the rest of Army logistics, providing that capable Medical Service Corps personnel—the corps has always had exceptionally able logistics people—were assigned to help run it.

It is essential to have a single source for support of the combat soldier. There may be exceptions to this rule, but I think we should guard very carefully the approval of exceptions. Aside from the separate logistical support agencies, at one point in Vietnam we counted twenty-three different pipelines coming into the country under control of different headquarters. For example, the 25th Division, which had been based in Hawaii, sent some of its requisitions back to Hawaii and was getting stuff in from Hawaii from people who weren't supposed to be supporting the division at all. Because they knew one another, they were going to take care of the boys in the combat zone. The Special Forces also had their own system. The Airborne had theirs. Fort Bragg, North Carolina, was supplying a certain amount of stuff directly to the 82d Airborne; Fort Campbell, Kentucky, directly to the 101st. These twenty-three different systems reflected a lack of discipline within the Army and its logistics system. We managed to provide logistic support well in most cases in Vietnam, but this indiscipline led to tremendous inefficiency and unnecessary costs.

It is highly doubtful that we could support such extravagance in future wars. Whether we can or not is beside the point; we should not allow unneeded "mass" to interfere with combat support. One logistics agency should manage and control the support of combat forces. This does not include exceptions for special task force arrangements, separate from the main battle area, but even special operations support should be governed by plans made in a senior logistics headquarters.

We never were able to formalize our support system for those allies who satisfied most or all of their logistics requirements through the U.S. pipeline. A specific plan should have been drawn up to provide the South Vietnamese, Thai, and Australian forces with the necessary supply and maintenance from the U.S. integrated pipeline, with their reimbursing the United States as normal customers. The method of funding, whether as part of a military sales program or a military aid program, should also have been worked out in advance. (Actually, from the viewpoint of efficient and economical logistic support, it would be far better to integrate the requirements of our allies into our own requirements and treat them as just one more customer for the logistic support system.)

In the case of engineer and signal logistic support, it finally worked out that they requisitioned most of their supplies through the 1st Log. These support agreements, although they started out slowly and inefficiently, soon became very satisfactory to all concerned. On the engineer side, the Pacific Architects and Engineers Corporation, responsible first to the 1st Log and then to the engineers, provided Army base utilities, construction, and other functions. The 1st Logistical Command was the single lead procurement agency and provided procurement support for contracting and negotiating.

When engineer and construction support is required, as it was in Vietnam, it is critical that base development plans be decided early. The waste that occurred because of a lack of planning put us at a terrible disadvantage. When we started out, Army base development was to be provided at three standard levels: one for field operations, an intermediate level, and a temporary level. However, the standard of living for troops in Vietnam was allowed to escalate almost totally uncontrolled. Also various construction standards were used as the basis for requirements for push shipments of construction material. This created considerable waste. The top-level, temporary standard for construction specified preengineered metal or painted wood semipermanent buildings with modern utility systems, including baths and toilets. Intermediate standards permitted wood buildings with limited utility systems, and the field standard included tents or wood buildings with minimal utility systems. As it turned out almost all plans finally were advanced to the temporary standard, and supplies were pushed in the pipeline to meet such standards. When it was realized that we could not continue to build at the top level, especially when we knew that we were not going to stay in Vietnam, the temporary standard was cut administratively and surpluses cropped up everywhere since so many of the push shipments were specified at that level.

Because special problems continued to occur that required aircraft experts and because of the rapid increases in the scope of Army aviation in Vietnam, the Aviation Materiel Management Center, organized and active in 1966–67, was assigned in 1968 to support all Army aviation in Vietnam. For example, where in 1965 there had been an authorized stockage list of 8,000 lines of parts for aviation, by 1968 this list had increased to 46,000 lines. Following the guidelines of the Logistics Offensive, the Aircraft Materiel Management activity had reduced the stockage list to 25,000 lines by the end of 1970. However, even within this parts list, some items were duplicated on the lists of the Aviation Materiel Management Center and the 1st Logistical Command. These items were primarily those common to aviation and other commodity areas. In view of the importance of aviation to combat in Vietnam, it was decided that the value of providing aviation units with a single point for obtaining repair parts outweighed the cost of duplicate parts and duplicate storage. Circumstances in Vietnam dictated this overlap, but I do not believe this approach should govern as a principle. Otherwise, we will end up applying this principle to other weapon systems like tanks and trucks. And the first thing you know—and this would be encouraged by program managers if we are not careful—instead of the seven systems under the Chiefs of the Technical Services before 1962, we will have a separate system for each type of weapon.

Common supply support was another difficult problem that lingered on unresolved in Vietnam because no one was anxious to push for common supply support to all services by one service or another. For example, the responsibility in Da Nang was taken by the Navy, but for the rest of Vietnam, except for unique aircraft items, supply support, although never clearly defined, became the responsibility of the Army. The Army worked things out pretty well with the Air Force in providing fuel oil, munitions, food, and other common supplies, but we did not do nearly as well with the Navy on food. This was because our menus were basically not compatible. One usually considers food a common item, but the Navy was using different foods at different periods of time and considered the diet needs of its personnel to be different from those of the Army and Air Force. One of the things we could do for the troops in the combat zone was to feed them well, and I believe that we really did that job to perfection, even though we could not combine food support with the Navy.

With the very few exceptions of combat teams that were involved in firefights in forward areas, the troops were served hot meals at least once or twice a day. The menus compared favorably with those in fine restaurants in the United States. In fact, I was once asked by a newspaper reporter how we managed so well. He asked because he had gone forward with a patrol, and at noon that day, while the patrol stopped and rested under some trees, in came a helicopter with a hot meal. The reporter asked the soldier sitting alongside of him, "What do you do when you don't get this kind of great support?" The soldier said, "I don't know, sir, we've never failed to get it." The reporter asked, "How long have you been in this outfit?" The soldier answered, "I just passed the 30th day." The reporter said, "You mean you've been here for a month, and you've been getting food service like this all along?" At that point, the reporter decided to find out how this was done. He eventually discussed the Army food system with me and wrote a fine article about our support of the troops. He sent it to the *Washington Post.* Several months later he told me his editor had considered it a fine story but not a sellable article because there would be no interest in a story on service support.

I reviewed the thirty-day menus that we set up each month. It was on the basis of this schedule that we requisitioned Class I rations. One month the food service officer told me, "We're now going to have three kinds of sherbet on the menu in addition to various ice creams." I said "Sherbet? You know when we send ice cream to forward areas, if it melts, we can at least say it's a milk shake; but if you send sherbet and it melts, all you can say is that that's colored water, and no soldier in a forward area wants to drink that. So, we're not about to add sherbet to our menus in the combat zone." That ended that.

Another problem was our failure to prepare our Vietnamese counterparts to manage their logistic support after we left Vietnam. In January 1969 I recommended what we called the Buddy project. This provided for American troops to work alongside ARVN troops in counterpart missions that we then knew would be taken over by the South Vietnamese when we were sent home. For example, we planned to have ARVN ammunition troops working with our ammunition troops in the same ammunition supply points (ASPs) and depot locations. The same pattern would be followed for maintenance units and all other combat service support units. General Abrams blessed the idea, but we made very little headway because there were those at MACV who felt that the 1st Logistical Command was attempting to take over MACV's responsibilities for the supervision of the advisory program. Each ARVN unit of any size generally had a U.S. adviser attached under the supervision of MACV. Our Buddy program was not intended to replace or disturb the adviser program. We simply wanted to provide on-the-job training for units to perform the tasks that the ARVN would have to undertake when U.S. combat service supply troops were withdrawn.

We made some progress at several locations with ammunition troops, but that was about it. Because of the lack of cooperation within the MACV staff, even though their boss had approved the project, we did not make nearly the progress we should have. I can't judge the extent to which this failure affected the capability of the ARVN combat service support troops, but I know that it did hurt in the long run.

This is just one more example of the fact that even when the boss approves something, the level of cooperation displayed by those required to carry it out can make the difference. If they choose to, lower-level bureaucrats can defeat an approved program by inertia if they are not closely supervised by the approving authority. Inaction can become a protective shield to preserve missions and provide job security. This is not a problem in combat operations, but it often occurs in the case of administrative orders. One might ask why didn't I point out this problem to General Abrams? Abrams had many problems, and I didn't feel this one needed to go to him. My staff and I kept working with his staff to try to accomplish our objectives, but it was so dragged out, so impeded by schedule postponements, that we didn't do the job we should have.

The Logistics Offensive would continue through 1972 and yield, as I have reported, benefits estimated at $9.3 billion. (For a midterm report, see Appendix B.) Of this total, $6.9 billion had a direct effect on the reduction of the Army's budget submissions. The result was reduced requirements for storage facilities, personnel, equipment, transportation, and utilities to support a more efficient logistics system. Even more important, these savings were accompanied by dramatic increases in logistics readiness in Vietnam and for the rest of the Army. Based upon unit reports, Army equipment on hand outside Vietnam increased 44 percent between fiscal years 1968 and 1972, while equipment deployability, or operability, increased 41 percent during the same time period.

## Other Command Responsibilities

Because of my Vietnam-wide command of resources, it became rather routine for MACV to assign me unique tasks not directly involved in combat logistics. For example, I was assigned to serve as host for a number of American celebrities including Billy Graham,

Terence Cardinal Cooke of New York, Bob Hope, Jimmy and Gloria Stewart, and Martha Raye. I got to know these fine people very well and saw how much their visits served to raise troop morale.

I particularly remember sharing a meal with the Stewarts when the celebrated actor asked where I would be going the next day. The Stewarts were in Vietnam for an informal "handshaking tour." I told them I was heading for the delta and invited them to accompany me to Can Tho where they could meet men from all the services. When they agreed, all of us flew down to Can Tho early the next morning. As it turned out the Stewarts completed their tour despite learning of the death of a near relative. Their decision to complete their tour allowed them to see their son, who would soon give his life for his country.

I must pay several personal tributes to soldiers in Vietnam. The first was my enlisted assistant, Sergeant Gordon. One night we were under attack at my quarters. I had instructed him to stay with his unit, thinking that was the best place for him. Nevertheless, when I got up in the middle of the night, at the most critical point of the enemy attack, I opened my door and there he was, lying across the doorsill.

We started a Soldier-of-the-Month Program in which soldiers were nominated by their units. The final choice of Soldier of the Month was drawn from the over 75,000 troops of the 1st Log. For four months in a row the winner was a soldier from a Reserve unit chosen by the sergeants major of the command. These selections were not in any way biased toward a reservist. The fact that a reservist won so often was particularly significant to me because of the frequent and mistaken warnings we had been receiving about the dedication and loyalty of Reserve Component units on their way to Vietnam.

Each Soldier of the Month served me as an enlisted aide, not to perform menial chores, but to carry out missions such as courier, messenger, and administrative assistant. It was generally my enlisted assistant who helped me with the Logistics Offensive inspections by determining the FSNs on containers. I then made it his responsibility to ensure that proper follow-up on our observations occurred. In fact, I asked these enlisted aides to check up on corrective action as we went through the 1st Log units. They did a great job in these tasks, under the supervision of my officer aide.

I refused to use officer aides solely for help in personal and protocol chores. They served as full-time assistants in all aspects of my command responsibility. As a result I believe they gained knowledge and experience that would help in future assignments. I was assigned two outstanding young officer aides: Capt. (now Brig. Gen.) Terry Scott of the Special Forces and Capt. (now on the brigadier promotion list) John Zierdt. Zierdt is the son of Maj. Gen. John Zierdt, an earlier, great Ordnance Corps boss of mine.

In Vietnam there was a close and wonderful relationship between the man doing the fighting and the man providing the support. In part this was because both were exposed to somewhat the same dangers and, unlike World War II and sometimes in Korea, there were no safe rear areas in Vietnam. In August 1968 Sgt. William W. Seay, a truck driver—a logistician—won the Medal of Honor for breaking up an ambush against his convoy on the road to Tay Ninh. He gave his life to save the lives of his comrades and the supplies for the men fighting in the Tay Ninh border area. In similar circumstances, another trucker, Sgt. Larry A. Dahl, gave his life defending his convoy from an enemy ambush on an exposed road near An Khe while driving an armored truck we had improvised. He too was awarded a Medal of Honor. Logisticians are proud of Sergeants Seay and Dahl and of the collective achievements they represented in providing the quality of support to the combat forces in Vietnam.

As our casualties increased it occurred to me that we should establish some sort of memorial. We created the First Logistics Association and collected $2 apiece from all who volunteered to become members. The primary purpose of the fund was to establish a memorial for former logistics soldiers who lost their lives carrying out their duties in Vietnam. Members of the 1st Logistical Command contributed almost $75,000 to create this memorial. Initially intended for a site in Vietnam, the permanent memorial was erected at Fort Lee, Virginia, which was becoming more and more the center of Army logistics. Completed in May 1974 and dedicated by Assistant Secretary of the Army for Logistics Eugene E. Berg, the memorial is located on the parade ground at Fort Lee. The parade ground itself is dedicated to Sergeant Seay. This 1st Logistical Command memorial, erected by soldiers for soldiers of their own command on a parade ground named for one of their many courageous members, is actually dedicated to all logisticians, past and future, who sacrificed themselves for their country.

The logistician's memorial also serves as a reminder, as General Creighton Abrams said, that the American soldiers in Vietnam were "among the best that have ever represented the United States in its entire history." The men of the 1st Log did their duty well and often heroically. We owe it to those men whose names are honored by the memorial to ensure that the young American of today remembers that they gave their lives for the benefit of future generations in trying to preserve our freedom through preventing the takeover of the freedoms of another nation. That purpose was basic to the dedication, motivation, and sacrifices of all ranks of the armed forces embroiled in Vietnam. In most human endeavors, especially in war, history shows a mixture of good and bad results. Combat support in Vietnam is certainly no exception. As Congress noted, supply support was a remarkable achievement. Also among the good things that are sometimes overlooked are the unpublicized constructive efforts which contrast with the well-publicized destructiveness of war. For example, voluntary efforts by U.S. servicemen on behalf of the Vietnamese in 1968 and 1969 included construction of:

| | | | |
|---|---|---|---|
| Schools | 1,253 | Churches | 263 |
| Hospitals | 175 | Dispensaries | 422 |
| Markets | 153 | Bridges | 598 |
| Roads (km) | 3,154 | Dwellings | 7,099 |

Much of this was accomplished by American soldiers in their non-duty time—showing again the humanistic qualities that the American soldier had displayed in earlier wars.

I am sure that there are many who might doubt my claim that my success as an individual results from how I reflect the great people with whom I have been associated. I would like to describe an incident that will prove that this is not false modesty. When I ran into General Abrams at the 1st Division headquarters in Vietnam after I had been told of my nomination to be Deputy Chief of Staff for Logistics, Abrams said, "Joe, you have the vote of every combat soldier in Vietnam." This statement illustrates what I have been saying about reflecting an image. In spite of the fact that I was on the go most of the time while I commanded in Vietnam, I certainly did not get to know many soldiers, nor did the soldiers get to know me personally. The fact is that I got credit for what thousands of personnel within my command did in providing the best combat support that the combat soldier has ever seen. They were dedicated to getting the job done, and so they had the confidence and the faith and the respect of all the troops in Vietnam. General Abe's statement reflected directly the image that each and every member of the combat support team had created in the minds of the combat soldiers in Vietnam.

## Farewell to Vietnam

In late July 1969 George Mabry got me over to USARV headquarters to hand me a message announcing that I was transferred to Washington to become Deputy Chief of Staff for Logistics and, further, that I had been nominated for the rank of lieutenant general. This was great news, but since good-byes were always so painful to me, especially considering the close ties I had made with men in the combat zone, I arranged to leave quietly and visit our logistics activities in Okinawa and Japan on the way home. But while still in the Far East I heard from my boss, General Mildren, who had been away, that I had to return to Vietnam. Back in Long Binh, I was told there was to be an official gathering that night at the USARV mess. I reported accordingly, only to discover the entrance to the mess hall blocked by many obstacles, including a large pile of telephone poles. I should have known what was coming.

They gave me a fine farewell party, and General Mildren presented me an award for my work in Vietnam. I can't deny that the pressure General Mildren exerted upon me to solve problems was very irksome at the time and caused me considerable worry. But, as I told him during my farewell remarks, if he had not been so rough on me, it is entirely probable that many logistics actions that were expedited during that year might have been delayed or skipped altogether. Later I came to realize that Mildren was a fine commander who used toughness to stir up subordinates to get an important job done. My departure became an emotional thing and strengthened what has become a continuing friendship with Frank Mildren.

The predominate figure during my Vietnam tour remained General Abrams. One incident in our close relationship lingers with me even today. Once in early 1969 I was at the 1st Division discussing logistic support with its commander, Maj. Gen. Keith Ware. We were preparing to visit a forward fire support base when I was called off the helicopter to answer a call from headquarters ordering me to report immediately to General Abrams. Ware left without me and was killed when his helicopter was knocked down by enemy fire. (Ware was a Medal of Honor winner and the first World War II enlisted man to receive a general's star.)

When I arrived at MACV headquarters, the MACV chief of staff told me that Abrams wanted me to hear a briefing by his deputy, Lt. Gen. Andrew J. Goodpaster, on the possibility of a quick move of the 1st Cavalry Division from up north in I Corps to block a movement by North Vietnamese regulars from the Cambodian border toward Saigon. From the rear of the room I listened to the dry run and, after Abrams came, to the official briefing. As usual Abrams asked some direct questions. Then he said, "I sent for Joe Heiser, is he here?" When General Goodpaster said I was in back, he asked, "The most important part of this is, can we do this logistically?" I said, "Yes sir, we can do it." With that he said, "If Joe says we can do it, we'll do it," and walked out of the room.

I was in a fortunate position that day because, while there were some problems in making such a move in less than the targeted seventy-two hours, I had the full responsibility for the resources we needed, except for the small aircraft carrier we needed to move the helicopters from the north. But I was not worried about arranging for the ship because I was sure the Navy commander, Admiral Elmo Zumwalt, would back me up. Thus it was not a very difficult problem for me promptly to say we could do it. The operation was successfully carried out with the help of many people including Zumwalt. Once again, and I can't stress this too much, I looked good because many people performed so well.

# CHAPTER 10

# Chief of Army Logistics

I am not certain how I came to be appointed Deputy Chief of Staff for Logistics (DCSLOG), although I believe Secretary Resor, General Johnson, and General Abrams probably recommended me to the Chief of Staff, General William C. Westmoreland. I had never met the Chief of Staff before I reported in to him for duty. I must say that General Westmoreland never once failed to provide me with appropriate guidance and, more important, never failed to give his personal support to needed logistics reforms. This showed a remarkable degree of trust because no Chief of Staff can be constantly aware of the Army's logistic resources. He must depend upon his advisers and most particularly his chief adviser, the DCSLOG.

Knowing this, I recommended to Westmoreland during our first meeting that I should advise him, at least weekly, of what was going on in Army logistics. He agreed. Westmoreland had not required periodic logistics briefings in the past unless he became aware of something unusual. Therefore, his staff had not included a regular logistics briefing in his busy schedule. My experience as a staff officer, however, had taught me the danger of leaving a boss uninformed about events that might involve him. In particular I was entrusted by General Westmoreland and Secretary Resor to take the initiative on the Logistics Offensive, parts of which some of the four-star commanders and staff did not really support because they were concerned that efficiency efforts might reduce readiness. Keeping my superiors informed of progress, even though in most cases I did so after the fact, was very useful to me, for when senior commanders then disagreed with my actions, my bosses already knew what I was doing and supported me.

On leaving my first meeting with General Westmoreland, I indicated to his various secretaries and assistants that I would need at least one hour weekly with the general to cover logistics matters. This request for time displeased them because of his already busy schedule. I finally had to tell them that the Chief of Staff had agreed to this weekly session. From that time on, throughout his tour, I spent a minimum of about forty-five minutes a week with him and the Secretary. It proved to be a sound practice because I was never criticized for not keeping the Chief or the Secretary informed. In preparing for these meetings I accumulated the relevant papers, mostly carbon copies of completed actions—sometimes in a pile six to eight inches thick. I took these papers with me when I briefed the bosses. After briefly covering the topic on each page I would throw the page on the table or floor as we moved on. This habit of strewing the floor with paper became my trademark both in briefings and in delivering speeches. It certainly helped to keep my listeners' attention!

I had never held such a high-visibility job before, and I got my baptism of fire early. Soon after becoming DCSLOG I decided to centralize the Army's food management activities at Fort Lee, Virginia, under a brigadier general. Food management had been entrusted to long-time employees in the Chicago and Washington areas who did not perform effectively and lacked top-level surveillance. My reorganization proved controversial when a congressman opposed the move. I briefed him on why the action was being taken, but I made no headway in changing his mind. Subsequently, it was revealed that he had a close relative and Saturday golfing partner who would have had to move from Washington.

About the same time I was accused by columnist Jack Anderson of robbing commissary customers of $80 million a year because I allowed food salesmen to contact commissary managers, especially overseas. Anderson said that these salesmen got a 10 percent commission for whatever they sold; and based on commissary sales of $800 million yearly, $80 million could be saved if the Army prevented the sales representatives from contacting the commissary managers. Even after a lengthy discussion, Anderson refused to recognize the fact that the representatives' contact with commissary managers was one of the ways the commissary manager was able to meet the requirements of his customers. Anderson dubbed me the "czar of commissaries" and accused me of taking this position on the issue because I wanted to become the head of the Defense Supply Association upon my retirement. He refused to see that, as a basic ordnance officer, I would hardly be interested in becoming the president of what was mainly a food processors association. What caused him to fix on the Defense Supply Association was the fact that all recent DCSLOGs, including myself, had become honorary vice presidents of the association. This position was entirely ex-officio with no actual relationship to the operation of the association. I recognized, however, that this role allowed for a perception of conflict of interest, so promptly resigned the honorary position.

Nevertheless, a congressional hearing was set up, and I was the primary witness. I was chastised, especially by Congressman Joseph P. Addabbo, whose questions implied his sympathy with Anderson's charges. He questioned me sharply, but on his way out of the hearing room he stopped by my seat and, kneeling on one knee, privately apologized for his sharp manner. He knew me well, he said, and had every confidence in my decision, but he had certain constituents who had compelled him to question me as he had. This was just about my only encounter with Congress in which I did not feel I had been treated very fairly.

This was also my only time as a congressional witness when the Army tried to guide my testimony. I was asked to accept responsibility for something that was to be passed off as an error by the Army. The allegation was false, and I said that if the Army was going to take the blame unjustly, then someone else should be assigned the task. As General Westmoreland later said in a similar situation, "Joe, you give them the facts," and that ended that. Food management operations were moved to the newly established Troop Support Command at Fort Lee, Virginia, and I did not become president of the Defense Supply Association.

As DCSLOG I had a chance to observe more closely the political aspects of military testimony on Capitol Hill. I found that if you try too much to factor in what you anticipate will be the reaction of the Congress, if you place too much emphasis on what Congress might want, you can undercut a real military requirement. The military should confine itself to true military requirements, whether right or wrong politically. When the military staff attempts to modify its position to meet political needs, it can end up with a recommendation that misses the heart of the question because it is not based on a military requirement. In other words, as I used to say to my staff many times, "Don't come in here to me with a recommendation that is influenced by what you think the political position is. That's the Secretary's responsibility, acting as an appointee of the President, to exert whatever political influence is necessary." Military personnel should state what they know is right militarily regardless of what they expect the political position to be, and any political positions should be taken at the secretariat level.

At the same time politico-military tensions arose now and then in the Pentagon itself when I was DCSLOG. Once the Assistant Secretary of Defense for Installations and Logistics attempted to set up standard policies and procedures governing such common services as food. The services objected strenuously, however, and in 1969 they got him to agree to their establishing a Logistic Systems

Policy Council (LSPC) to set standards rather than have OSD staff members attempt to dictate them.

The council, under the guidance of the assistant secretary and with the participation of the deputy secretary, conducted studies that resulted in agreements on defense logistics policies covering all services. At that time David Packard was deputy secretary and Barry Shillito the assistant secretary. The system worked very well at first, even though Shillito's staff was unhappy because it felt that the LSPC was taking over the staff's responsibilities. Packard, however, was not content with the pace of the reforms. It was difficult to win the services' agreement to a standard system that would require changes in service policies and procedures (and would reduce service budgets, something that causes the greatest friction in the Pentagon between the services). For example, the council considered establishing a standard defense depot system against much service opposition. Packard was displeased with what he considered the uncooperativeness of the service representatives. In time the LSPC was gradually disbanded. This was allowed to occur despite the fact that the Defense Department told Congress in 1971 that the LSPC had the critical assignment of standardizing military logistics.

## The Worldwide Logistics Offensive

When I became the DCSLOG there was a supply excess not only in Vietnam but throughout the service. We had over 1 million different stockage list items. I was convinced that this was at least five to eight times greater than it should be. Yet field commanders considered it necessary to support their logistics people in holding on to what they had. It was difficult to convince four-star commanders that they should reduce their stockage to such a great extent. But it simply had to be done to ensure the effectiveness of combat support. I had set what I considered a practical objective: reduce the June 1969 stockage list (items on hand or on order) of 1,063,000 items to 509,000 by June 1970 and to below 200,000 by June 1972. I promised that to Congress! This meant, for example, that I was telling USCINCEUR to reduce his 200,000-item stockage list to 60,000 items in three years.

This policy meant not only disposing of many items from the worldwide stockage lists, but also stopping any further requisitioning for those items unless a specific need showed itself. I was backed by General Westmoreland and Secretary Resor every step of the way. An example of their support occurred at the commanders' conference in November 1969, when the air defense commander, Lt. Gen. George V. "Bud" Underwood, Jr. (he was in charge of, among other things, all the vital NIKE sites throughout the United States), told Secretary Resor that "Joe Heiser, a friend of mine, is hurting my readiness because he is requiring that we turn in 32,000 of the items in our stocks, more than half." The Secretary turned to me and said, "Joe, what about this?" I was forced to reply, "Sir, I'm sorry if Bud Underwood believes we're hurting his command readiness. Actually we will improve his readiness by eliminating unnecessary management and control of useless items." I went on to explain that there had not been a single demand for any of those 32,000 items for over ten years, not even by mistake. I even preached a little, telling both the Secretary and Bud that "I doubt very seriously that there is a reduction in readiness. Rather, my friend will find that his readiness will go up because, after turning in this excess, he will be able to have a better knowledge of what he actually has on hand and what he may require if not there."

We called this program to cut unneeded stockage "DA Clean," and, in fact, we reduced excess stocks by over 3.6 million short tons, achieving a $9 billion savings during the three years I served as DCSLOG (*see table*). I don't want to leave the impression that we ever solved the problem of excess stockage. It continued through the buildup of the 1980s, and it continues today because it still appears far easier and less risky to commanders, program managers, and production contractors to put support in the field that *may* be needed rather than to use their knowledge and experience to decide what is the actual, needed level of support, including provision for unexpected requirements. The problem is that program managers and contractors get blamed only for shortages, not excesses, of support.

As a result of experience gained in Vietnam and elsewhere, we embarked upon an Army-wide Logistics Offensive in DCSLOG. I directed the staff to review all the programs/projects that we had initiated in Vietnam and to include them in all future departmental policies and directives for Army-wide implementation and control. Should a senior responsible person determine that Army-wide application would be inappropriate, I would review the case to see what we could do instead to increase efficiency. (A partial summary of the Army-wide Logistics Offensive is contained in Appendix D.)

In order to understand how the many projects and programs in the worldwide Logistics Offensive were tied together, we found it necessary to establish a logistics master plan (LOGMAP). Where before all our managers worked on various separate projects, unsure how each was being integrated into a total plan, now the

## DA CLEAN
## Theater Authorized Stockage Lists (TASL)
Task—Maintain TASLs with Objective Range (LOGMAP OBJ 2–8–2)

|  | Actual 30 Jun 69 | Actual 30 Jun 70 | Actual 30 Jun 71 | Actual 30 Jun 72 | Objective 30 Jun 72 |
|---|---|---|---|---|---|
| Vietnam............ | 155,000 | 101,300 | 67,785 | 19,989 | 40,000 – 50,000 |
| Okinawa........... | 158,000 | 114,000 | 60,582 | 46,972 | 30,000 – 40,000 |
| Europe............ | 171,000 | 85,600 | 67,000 | 51,000 | 55,000 – 70,000 |
| Korea............. | 155,000 | 101,300 | 67,785 | 19,989 | 40,000 – 50,000 |
| Alaska............ | 65,000 | 52,200 | 49,577 | 21,065 | 15,000 – 20,000 |
| Hawaii............ | 74,000 | 32,000 | 20,510 | 29,979 | 15,000 – 20,000 |
| Japan............. | 159,000 | 11,200 | 7,849 | 4,483 | 8,000 – 10,000 |
| Thailand.......... | 48,000 | 20,600 | (¹) | — | 10,000 – 15,000 |
| Canal Zone........ | 53,000 | 25,000 | 8,845 | 11,983 | 10,000 – 15,000 |
| Total........ | 1,038,000 | 543,200 | 349,933 | 205,460 | 223,000 –290,000 |

¹Data now included with Okinawa.

*Analysis as of 11 Aug 72 (Data as of 30 Jun 71):* Progress in worldwide TASL reduction continues at a favorable rate. While the decrease in USAREUR TASL is not solely attributable to DSS, this new system has had impact on the reduction. USARV continues to drop in conjunction with the phasedown. USARHAW is being queried regarding failure of that command to meet FY 72 objective.

LOGMAP clearly demonstrated how every project and program was contributing to overall objectives. I believe this was an important step in the administration of a tremendously broad and complex program. Also of great help was publication of the so-called gold book. As a result of my dealings with the Holifield committee and our continuing excellent relations with the GAO, I broke with the Army's previous hesitation to voluntarily inform the GAO of our policies and published quarterly a compilation and description of each project and program in the Logistics Offensive. More important, we met with GAO representatives each quarter, either in the DCSLOG office or in the GAO, and frankly discussed our problems and our successes. As a result both sides quickly agreed upon the facts of the logistics situation and what needed to be done. These meetings proved to be very useful for all concerned, including congressional committees, to whom the GAO reported. This valuable practice continues today.

I also determined that we needed better means to communicate logistics policy to the field. We decided to establish a logistics policy council of all senior logisticians throughout the major commands as well as other senior logisticians on staffs and in logistics commands. These councils lasted approximately two days and were highlighted by talks by the Secretary and the Chief of Staff. The agenda covered any important changes and any new projects being initiated that would eventually affect the various commands. These councils helped to establish a unified understanding of what we were trying to do. We not only gave the word from Washington, but we also received the reaction of those from the field who were responsible for implementing the action. Under a different name the council meetings continue today with great success.

All this activity put great demands on the DCSLOG staff. Accordingly, I held a seminar for all the spouses. I assured them that while we required hard work, I did not want soldiers spending more time at work than was necessary—no working on weekends, for example, unless it was necessary. Anyone working overtime would be required to obtain the approval of the DCSLOG to do it. I told the spouses that when they heard that their logistician had work to do on Saturday, Sunday, or late in the evening, they should ask, "Does Heiser know you are going to do this work?" If the answer was uncertain, someone should ascertain that such nonduty-time work had been approved. I personally took walks through the DCSLOG portion of the Pentagon in nonduty time to see who was working and why their work was necessary. I believe, in the long run, this policy raised morale because it allowed more time to be spent with families. This was important, especially since those who were likely to overtax themselves were, in most cases, the outstanding people within the organization.

Supervisors and commanders should demand that work be done efficiently during duty hours, thus avoiding much of the overtime particularly associated with staff work in Washington. I was a demanding supervisor, but I always tried to make it clear that I did not expect personnel unnecessarily to deprive themselves and their families of adequate and deserved nonduty time.

As DCSLOG I quickly rediscovered unnecessary tasks that I should have remembered from previous Pentagon tours. Too often a staff officer briefed his supervisor, who then briefed his supervisor, and so on up to the final briefing given at the decision level. It was normal Pentagon procedure for a general officer to come in and brief the DCSLOG, but many of my questions could not be answered by that individual because the questions had not been raised in the dry run of the briefing he was to give me. Consequently, I directed that action officers give the briefing, with the senior officer retaining overall responsibility. Such practice teaches junior personnel how to keep their superiors informed, and it gives senior officials the chance to talk with those actually doing the work. It also eliminated the inevitable dry runs that consume so much of every staff officer's time.

## Automation, Accountability, and Resupply Requirements

One of the continuing problems in DCSLOG has been the effective utilization of computers. The computer industry is very dynamic, and users often discover that programs need to be revised, modified, or replaced as time goes on. They also find that they can do much more with the computer than originally intended. All this adds up to a complex problem of management. This is especially so in logistics, where so much data is involved. In DCSLOG we had to develop and define our computer requirements in terms of what the logistician and the logistics system needed. The logistics manager had to decide what support or information he needed at what point in the logistics structure. This was difficult to do for two reasons: logisticians in the past had not needed to define their information requirements as precisely as was required for a computer program, and the computer programmer, unless closely associated with the functional aspects of logistics, tended to include in the logistics computer program what he, the computer expert, thought was necessary. In many cases the computer designer would not know what the logistics manager needed at various points in the system, and thus the resulting system would not produce what the logistics manager really needed. The problem was not one of technology but of management.

Despite much reform, this general problem of effectively harnessing automation continues today. We must ensure that the computer and its programs will provide what logistics managers in all parts of the Army structure need. I and other senior officials have made promises to our superiors, including Congress, that we failed to keep because of unexpected problems in the design, installation, and use of computer programs.

The first time as DCSLOG that I talked at the Command and General Staff College at Fort Leavenworth, I enjoyed some success, and I was treated royally by the staff. They even put a picture of my own Leavenworth class of 1950 under the glass top of the desk I used backstage. When I returned the next year to speak, I was again provided with a desk, but in place of the picture of my old classmates I found a note that read, "To err is human but if you really want to screw up, you need a computer." I think this pretty well summed up our own frustration with some of our automation problems in DCSLOG. Automation has provided logisticians with a wonderful tool, but one that can produce disasters if not designed, programmed, and controlled properly.

While DCSLOG I had a serious disagreement over computers with the Assistant Vice Chief of Staff, General William DePuy. DePuy wanted to eliminate logistic computers at certain command levels, particularly field corps and CONUS army commands where I thought it was necessary to have computer support. Especially when an Army field command had many subordinate commands that maintained significant levels of inventory for the support of units within that command's responsibility, I stated, the corps and army commanders needed to have computers. These would provide them with immediate information on what was in hand, on order, or in excess so that unnecessary requisitioning could be avoided by cross-leveling within the command itself. DePuy, who for good reasons wanted to restrict the number of computers, disagreed. I almost decided to take the problem to the Vice Chief or Chief. I regret that I did not because it might have avoided many problems the field corps experienced later because they lacked proper computer support. In the case of the CONUS army commanders, their missions later changed, along with the necessity for computers; to some degree, however, their current responsibilities for Reserve logistic support would also be facilitated and made more efficient through an automated capability of knowing what was in the hands of Reserve units.

Computers figured in another Army-wide logistics problem, the maintenance of asset accountability. In the logistics business it is difficult to count. The greater the volume, the more difficult it is to maintain the credibility of inventory accounting. It takes a well-trained, highly experienced group of people to maintain an inventory accountability acceptable to those responsible. Our overseas depots have been particularly troublesome in this regard because we have not had the level of expertise nor the facilities and other resources required to maintain accurate inventory accounts.

When I became DCSLOG the Army still assumed that rapid resupply would be questionable in wartime, so we continued to build overseas depots containing masses of supplies which we couldn't count, keep in the proper condition, or ship efficiently within our commands. This is a disastrous idea. Having a mass of anything can be very deceiving and cause more trouble than any of the practical advantages that might be achieved. We have proved this to ourselves many times over in peace and war. We needed to rid the logistics system of its excesses, and one important element was the elimination of overseas depots—excluding Class V, Ammunition, and Class III, Petroleum, Oil, and Lubricants (POL)—and the establishment of a direct support system between CONUS supply agencies and general and/or direct support supply units. I knew we needed to do away with the depots, but overseas commanders were intuitively happy with their depots and other storage locations with masses of supplies. I tried to convince them that, using the advances in transportation, communications, and automation, we could eliminate overseas depots and still provide effective resupply. We had proved this in Vietnam, but it was tough to gain acceptance of the concept. CINCUSAREUR was dead set against it. I finally got him to agree to a test to see if we could save him enough money so that he could double his tank training, which was severely limited by the cost of petroleum, oil, and lubricants. Since he was a tanker, he really wanted funds for more POL. The results of the test finally convinced him to eliminate his depots. But if we're not careful, depots will continue to be built overseas. It's simply very comforting to commanders to have masses of stocks, under the false perception that "if I've got a lot of stuff, I'll have the support I need."

This perception was part of the problem of maintaining a credible asset-accountable system of control. Achieving an acceptance by field commanders of an asset-control system, which would enable the Army to maintain a service-wide inventory of major items and components, was very difficult. They opposed the system because they felt that items issued to them, in some cases purchased out of their consumer funds, were owned by them. They believed that if they had to report on the status of these stocks, they would lose control of the materiel, which would become subject to redistribution by the National Inventory Control Point, the Army agency controlling the asset report. It was difficult to get across the idea that the field commander did not own the inventory. He only had it on loan as long as it was in his accountable area.

At best, inventory accuracy and accountability were difficult. Once we divided the assets into many different distribution pockets, it was impossible to achieve a credible accounting. Yet many decisions, including use of resources, were necessarily based upon the total asset picture, not a part. With improved automation and communication we had no excuse for the degree of inaccuracy and ignorance that we allowed in asset accountability. We faced situations where we had little account credibility for even major items, such as tanks. Yet decisions had to be made with regard to the use of resources in support of these assets. So assumptions were made based on a faulty degree of accuracy and credibility. Of course, this situation is bad enough in terms of peacetime readiness and economy. In time of war such a lack of knowledge is clearly unacceptable for operational reasons.

Related to the problem was the issue of controlling war reserves. Advances in automation aided in asset accountability here too, but the immediate question I faced when I became DCSLOG was whether we had determined the needs for war-reserve stocks effectively and efficiently. My early review indicated that the determination of requirements was weak. Early in 1970 I therefore initiated a project called Strat (for strategic) Requirement to validate or recommend for revision the methods and principles used in the determination of war reserves and their supply requirements. This review was completed in the fall of 1970 and resulted in a reduction of almost $300 million in what had previously been indicated as the valid war-reserve requirement in repair parts, etc., excluding ammunition. Much of this requirement had been procured and stocked; more was in the process of procurement. As I recall, this reduction in approved requirements reduced the war reserve to a little over half of what it was at the start of calendar year 1970. A recent study prepared by the Logistics Management Institute for the Office of the Secretary of Defense found that the weakest link in the logistics chain remained the basic problem of determining requirements, including requirements for war reserves, on both an Army-wide and DOD-wide basis.*

Also directly related to the supply problem was the need to update maintenance policies and procedures. The maintenance system in place when I became DCSLOG, the Logistics Support Analysis (LSA), merely outlined processes for the "front end" analysis of equipment as it came off the production line. We urgently needed to publish new procedures that reflected the maintenance actually being used for equipment already in the hands of troops. As part of the Logistics Offensive we launched a project called Maintenance Support Positive (MS+) which in effect updated the LSA by establishing maintenance procedures, especially the procedures governing the modular replacement of equipment parts, which was rapidly superseding the old piece part replacement system. MS+ covered, for example, changes in doctrine, regulations, maintenance allocation charts, skills at various levels, and maintenance management processes. Like a number of other initiatives in the Logistics Offensive, MS+, renamed, continues today as part of the Army's Logistics Systems Analysis.

## Acquisition

Although AMC first comes to mind in any discussion of research and development and acquisition, DCSLOG retains important procurement functions, as stated in the Army's mission statements. Further complicating this organizational mix when I was DCSLOG, the Assistant Secretary of the Army for Installations and Logistics also maintained an acquisitions organization headed by an Army logistics general. I proposed to the Chief of Staff and the Secretary, with the agreement of Assistant Secretary Ron Fox and General Chesarek of AMC, that the DCSLOG not attempt to duplicate the expertise found in these two organizations, which were the actual acquisition managers for wholesale logistics and where the major acquisition process was performed. We agreed that the DCSLOG would assist the acquisitions people in Assistant Secretary Fox's office. I assured the Vice Chief of Staff that we could get the acquisition function performed best through the cooperative efforts of these three agencies. We did this during the entire period of my tenure as DCSLOG with no difficulty whatsoever.

---

*LMI Briefing to the Office of the Secretary of Defense, 1989, sub: Readiness for Transition to War.

On a personal level, I lacked the specific background in the major tasks associated with the acquisition process, namely research and development and industrial procurement operations. It was for that reason that I had convinced General Chesarek that Hank Miley, not I, be made his deputy at AMC in 1969. Miley had a very strong background in these areas that are so essential to AMC's mission, and he subsequently performed outstandingly as General Chesarek's successor.

## Doctrine, Training, and Career Management

During my years as DCSLOG one of our greatest concerns involved the overall supervision of the training and career management of the Army's logisticians, including both soldiers and civilians. When I arrived in Washington, I found that the McNamara reorganization of 1962 and subsequent reorganizations had tended to cloud DCSLOG's responsibility both for supervising logistics training and developing logistical doctrine. Until the 1972 Army reorganization, chaired by General DePuy, development of Army logistics doctrine as well as training and career management had been conducted at various places under various authorities. These included facilities under the Army Materiel Command, the technical service schools and the combat arms schools, both under the Continental Army Command—shortly to be redesignated the Training and Doctrine Command (TRADOC)—and the Office of the Deputy Chief of Staff for Personnel (DCSPER). DCSLOG itself also had a small doctrine and training center, the Logistics Doctrine Systems and Readiness Agency (LDSRA) at New Cumberland Army Depot, Pennsylvania. Along with establishing a Center for Combat Doctrine at Fort Leavenworth and the Personnel and Finance Center at Fort Benjamin Harrison, Indiana, the 1972 reorganization also created the Logistics Center at Fort Lee.

I participated in planning this reorganization and was instrumental in establishing the center at Fort Lee. With DePuy's agreement and the Chief of Staff's approval, AMC's role in the new logistics center was restricted to wholesale support, while TRADOC retained general oversight over training and doctrine and DCSPER coordinated the supervision of all logistics career management. But most important, in establishing the Logistics Center and setting its mission, the 1972 reorganization recognized in peacetime what the Army practiced in wartime: DCSLOG's close and direct participation in all planning and decision making pertaining to training, doctrine, and career management of all logisticians in the United States Army. To get the new Logistics Center going, I arranged for the transfer of 125 spaces from LDSRA to form the organization's basic cadre.

The reorganization called for what we at the time termed a "solid-dotted line" command arrangement for the Logistics Center. This setup recognized that while the Logistics Center was organizationally part of TRADOC, there would also be a direct supervisory relationship between the DCSLOG and the center with the full understanding and cooperation of TRADOC. Furthermore, a similar solid-dotted line agreement was reached between DCSPER and DCSLOG on their cooperative responsibilities for logistics career management. To some extent this objective was achieved. However, as the years have passed, DCSLOG's responsibilities have been curtailed. Further changes and agreements are needed today to correct this counterproductive restriction in DCSLOG's responsibilities.

As DCSLOG I worked hard on logistical training, but I must confess that our success was limited. Much still needs to be accomplished in this area. I believe that logistical training for enlisted personnel in the early 1970s was probably as good as or better than any given since that offered in the small pre–World War II Army with its legendary "ordnance sergeant" in every unit and post, camp, and station. My concern focused on our enlisted reservists, who will bear the logistical brunt in any future contingency. I was not at all sure that their training was at an acceptable level, primarily because I was not sure that they could participate in the improved active enlisted training because of lack of time and facilities. We had good results in improving training for enlisted reservists, although even today I believe that much further improvement could be made.

In the early 1970s we concentrated on the training and selection of warrant officers in the logistics field. In the past much of our ability to do the technical logistics job could be traced to a very strong corps of warrant officers who had gained considerable experience as noncommissioned officers before receiving their warrants. By the time I became DCSLOG most of these men had retired. Logistics needs this practical expertise, and the warrant officer program needs continual strengthening.

With regard to commissioned officers in logistics, I have often indicated my belief that we have no room for company grade generalists in the logistics area. Our lieutenants and captains need to learn leadership and a commodity know-how on which they then can base the rest of their career. At the grade of major and above, it's perfectly appropriate that the officer become more of a generalist, using his or her experience and training in the company grades as a base for the general and functional responsibilities open to field grade officers. This, by the way, does not mean that all logistics commissioned officers should spend all their company-level career in logistics. My own experience demonstrates the advantages of combat arms duty for young logisticians. Such experience leads to a greater awareness of the needs of the combat arms. The melding of logistics knowledge with that of the combat arms results in optimum logistic support.

In fact, as DCSLOG I worked under the assumption that all logistics officers needed an assignment with the combat arms early in their career. After that, I believe, attendance at basic and advanced courses at logistics schools should be mandatory. At this level officers gained their last formal training in logistics, unless they were fortunate enough to attend such training centers as the Army Logistics Management School at Fort Lee. While it is important that logistics officers attend the senior schools as well as Fort Leavenworth's Command and General Staff College, we shouldn't be deceived into thinking that these senior schools further logistics training. At best, these schools can provide an understanding of how logistics fits into the overall mission of the Army.

Training outside the sphere of military schools is also essential for logistics officers. As DCSLOG I worked with DCSPER to make such a training pattern standard for all logistics officers. The current masters course affiliated with the Logistics Executive Development Course (LEDC) is an example of our efforts. I wish that I had been able to restore the practical executive training I received with industry and at the University of Chicago. I believe that the logistics community should continue to press for such training, which at a relatively small cost to the government is of great value to the Army.

I should add here that as DCSLOG I retained my belief that it was unfair to the officer, to the logistics community, and to the Army to place combat arms officers in senior, responsible positions in logistics. At those levels of command, especially during times of crisis, the Army needs logisticians who also know the combat arms and understand exactly what is required to support the combat soldier. If a combat arms officer desires to fill a senior logistics position, especially positions at the general-officer level, he should be willing to invest in logistics assignments earlier in his career so that his experiences will better fit him for filling the top logistics positions. There is a common misconception that not much leadership ability is required in logistics. In fact, it requires a great under-

CHIEF OF ARMY LOGISTICS 183

standing and practice of leadership because a logistics commander faces decisions requiring a comprehensive understanding of many complex logistics alternatives.

This problem came to a head as I neared retirement. General Abrams, who by then had become Chief of Staff, indicated that he might assign as my successor a combat arms officer—well acquainted with logistics, but not a logistician. I advised against it and suggested a more appropriate assignment for the officer involved. In addition to the considerations mentioned above, I explained that the DCSLOG was the career focal point in logistics and to assign a nonlogistician to this position would demoralize logistics officers. General Abrams agreed and said, "Okay, give me a list of the top potential officers in the logistics community of the Army."

I was ready for the challenge. During my tenure as DCSLOG I had worked with commanders all over the Army, getting them to provide me informally with the names of top-caliber logisticians with notable potential in their commands. I passed these names along to the promotion boards, not asking them to promote specific individuals, but thereby assuring that these highly recommended individuals got careful consideration. Nobody ever called me down for doing this, and because of this relatively intimate knowledge of logistics officers around the Army, I was able to answer General Abrams' request quickly and, I think, without bias. I was both surprised and admittedly pleased to see that the officers promoted to top logistics positions during the next eight to ten years closely matched the recommendations that I made to General Abrams in 1972.

One of the names on my list was that of Maj. Gen. Jack Fuson, who headed the transportation directorate when I was DCSLOG. He was one of the Army's smartest officers, and I expected in time to see him become the DCSLOG. But Jack needed some broadening experience outside transportation before he could be considered fully eligible for the job, so I arranged for his transfer to USARPAC to learn something about other aspects of logistics. Unfortunately, news of the transfer broke on the heels of one of our heated arguments over target dates for certain DCSLOG automation initiatives, and I have always been convinced that Jack concluded that his transfer was on account of our differences. That was not the case, and as it turned out, he served with great distinction, both as the J–4 at MACV and later as the DCSLOG of the Army.

In all my recommendations to General Abrams about personnel, I sought to stress that matters pertaining to logistics training and career management must be directly influenced by the Deputy

Chief of Staff for Logistics in order that the total logistics job can have the kind of people who are needed to perform the many and various complex duties within the logistics mission field. Leaders in time of crisis understand this much better than those who have not had such experience.

## Spreading the Word

I considered that one of my major tasks as DCSLOG was to explain to Army audiences and, when requested, to the general public the Army's roles and missions, especially its role in the Vietnam War. I called it "spreading the word," and I took this duty very seriously. In order to spread the word not only in the Office of the DCSLOG but throughout the logistics community, I also used a system of DCSLOG guidance bulletins (see Appendix C for an example).

I was asked to make quite a few speeches at universities and many other organizations to promote a better understanding of the Army's mission in Vietnam and elsewhere. By being straightforward, simple, and sincere, I avoided any difficulties with students, a fact that surprised many of my hosts. My point was simple: peace, love, and freedom, important concepts often displayed on the signs carried by antiwar activists, could only be achieved by dedicated persons who also subscribed to three other values: duty, honor, and country. Audiences had no difficulty understanding this, even though I am sure they did not always agree with the nation's policy.

From the reaction of many student audiences I became convinced that as long as I stuck to the facts and spoke from the heart I would get a favorable reception. After one student protest leader at Notre Dame University told me that my discussion had prompted him to rethink his previous opposition to all things military (especially ROTC at the university), I decided that what had been missing all along was a clear presentation to the students of the Army's side' on many of the issues of the day. I believe that we in the military had failed to take the initiative or had not been allowed to state our case. As a result we had lost the understanding of many young Americans.

I never read a speech. My talks appeared extemporaneous, but I actually prepared very hard, with a careful outline and a clear idea of what I was going to say about each topic. (For examples of my speech material from this period, see Appendix G.) I used crutches to help me—if slides or vugraphs were available, I used them, or I used a blackboard and chalk, or papers and articles on my intended topics and visibly referred to them one by one. Then after using them, I'd throw them on the floor. At times it looked like I had made a trash basket out of the surrounding stage. I found that in talking about logistics, leadership, and management, I had to use every trick of the trade to keep people's attention. Logistics is not a very glamorous subject, and you must liven it up with whatever means are at hand.

I don't want to leave the impression that all my dealings as DCSLOG with the high and mighty were pleasant. During the Nixon administration the White House emphasized converting public lands to public use as parks, especially in low-income areas. This was a well-intentioned program, I'm sure, but there were those in the White House, including H. R. Haldeman and John Ehrlichman, who wanted to convert active Army posts like Fort Meade, Maryland; Fort DeRussey, Hawaii; and the Presidio in San Francisco into public parks. As the DCSLOG I was responsible for Army real estate, and therefore I had to accompany Secretary of Defense Melvin R. Laird to the White House in an effort to convince Haldeman and Ehrlichman that the Army should retain the posts in keeping with its mission. It was not a happy experience. The discussion became heated when the White House group accused the Secretary of Defense of disloyalty to the President. At that point the Secretary walked out. In the end the Army got to keep its posts with the proviso that the public be granted greater access, that a planned rest hotel for returning Vietnam veterans on the beach at DeRussey be sited differently, and that "happy face" signs be installed throughout the military reservations. But I must say all my dealings with ammunition fires hardly prepared me for that day.

The logistician's nightmare. A POL fire following a Viet Cong rocket attack at Tan Son Nhut, April 1966.

Overcrowding led to a lack of supply accountability at the Saigon Port Activity and demonstrated that the Zone of Interior can always overload an objective area. *Top left,* the Fish Market in 1966, a thorny problem for the logistician; *top right,* field depot, Thu Duc storage area, five miles north of Saigon, showing the results of increased planning control and accountability. Logistical support was a continuing concern of the senior leadership; *right,* General Abrams, the MACV commander, visits 1st Logistical Command headquarters accompanied by Generals Mildren, Ramsey, and Heiser.

Important facets of the log mission. Repairing T–53 helicopter engine on the USS *Corpus Christi Bay,* December 1969; *below,* cleaning rifles prior to wrapping and shipping for retrograde, November 1971.

Sea-land vans used to transport supplies; *below*, an Army artist's rendition of the dangerous resupply routes through the mountains of Vietnam.

Assistant Secretary of Defen[se] Thomas Morris (*center*) in co[n]ference with 1st Log staff, Vi[et]nam, November 1968.

Equipment maintenance in Vietnam. Logistics personnel remove the engine from a 5-ton truck for repair.

"Well, we needed tail rotors more than telephone poles, didn't we?"

A cartoonist's solution to t[he] 1st Log's problem with e[x]cess materiel.

The 1st Log commander reviews logistics operations, 1969; *below,* computers provide inventory accountability in all direct support units in Vietnam, 1969.

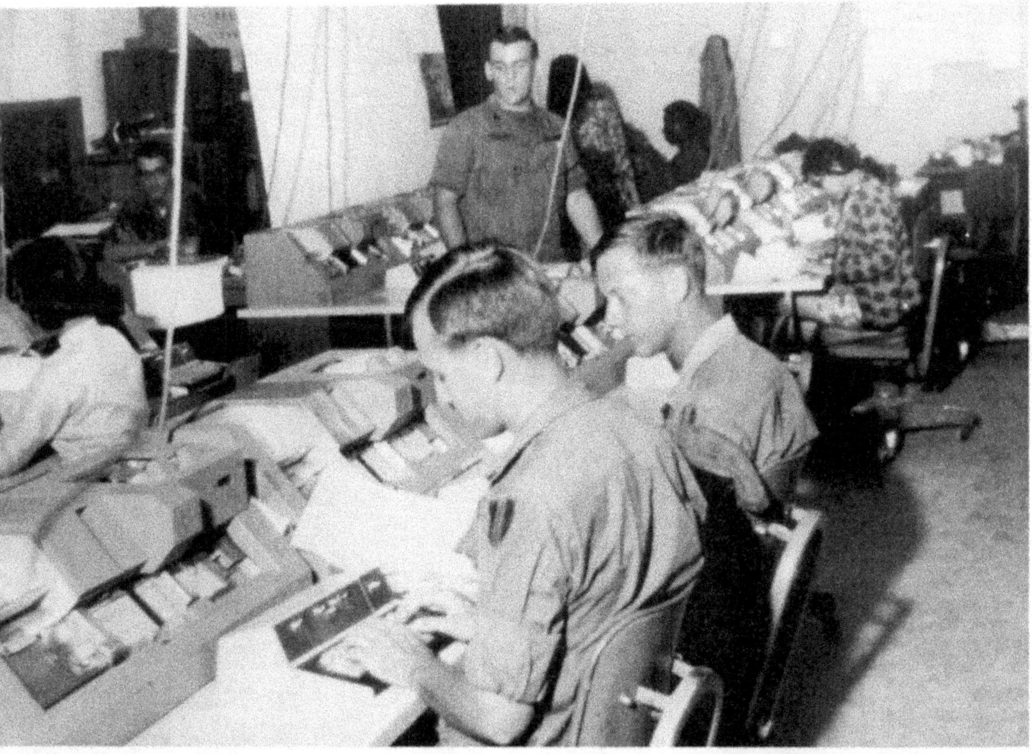

A CH–47 Chinook helicopter airlifts supplies to a battalion of the 23d Infantry Division (American), west of Tam Ky; *below,* artillery ammunition prepared for sling loading by helicopter.

The Sheridan M551 arrives in Vietnam. General Heiser speaks at a demonstration exercise at Long Binh Depot before issue to Col. George Patton's 11th Cav; *below,* armored gun truck for logistics security. A 5-ton M54A2 mounted with the stripped-down hull of an APC like that driven by Medal of Honor winner Sgt. Larry A. Dahl.

VIP support, a continual responsibility of senior logistician Heiser in Vietnam and elsewhere. *Clockwise from above,* Archbishop (later Cardinal) Terence Cooke; actress Martha Raye; Rev. Billy Graham; Mrs. Ethel Kennedy; and comedian Bob Hope.

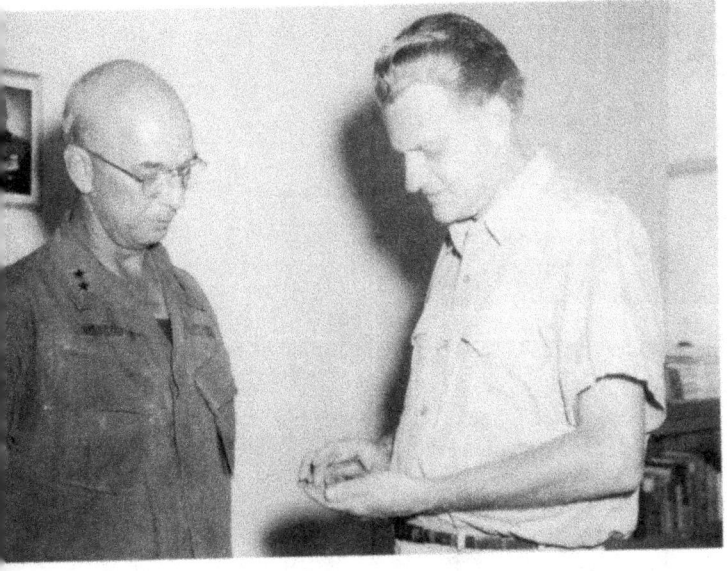

Off-loading lumber and steel at Newport, a modern facility built by the U.S. Army and capable of handling four deep-draft and nine smaller vessels simultaneously; *below,* an Army reservist receives the 1st Log Command's coveted Soldier of the Month award, April 1969.

PART IV

A Continuing Commitment

# CHAPTER 11

# Retirement

Normally, lieutenant generals retire at the age of 59, but I had been led to believe that even though I would reach retirement age in January 1973, I would be retained on active duty for another year to get the Logistics Offensive on a firm footing across the whole Army. To my surprise I was informed the summer before that I would have to retire by my birthday, 22 January 1973. I must admit that this was one of the worst days of my career because I had been counting on further duty as the DCSLOG, especially since I would be working under General Abrams, who was just returning from Vietnam to become the Chief of Staff.

My retirement exactly on schedule instead of an expected extended tour was probably the result of several factors. First, Secretary Robert F. Froehlke told me after a tennis match one day during his first week on the job that he intended to reduce "Army brass" immediately. Shortly thereafter, thirty-two major generals were given notice of early retirement. To extend someone like me at that time might have appeared unfair to the others. Second, I had not supported all of the reorganization concepts advanced by the Assistant Vice Chief of Staff, General William DePuy. I had also opposed the dictatorial manner in which automation planning (including automation of Army logistics) was being carried out. General DePuy and those in control of this planning often disregarded the advice of those operationally responsible. Finally, I had opposed Secretary Froehlke's decision to relieve a lieutenant general rather than face a congressional investigation because the general unjustly incurred the ire of a senator investigating property disposal operations. I defended the general for acting in accordance with good judgment and proper authority. (The general, incidentally, retained his command.) I'm not sure which of these three factors led most directly to my retirement, but I took the appropriate action and retired in January 1973.

## Farewell to the Army

My wife and I wanted to avoid the usual retirement parade by the 3d Infantry at Fort Myer. Having been an enlisted man, I knew full well the reaction of troops ordered to pass in review before an officer with whom they had not served, particularly in midwinter. To avoid good-byes, I scheduled previously delayed talks at many training centers with General Abrams' approval. These kept me away from Washington during my last month on duty. I arranged for my successor, Lt. Gen. Fred Kornet, to assume the DCSLOG's duties a month ahead of time while I lectured at the twelve senior schools, presenting a summary of what had been recently accomplished in logistics and indicating what I thought was needed to set the pace for logistics to the year 2000.

When General Abrams heard of my request to skip retirement protocol, he said, "You and Sug are going to accept an invitation to dinner at my home. You invite whomever you want." It was scheduled a few days after the Abrams moved into the newly remodeled Quarters One at Fort Myer. We invited all of my previous superiors and peers who had given me the experience and inspiration that had helped me through the years. After dinner General Abe presented me with a second Oak Leaf Cluster to the Distinguished Service Medal and Sug with a gold bracelet with miniatures of the insignia of each of the ranks that I had held from first sergeant through general officer. In making these presentations Abrams talked about me, but he was really giving the distinguished guests a brief homily about an important aspect of leadership. He recounted the story of the 1st Cavalry Division's need to block an enemy attempt to take Saigon when the capital was only lightly defended. He wanted me to assure him that the 1st Cav could be moved in 72 hours from I Corps in time to block the enemy attack. He remembered all the details and said, "I want everyone to understand that working with Joe Heiser taught me that Joe would tell the truth about any matter. Therefore I knew that if Joe said we could do it, we could do it. When he told me we could move the 1st Cav quickly, that ended the matter. I approved the 1st Cav plan!"

Integrity is important in the Army, and obviously General Abrams depended on it in his subordinates. In the military we have to level with our peers, our superiors, and our juniors. We should try to be tactful, but in the last analysis, we cannot let those making important decisions for our country make them without all the pertinent information we have available. The word integrity means that we should not be untruthful, but it also means that we should not avoid telling the truth, even though we are not asked. It is our duty to be sure that every decision that is made looks all pertinent facts in the face. To do less is to shirk our duty.

There have been at least a dozen significant times in my career when I had to state what I knew to be facts even though I knew that my audience wished that they might be different. I tried to be tactful, but I didn't mince words. I would lay the unvarnished facts out as I saw them. As a result of this approach, in the short term, I may have left some meetings concerned that I had reduced my influence, but I never had to feel guilty about not doing the right thing. I never took such action without being sure I knew what I was talking about. There were times when, as a result of a truthful statement, I was asked, "Is that all, captain?" (or whatever my rank happened to be), and when I said, "Yes, sir," I was told on at least three occasions, "All right, you're dismissed." In the short run, I had to wonder if I had lost favor, but in the long run, it appears that what I did without seeking favor caused me to gain the respect and understanding of those who knew me. I believe that all the people with whom I served knew that they could count on me to state the facts.

After a recent talk I gave at the Armed Forces Industrial College, a Marine Corps colonel asked during the question-and-answer period, "General, you've leveled with us more than anyone who has been in here all year. Why don't other senior people do the same thing?" I could not agree with his implication that other senior officers did not level with people on things they knew. In fact, as I told the audience, I could count the general officer dissemblers that I knew on one hand. But there is a great deal of difference between a senior official stating what he knows to be the truth from his own experience and one speaking without the background and experience to acquaint him fully with the facts. This underscores the importance of a commander's staff. Senior people really want the truth 100 percent of the time, but they must depend on their staffs to provide it. As you become more and more senior, you have to develop the knack of determining those subordinates you can look to for the plain truth. This need to level with the boss is a very important principle to be understood and adhered to. Often the lives of troops and the welfare of our country depend upon our fulfilling this responsibility.

I must emphasize that the greater the crisis situation in which we find ourselves, the greater the need for honesty. This is so in spite of the fact that at times we wish that in being honest we could give a more optimistic picture of a situation. However, we must state the facts, whatever they are. People in logistics are often accused of being negative because many times we must tell our bosses that their logistics capabilities limit the actions that they want to take. We must be able to present a constructive plan for the situation as quickly as we give a negative report. But regardless of the effects of the facts, we must be honest and resist the natural temptation to "make points."

While speaking of the problems of leadership, I believe that to exaggerate the old principle of Rank Has Its Privileges (RHIP) is harmful to the morale of Army units that are subjected to it. The behavior of Paul Galvin, head of Motorola, which I have described earlier, was the opposite of RHIP. I am sure that the use of rank, whether for traditional reasons or as a form of leadership technique, depends upon the personality of the officer. I served with British units briefly before D-Day. I admire and respect the British Army, its officers, and its practices and traditions, but as an American I could never feel comfortable with the unbridgeable gap I observed between its officers and enlisted men. It is different in the U.S. Army. While not democratic, neither is it autocratic, nor does it have to be. Since the Revolutionary War our Army has treated men in the ranks differently than do our British cousins. There is no unbridgeable gap between our enlisted men and officers. You can hardly tell an officer from an enlisted man under certain combat conditions. In fact, on occasion I have had to raise Cain with troops in combat who were determined to come to attention and salute even when fragmentation was flying. Such action, I believe, was subconsciously recognizing that in combat the lives of enlisted men depend to a great degree upon the capability of the officer leading them. To relax such outward signs of discipline does not mean that discipline disappears.

There are times to "pull rank," but in my experience the few times I have found it necessary were because of the poor attitude of the soldier involved. I can remember less than ten occasions in all my years with troops when I found it necessary to do anything approaching "pulling rank," and half of those times I was probably doing it unnecessarily. I certainly did get riled when I perceived a poor attitude.

The old RHIP syndrome led at times in the past to some senior officers' abusing their right to have enlisted aides. Generals used to be assigned one enlisted aide for each star. I would use my aides to help my wife when, for example, we had to serve as official hosts, but we couldn't help be aware of a next-door neighbor with nine enlisted aides—which was preposterous in itself—who performed all sorts of menial domestic chores. Toward the end of my active-duty career I raised this subject in an Army Policy Council meeting, but my attempt to call attention to the abuse was unsuccessful. I was questioning one of those traditions which most people fear to deal with. My suggestions were left lying on the table. The abuse continued until Congress took most of the enlisted aides away, thereby depriving conscientious senior officers of genuinely needed assistance in the performance of official duties.

I have seen spouses of general officers who attempt to "wear their husband's rank" and give orders to other wives. I know of cases of wives who have said that, unless they got another wife's cooperation, the efficiency report of the latter's husband would reflect this lack of response. Needless to say, this behavior is deadly and not the Army way. As a team Sug and I may have been deficient in some of the social graces. Sug is a "plain ole country gal" who had to fight for a high school education. We had little training or experience, nor really much desire, to participate with any great frequency in the social scene. But she never used my rank in her relationships with others. In fact, I am not sure she knew or cared exactly where my rank stood in the pecking order. As a result many people who knew her told me, "She's the way a general officer's wife ought to be." I believe meeting that kind of standard is about all that one can ask of a spouse.

I don't think there are general policies and procedures for using rank that will fit every officer in every situation. Leadership is necessarily personal. An officer needs good judgment and perhaps an ability to take counsel from his colleagues to decide how best to use rank to get the job done. Prudence is the key word in using rank, as it is in all decisions, personal and public. In my specific case, I honestly do not know whether my approach to rank had to do with my personality or my background and experience, including having served as an enlisted man. What I do know is that I was able to achieve better results more pleasantly by dealing with enlisted personnel and junior officers with little or no thought of rank.

I seldom had to give a direct order. Most of my direction was given by making requests or suggestions, and those who knew me knew that that was the way things were done in my unit. In times of stress I didn't hesitate to say, "Do it." On the other hand, they knew that when I did give such a direct order I was not trying to pull rank. It was just a case of getting the job done. One can't temporize in combat, and a leader must understand that leadership does not always allow one to make decisions that everyone likes. Military leaders cannot always win popularity contests. Nevertheless, a leader must strive to gain the understanding of his people by letting them know why decisions are made and how they fit into the objectives.

I admit I have a quick temper. As a result many times I did not "mince words" when giving orders to subordinates or arguing my position on staff decisions among my peers. But I have a principle to which I adhere to this day: whenever I lose my temper, especially if it is centered on one individual, I make it a point before the end of that day to get in touch with that person to let him know that I am sorry I lost my temper. Maybe I was right, maybe I was wrong, but I want him to know that it was not personal. I believe that most people who served with me knew that this was the way I was, and as a result, they accepted my apology when I told them that I was sorry that the discussion turned out as it did. I tried especially hard to acknowledge when I was wrong.

When thinking about this habit of apologizing the same day, I think back to my old boss in the COMZ, General Andrew O'Meara. O'Meara was a fine commander and a great planner, but he was also a very stern disciplinarian and not easy to work for. Long before it became popular, O'Meara emphasized physical fitness in his command. He was a positive bear about overweight soldiers. Once while touring the COMZ aviation maintenance center in Sandhofen, Germany, we were joined by the center's commander who, unknown to O'Meara, had been disabled in Korea. As a result he had put on weight. When we climbed to the second floor of the command building for a briefing, the always energetic O'Meara moved ahead. When he reached the top, he looked down on the slow-moving colonel and made a loud comment about out-of-shape officers. After leaving the unit I told O'Meara about the officer's leg problem and how he was desperately trying to stay in service. O'Meara ordered the car stopped and quickly phoned the colonel to apologize. I always remember that incident and have tried to learn from it.

My technique of relating to others can be used only if it fits an officer's own personality and style. But of one thing I am certain: any credit I got was because the people who worked with me got the job done. Because I readily admitted this fact, I could generally depend upon others to do what I asked. The job was done, and they probably did it far better than I expected or could have done by myself. I believe my dealings with people were successful, but then I have a somewhat "screwball" personality. I don't know whether others can do all the things that I tried, but certainly some elements of my general approach are worthy of consideration by all officers who deal with others of whatever rank.

# RETIREMENT

Officers are part of a community that is larger than the units and the soldiers who form those units. Except during wartime, families usually accompany officers and senior enlisted personnel during tours of duty. These families are part of the Army community. All members of this community must be prepared to cooperate to assure the well-being and happiness of each other, often in various parts of the world. They must learn to get along with and support one another. This also means that they must participate in the social activities that make a group of Army personnel much more than just a group but a cohesive community. Naturally, there are traditions, customs, and procedures that have grown up over the years to provide the basic elements of the community's relationships.

The community includes such things as enlisted, NCO, and officers clubs; thrift shops; welcoming teams; and places where a soldier can borrow money or other resources for needs when the Army family has just arrived, or where the family can borrow when a soldier has just departed. There are places to go for help when someone needs assistance beyond his or her own resources, to include formal organizations like the Army Emergency Relief and United Services Organizations (USO) and informal organizations that grow up in each community to provide help to one another when needed. In modern times, many Army wives are career women. Thus their availability to do community work is restricted. Army community life must accommodate such changes and yet still provide the optimum social support.

At the top of this community are the commanding officer and his wife. To a large degree they are the forces that turn that community into a wonderful place to be—or something less, depending on how well they do their job. This is a very important responsibility, not only for the commander himself but for his spouse. Each contributes to the vitality and the value of a particular Army community. This is especially true of commanders of high rank. It takes specific training and know-how to assume these responsibilities and carry them out properly. In my experience the implementation of these responsibilities has differed with the personalities of each general and his spouse. I have seen this duty performed very well by most commanders and their spouses. On the other hand, I have seen Army communities that really were not happy because of the problems emanating from the way the general and his wife carried out their duties. It takes tact, understanding, persuasion, and prudence.

## The Consultant

When news of my retirement became public, I was offered many opportunities in industry, but I declined them all to avoid any hint of conflict of interest. I quickly discovered that firms rarely approach a retired general officer to help them improve their management. Rather, they want to make more money by using his knowledge of people and connections. Even the Army Ordnance Association was not immune to exploitation. That group (now the American Defense Preparedness Association) invited me to attend its annual dinner after my retirement. I then got a letter from a contractor telling me that he appreciated my being his company's guest and asking me to take part in their hospitality-room proceedings before dinner. I was to be their guest, apparently, even though I was to sit at the head table. I called a personal friend at the association and said, "Look, I can't accept under these conditions. This wasn't what you told me." Unfortunately, I haven't had a polite conversation with that gentleman since.

I decided, with my wife's agreement, to use my background, training, and experience in the interest of the Army and the country to whatever extent I could. I've never sought work, but until today I have never been left idle. Very quickly, General Abrams, the General Accounting Office (GAO), and several other government agencies, including the White House, began requesting my help on an on-call basis. I readily agreed to such arrangements, which are still, seventeen years later, my first priority.

I am continually surprised at how long this working arrangement has lasted. I thought my value to the Department of Defense and others would gradually decrease within two or three years and quietly cease. Accordingly, I accepted a vice presidential position with Wilbur Smith and Associates, an engineering consulting firm in Columbia, South Carolina, not then involved in government contracts. But requests for help from government agencies, especially the GAO, took up almost 100 percent of my time, and I left Wilbur Smith and Associates with my apologies after just three weeks.

One of my earliest summonses to Washington came from the White House Executive Office and the Office of the Secretary of the Interior to assist in a fuel allocation problem caused by the 1973–74 fuel crisis. Working on fuel allocation to an oil-starved nation would have been a challenge, but after reviewing the situation for a week with the principals, I declined the offer, wisely I believe, because it would have put me in the center of a political fight within the administration that would have hampered my ability to

# RETIREMENT

get the job done. I did, however, agree to help out for two months in setting up a control organization which eventually evolved into today's Department of Energy.

Since January 1973 I have worked on many occasions with officials in the GAO. I have appreciated both the objectivity of that group of officials and their willingness to overcome the traditional antagonism that has existed between the GAO and the armed services. Some tension is natural between these agencies because the GAO, as "the eyes and ears of Congress," must review how defense officials execute the law in their area. I feel the atmosphere and rapport between the GAO and the armed forces are much better today, perhaps to some degree because my personal efforts have been useful and constructive.

Actually my close relationship with the GAO began during the Holifield committee hearings in 1968–70. Toward the end of those hearings, a news release was put together by Holifield's staff. I thought, frankly, that the draft did not give adequate credit to the Army and DOD for the expedited logistics actions and the good results that had been achieved. I got through to Congressman Holifield before his departure for California and told him of my concern. He told me to call his administrative assistant, give him my version, and "tell him that I've okayed it as long as he doesn't have any violent objection." As a result my version was issued to the press. Earlier I had gone on record that the Holifield hearings on Vietnam support were an outstanding example of the kind of cooperation that should exist between GAO auditors, Department of Defense representatives, and a congressional committee. I suspect that my work in relationship to the Holifield committee led to my becoming a GAO adviser soon after retirement.

My first consulting task for the GAO was to produce a videotape for dissemination throughout the agency on how the armed services felt about the GAO. There was little understanding and respect for the GAO by people in the services because of GAO's general lack of knowledge about defense problems and the somewhat arbitrary attitude of some of its officials. One direct result of this effort was that Elmer Staats, the Comptroller General, through his deputy, Tom Morris, asked me to help rewrite GAO policy, to include: "Promotion points will not be gained by the number of deficiencies found in an agency, but only by the constructive progress that results from the review."

Some in the Pentagon did not look favorably on my GAO duty. They'd say, "Holy mackerel, Joe, you know where all the bodies are buried." I knew that my loyalties transcended any single government agency, and I can say after seventeen years of duty with the GAO that I have never been put in a position of conflict of interest. I simply gave the best advice I could, and I believe that it worked to the benefit of all.*

In 1975 I was asked by an Assistant Secretary of Defense to work on a logistics reorganization plan for OSD. This was an internal study directed by Deputy Secretary of Defense William P. Clements, Jr. Under consideration was the combining of several of the assistant secretary positions, including a proposal to combine research and development with logistics. Logisticians were opposed to such a merger for very good reasons, and in an effort to block the move, we proposed instead that logistics be combined with personnel under one assistant secretary. We assumed no one would consider such an outlandish move, because in an emergency it would mean that manpower and logistics—two of the most important defense functions—would be controlled by one assistant secretary, leaving the Secretary of Defense with little to do. But we were fooled. Logistics and personnel were subsequently merged under one assistant secretary for many years. My appointment to this reorganization study, actually the location of my desk, seemed to cause a little discomfort in OSD. It was just after an assistant secretary for installations and logistics had departed, and his principal civilian deputy, John J. Bennett, had been named his acting replacement. Jack continued to occupy the office next to the assistant secretary's office, while I was placed on a temporary basis in the assistant secretary's office with that official's secretary, car, and driver. To many (but certainly not to Jack Bennett, the apparent nominee) this treatment was clear evidence that I would eventually be appointed to some high position. Although I was approached on several occasions concerning a senior civilian job, it was never in the cards for me. I was simply a consultant temporarily using that office.

## Iran

In 1975 I was asked by the DCSLOG and the Army Aviation Systems Command (AVSCOM) to participate in a review of an industry contract with the government of Iran to furnish 1,000 heli-

---

*Any mention of my work at GAO calls for special tribute to a number of exceptional civil servants: Kenneth Fasick, Fred Schaeffer, John Landico, Richard Helmer, Rich Davis, Paul Math, Donna Heivilin, Rosa Chavelier, Bud Connor, Julia Denman, and all those others at GAO who deserve recognition. These people, under Elmer Staats and Charles A. Bowsher, treated me royally, and I believe they have the defense of our country at heart. I find in these men and women a dedication to duty which rivals that found in the Defense Department. Among civilians, they stand at the top of the list.

copters and the logistic structure and pilot training to operate and support them. Under the terms of this complicated contract, Bell International, a subsidiary of the Bell Helicopter Company, dealt directly with the government of Iran under the close supervision of AVSCOM. Instead of bringing in a government team to do the in-progress review, the Army contracted with Col. Joseph Franklin, an experienced logistician who, now retired, headed his own consulting business. I was asked to ascertain the appropriateness of the logistic support and to recommend any necessary improvements.

Once on the scene we quickly learned that, because Bell did not have sufficient staff to manage the contract with Iran, they had hired many new people. They found some good people, but in almost every case these specialists in avionics and avionic support were put into positions that required far greater breadth and depth of authority and responsibility than anything they had done in the past. This led to problems and improper decisions, including a massive oversupply of spare parts. Part of the problem could be blamed on the Iranian government. We pointed out to the Iranians that the separate organization they were setting up to support helicopters was unnecessary. If this support were combined with other logistic support, many common functions and items could be integrated, thus avoiding unnecessary, separate management. I quickly learned that they did not want an integrated system. Part of the problem, as the Shah saw it, was the need to avoid putting too much power in the hands of any one person or organization.

Our review also indicated that the Iranians were establishing a logistics base to support the helicopters based upon an initial estimate of 150,000 line items for support. This compared with the 40,000 line items that AVSCOM required as the stockage objective for support of all U.S. Army aircraft, including helicopters and fixed-wing aircraft. The Iranian contract, on the other hand, supported just one helicopter type. Iran in turn was using the 150,000 lines as a base figure to determine how much storage space was required. It turned out that the estimate of 150,000 was at least three times greater than required, and the storage requirement was leading to construction of warehouse space that was at least double, if not triple, that required.

The Shah's operation was repeating all the errors that we had fallen into, and in many cases corrected, in our support of helicopters in Vietnam. These mistakes included lack of appropriate cataloging, lack of identification of parts, excessive dependence on contractor support, and inappropriate requisition objectives. Furthermore, Bell's inexperienced staff was supposed to train the Iranians so that in three years they could take over the logistic support for this fleet of helicopters. But whenever Bell identified an outstanding Iranian trainee, the government would promptly transfer him to some other job where his training and knowledge could be put, it was thought, to better use.

We recommended changes to avoid wasteful expenditures. We urged the Iranians to reduce their helicopter parts requisitioning objective because it was based upon too many years' parts requirements and included many parts that should never have been requisitioned at all. We were rebuffed in our efforts to get this requisitioning reduced, however. As the Shah put it, "I need as much as thirty years' worth of parts because I can't depend upon the United States to continue its support for the long-range future. I have got to have a safety level to ensure my continued support." We tried to get the Iranians to buy from DOD inventory as part of their standard system. That would have allowed them to greatly reduce the annual cost for repair parts, because they would have been treated as a claimant on the inventory available in U.S. stocks, as we were treating Israel, Germany, and others. But again the Iranians would not agree because of their perception that we could not be trusted to continue our support. In my view this perception still lurks behind a large part of our dealings with our allies, including those in NATO.

During my approximately two months in Iran I had the opportunity to meet the Shah and Shahbanu on the tennis court because of my acquaintance with their tennis instructor. The Shahbanu once asked me if it would be possible for some of the women professional tennis players in the United States to travel to Iran for exhibition matches. She was trying to elevate the position of women in Iran and to that end wanted to get Iranian women interested in playing tennis. I thought it entirely possible, and when I returned to the United States, I did enlist several professional women tennis players to participate in an exhibition in Iran. However, as it turned out, the Shah and his wife went into exile before the matches took place, and so that ended that.

## Cambodia

In November 1979 I had just returned to my home in Columbia, South Carolina, in the small hours of the morning when I was awakened by a call from the White House. It was presidential assistant Zbigniew Brzezinski telling me that President Jimmy Carter wanted me to accompany his wife Rosalynn to the Far East to deter-

# RETIREMENT

mine what could be done to avoid starvation in Cambodia. Brzezinski told me that the President had planned to go himself until the hostage crisis in Iran intervened. He had prevailed on his wife to go instead, promising to provide her with the best available logistician to advise her on the logistics of solutions to the hunger problems.

I told Brzezinski that I would be glad to be of assistance, but, because I was unfamiliar with the situation in Cambodia, I asked for a briefing prior to departure. Brzezinski replied that Mrs. Carter was leaving on Air Force One from Andrews Air Force Base that evening, and I had to be there. I promptly said, "I'll do my best" and hung up. I immediately contacted Fort Jackson to schedule the necessary inoculations and an Army aircraft to take me up to Andrews by 1800 hours. I then remembered that my passport was at the State Department for renewal. When contacted about the problem, Brzezinski's office promised my passport would be on the aircraft. (It turned out that an assistant secretary of state hand-carried my passport.) I arrived at Andrews just in time to board Air Force One as the President's helicopter arrived.

The plane was loaded with Secret Service and media personnel. Its forward compartments were reserved for Mrs. Carter and her party, including U.S. Surgeon General Julius B. Richmond; Assistant Secretary of State Richard C. Holbrooke; former Senator Harold E. Hughes; Mrs. Andrew Young, the chairperson of the United Nations International Year of the Child; and Mrs. Carter's secretary, Madeline MacBean. I immediately began hearing rumors that there was a plan that I would remain in Thailand/Cambodia to supervise relief actions after Mrs. Carter's departure. I certainly was not prepared to remain for any length of time in the Far East, and so I asked Madeline MacBean to make sure that I would be on any plane with Mrs. Carter going back to Washington. This young woman thus became my "guardian angel."

We took a direct flight to Bangkok, with two complete aircraft crews so that, except for refueling, there would be no delays en route. In the air I was briefed on the plan and objectives of the trip. Assistant Secretary Holbrooke indicated that he wanted to arrange air shipment of trucks to Cambodia to carry food. I had to set things straight with him quickly. I said, "Mr. Secretary, I cannot recommend airlift of trucks, because we do not know what the problem is yet. As soon as we ascertain the problems then I will submit my recommendations, which may include an airlift of trucks, but that will have to depend upon what we find the problems to be." That clarified my position, and thereafter I had no further problems with any preplanned recommendations.

It was of great interest to the reporters in the rear of the aircraft when they discovered that a general was going along to advise Mrs. Carter. In an impromptu press conference I explained simply that logistics is logistics. If people need food, transport, or whatever other resources, a trained logistician should be able to figure out an effective and efficient plan of action. The fact that I had military logistics training made it even more appropriate that my experience be used in a time of crisis. My explanation was generally accepted, and the question was not raised again.

During the twenty-hour flight I had the opportunity for several informal talks with Mrs. Carter. I indicated my surprise at being asked to participate because, as I told her, I had not voted for her husband. I said it humorously, but I really did wonder why I had been selected. Mrs. Carter replied, "We weren't interested in what party you belong to or for whom you voted; we were interested in getting someone capable of advising myself and the President on what we could best do to solve the logistics problems that we would find in Cambodia and in those countries bordering on that sad state." That cleared the air and allowed me to get to know the First Lady as a person.

In our personal discussions on the lengthy trip she told me how she was afraid when she came to the White House because she knew she would be expected to entertain royalty and other dignitaries from around the world. Her previous experience was limited to the role of a governor's wife, when she had been surrounded by friends and politicians she knew. The White House was obviously a great deal different. To her surprise, she told me, she found that the people she thought would frighten her turned out to be just as fearful of her and the President. When she discovered this, she had no further problems. She proved to be a delightfully frank person as she talked of life in the White House with Amy and with the President, their difficult and often conflicting official schedules, and how they had to arrange family meetings to prevent their schedules from taking over their lives.

It was agreed that Mrs. Carter's schedule would be devoted mostly to official meetings, in visits both around Bangkok and in refugee camps near the Thai-Cambodian border. We decided on a separate itinerary for me so that I could meet with representatives of the Thai government, United Nations agencies, and private charitable organizations, all of which were attempting to solve the problem of starvation in Cambodia. I sent a message to Ambassador Morton I. Abramowitz asking that I be assigned a knowledgeable U.S. official to accompany me to these meetings.

# RETIREMENT

Immediately upon our arrival in Bangkok, the taxing schedule started. We had very little time for sleeping or eating. The Carter party was on the go traveling around Thailand for almost five full days. In my case, with the help of Ambassador Abramowitz and his staff and that of the U.S. Agency for International Development, I was given some flexibility in arranging meetings. Individual discussions and group meetings involving all those engaged in the valiant effort to feed the Cambodians were valuable and allowed me to get a better feel for the actual problems.

One of the major problems was one that often affects groups of people trying to help: communications. People were just not talking to each other. There was little or no joint effort to try to solve the food problems of those who had crossed into Thailand or those still in Cambodia. It was not that the groups were uncooperative, but each was dedicated to solving the problem using its own resources in isolation from the others. One of my scheduled meetings marked the very first time that representatives from at least twenty-five different agencies had sat together to discuss common problems.

At the outset of that meeting I asked each representative to outline his problems as he saw them and his agency's capabilities and limitations to meet the problems. After they all spoke, quite candidly, it became evident that all had limited capabilities. For example, some organizations needed transport; other organizations didn't have a problem of transport. Some organizations were feeding groups of evacuees who were also being fed by other organizations, meaning that some people were getting more than enough rations while others were still not getting enough. This same imbalance existed for health care and medical supplies.

It also quickly became apparent that very few organizations, including the United Nations, were being favorably received by the government of Cambodia. They were willing to accept the food, but they didn't want any outside support or supervision of the distribution process within their boundaries. Thus the United States, Thailand, and other governments needed to push negotiations to convince the Cambodian government to allow the required help within its borders.

It was readily apparent that there was in Thailand a considerable supply of rice but that the funds to obtain this food were not available. Thus, at least temporarily, money was needed to buy the available rice for the refugees. When the discussions turned to constructing base camps for evacuees with adequate sanitation, food service, and health care, the Surgeon General and his assistants provided invaluable advice.

Starvation, the basic cause of the death of so many Cambodian refugees, has been practically eliminated since the Carter visit, which proved to be a catalyst for progress. Before the Khmer Rouge came to power Cambodia was known as the breadbasket of the Far East. The constructive action that really began with the Carter team visit proved of long-range value. As the result of the actions it recommended to the President, the Cambodians, beginning in about 1979, were able to resume rice production. But many problems continue to exist in that war-torn nation. The government and the people of Thailand deserve considerable credit for the help they continue to give to refugees who cross their borders.

CHAPTER 12

# Coalition Logistics

> Co-ordination is all very well, but eventually somebody has to get on and do the job.
> *NATO Logistics Handbook, 1989*

Since my retirement in 1973, much of my attention has been focused on the logistical situation in the North Atlantic Treaty Organization. NATO is now forty years old. That's a long time for sixteen independent nations to remain banded together against a common threat. I believe our alliance has been remarkably successful. To a great degree it has been a deterrent to war in central Europe. It also has continued to be a key element in planning for a new military and political order in Europe in the 1990s. At the same time this vital coalition has had significant problems, some of them closely related to the logistical aspects of war.

I believe that our experience in NATO provides an understanding of alliance concepts that can be applied around the world. Membership in NATO, as in any military alliance, demands that each nation relinquish some of its authority in order to gain the objectives of the whole alliance. Each nation and its citizenry must understand this commitment. Unfortunately, until a crisis each nation, including the United States, tends jealously to guard its sovereignty. In fact, my deputy in the NATO Logistics Task Force in 1976 (a Belgian major general) would needle me occasionally by asking, "When is the United States going to join the alliance?"

To work successfully, such an alliance demands that its members allocate much of their national resources to provide a logistical base. But the sixteen nations of NATO have resisted delegating control of their national logistics. One of the greatest problems in NATO is the common perception that logistics remains a national responsibility. Such an assumption runs directly contrary to the basic definition of a military alliance. Some members of the alliance ignore the founding principles of NATO and avoid following them.

Concern about such matters has led NATO and American officials to ask me on four separate occasions since 1975 to study the logistical situation in NATO and recommend necessary reforms. In 1975 I conducted a logistical survey of NATO forces for General Alexander Haig, the Supreme Allied Commander, Europe (SACEUR). In 1977 I headed the logistical committee in a major review of NATO's defense plans conducted by the NATO ministers. In 1980 General Frido von Senger und Etterlin asked me to review logistics in Allied Forces Central Europe (AFCENT), one of the three major NATO land forces. Finally, in 1988 I was asked by the Comptroller General of the United States, Charles A. Bowsher, to participate in an examination of issues relating to the balance of forces between NATO and the Warsaw Pact.

During much of this time I was doing other consultancy work for the GAO and other governmental agencies. The almost full-time nature of the NATO work, especially service on the NATO task force in 1977–78, required a modification in my status as a part-time government consultant. Accordingly, at the behest of Secretary of Defense Harold Brown, I became a member of the consulting staff of the Logistics Management Institute (LMI), a prominent defense management research center, which in turn contracted out my services to the Department of Defense. I had always been leery about working for defense contractors, but since the arrangement had been suggested by the Secretary of Defense and since the president of LMI, Hugh McCullough, was a personal friend who agreed that LMI's connection would be limited to providing editorial and other administrative assistance, I gladly signed on. This arrangement has lasted some fifteen years and, I believe, has worked well.

The opportunity to work for General Haig came about because Haig asked Secretary of Defense Donald Rumsfeld to provide an experienced person to review the logistic status of the Allied Command Europe (ACE). One of my National War College classmates, Air Force General Theodore Seitz, the Supreme Headquarters, Allied Powers Europe (SHAPE), Chief of Staff, knew of my logistics background and supported my nomination. In fact, Haig didn't know me well personally, but he depended on the advice of Ted Seitz and others. I consider the work I did for Haig as valuable as anything I have done in my entire life. Many of the things I learned while evaluating the ACE logistics situation for the Supreme Allied Commander formed the basis for all subsequent work I did in NATO.

General Haig asked me to get out with his local commanders and talk freely with them about their logistics problems. My tour was not that of an outside inspector reporting on the limitations and deficiencies of local commanders. I was accepted as a fellow practitioner anxious to help correct any military problems. None of us was inhibited by the need to represent national positions or observe diplomatic niceties. We were fellow soldiers discussing the common logistic problems of deterrence and/or warfighting.

I quickly discovered that SHAPE had many senior officers of many nationalities who were deeply concerned about problems with lines of communications, interoperability, transportation management, and retrograde and sustainability operations. They wanted to solve these problems but were inhibited by the continued reluctance of member nations to relinquish control over national resources, which more often involved national pride than availability of resources. They shared their concerns and made it easy for me to prepare a survey of their logistical problems with recommendations for improvement in the logistical base of the alliance.

I also visited each of the ministers of defense of the NATO allies and talked with all the military and civilian representatives of the allies and members of the NATO secretariat at the Brussels headquarters. Discussions with these officials went all the way back to the directives contained in the original NATO charter and their subsequent implementation, so that the resulting study was not only thorough but based on the experiences of all types of NATO authorities.

I drew up my frank conclusions about logistic weaknesses in ACE in a secret personal report for General Haig. Haig agreed with my recommendations for reform, but he also knew that his was a strictly military reaction to the report, which would likely get a very different reception at the NATO ministerial level. After I briefed him on the subject, he asked me to prepare an edited version—eliminating those things of direct interest to the United States alone—for his distribution to the allies. The concerns and recommendations in my report formed the basis for my subsequent work in NATO and will be discussed in detail below.

## NATO's Long Term Defense Program

About the time I finished my study for General Haig, President Carter, supported by Robert Komer, Special Assistant to the Secretary of Defense for NATO Affairs (later Under Secretary of Defense), decided that NATO's defense plans needed strengthening in ten different areas. This led to NATO's initiating a Long Term Defense Plan (LTDP). Ten task forces were organized in relation to this plan, and Bob Komer asked me in September 1977 to head the one on Consumer Logistics. The heads of the task forces were selected from among senior NATO officers and government civilians. I gather it was not easy to fill all the billets. Our objective was to prepare recommendations on the LTDP for review and approval by NATO heads of government at their meeting in May 1978. My earlier experience with General Haig proved of immense value in developing the logistics portions of the LTDP.

The logistics task force included senior military and civilian officials from among our allies. Each was assigned to examine a logistics subcategory and prepare reports and recommendations. While their perception of the problems was almost always on the mark, their willingness to recommend necessary reforms was not so often forthcoming. One colleague, for example, who prepared a splendid draft on fuel problems, submitted a final report significantly different because of objections by his home country officials. Although I refused to retreat from my conclusions, I too did not always receive full support from the U.S. Defense Department when it came to our task force's recommendations to the NATO ministers. In the end I personally visited each national capital and explained the content of our proposed recommendations. As a result of such visits recommendations were modified or added. Even those recommendations not agreed to officially had the private support of logistics officials in those nations where political reasons prevented agreement. This is a hazard in any alliance: until a crisis occurs, the protection of perceived sovereign rights of a nation tends to take first place. I prepared the final report myself, based on the work of the subcommittees, strengthening their recommendations when and where appropriate.

## A NATO Logistical Command

One of the Consumer Logistics Task Force's major recommendations concerned the establishment of logistics commands in Allied Forces Central, Northern, and Southern Europe. What may appear a relatively straightforward proposal was actually extremely complicated because it involved consideration of lines of communications (LOC) and communications zones. Most people in the United States, for example, talk of a line of communications across central Europe as if it were a proprietary service. There is no U.S. line of communications in Europe. We share with all other allied nations what is really a NATO LOC. We have no real control over the LOC we use to support our forces in central Europe. Each country remains sovereign within its national

# COALITION LOGISTICS

boundaries and retains its national prerogatives. What is important is to obtain the highest degree of cooperation in order that integrated logistics functions such as transportation and communication can be operated effectively and efficiently, especially in time of crisis.

At first in my discussions with NATO officials I used the word "integration" in regard to the LOC within NATO. I found, however, that various countries were intolerant of my use of the term "integration of logistics functions" because they perceived that it meant that the United States would take over the LOC and impose U.S. procedures on each of the countries involved. This was never our intent; that's the conclusion they drew. So we substituted the word "coordination" in discussing the efficiency necessary for an effective LOC across the NATO countries.

The task force also had to clarify a point that is not too well understood—the difference between the line of communications and the communications zone. I discovered in my work as task force director that it was necessary to separate clearly the two terms. They are not interchangeable. The line of communications is a line of networks consisting of roads, railroads, ports, airports, and sea lanes that provide the means for moving the troops and supplies needed in the combat zone. The communications zone is the organization that covers what are called, today, echelons above corps—that space between the corps rear area and the theater ports of entry. The communications zone includes the lines of communications as well as the means to move men, women, and supplies along the lines of communications. It also provides the service activities that take place behind the corps boundaries to provide support to the forward combat units.

It is essential to understand this difference in order to understand the importance of command and control within the communications zone. One of the biggest problems in all three wars in which I have served was the determination of appropriate headquarters for the operation of a communications zone. For example, in World War II in Europe the number of headquarters and the sizes of those headquarters were indefinite. Many times it seemed to be determined on the basis of how loudly the wheels squeaked.

Because of this problem, after World War II the Army organized TO&E logistics commands and established an appropriate command in the various communications zones depending upon their needs and responsibilities. In my own experience, in 1950 I was the first person assigned to the 2d Logistical Command activated in support of Eighth Army during the Pusan Perimeter campaign in Korea. In 1962 I was assigned as G–4, and then as Chief of Staff and Deputy Commander, of the 4th Logistical Command, which was responsible for operating all depots and other activities within the communications zone across France and Germany, and later to the 3d Logistical Command, which was the base TO&E for Headquarters, COMZ, in Orleans, France. During the Berlin crisis, when the European theater was reinforced with men and equipment, the 1st Logistical Command, a planning agency at Fort Bragg, had been ordered to France to assume responsibility for the operation of the southwest part of the communications zone in France. When the crisis subsided, the 1st Log returned to Fort Bragg. Later it became the logistic support command headquartered in Long Binh to support U.S. Army forces and to some degree all U.S. forces in Vietnam. The 2d Logistical Command went to Okinawa and, in essence, became a part of the communications zone in support of the 1st Log in Vietnam. Actually, the 1st Log was more like what used to be called a Field Army Support Command. Most of the 1st Log's operations were direct support, while most general and depot support was performed in the communications zone primarily composed of the 2d Log in Okinawa, the U.S. Army Depot Command in Japan, and the Taiwan Maintenance Activity.

It is especially important to understand that U.S. forces in Vietnam never had a typical (Continental) communications zone. The communications zone responsibilities were carried out by the three agencies mentioned above. Thus while there was no geographical area designated a communications zone, the fact is that a communications zone existed, with part of it under the U.S. Army, Vietnam; part under USARPAC, to include Okinawa and Japan; and part of it, the Taiwan Maintenance Activity, under the AMC.

The example of the Taiwan Maintenance Activity's rear-area support was later completely ignored by those involved in NATO planning, who took the position that the support was rather easily accomplished, maintained, and secured basically in CONUS. Some of this thinking can be traced back to Secretary McNamara's mistaken belief that a surface LOC in the age of aircraft transportation and fast communications was no longer needed by the Army. By contrast, I would strongly urge anyone involved in logistics planning to study the detailed histories published by the U.S. Army. They should convince any thoughtful person of the ongoing necessity to pay close attention to the planning and organization of possible wartime communications zones, to include command and control of the lines of communications.*

This attention is particularly important for the United States and its NATO allies. Beyond our own shores the United States today does not have its own line of communications. It must share the lines of communications in NATO with its allies based on various bilateral agreements. As many as a dozen nations have a right to use the same roads, railroads, barge canals, and communications systems as the United States. The operational details, covered by the bilateral agreements in most cases, clearly have to be worked out in advance. So far they have not been. To this day the United States does not have its own organized LOC in any part of the world but is dependent on allied support. This is true today in the Arabian peninsula and will most likely remain the case for the indefinite future.

Theoretically, the bilateral agreements that cover the NATO communications zone appear to work well. It is only when we stage maneuvers and tests that the agreements come into play and we can begin to see what the complexities really will be. Unfortunately, tests generally demonstrate how everything would work if everyone cooperated. REFORGER, the annual NATO training exercise, is an example of such a demonstration, as is the WINTEX command post exercise. But even these artificial exercises highlight certain problems. If we closely scrutinize the lines of communications NATO forces plan to use, we can clearly point out some of the obvious roadblocks and choke points that will cause trouble. We can learn a great deal by taking a close look at likely problems and working out alternatives to the conflicts that are likely to occur.

It is especially important to recognize what logistics command and control is needed first to make quick and timely decisions in wartime. I go back to Mr. Galvin at Motorola, who said you can't make decisions of this kind by committee. You have to have a single commander with the proper information who can make a timely decision. Of course, the commander depends on completed staff actions to give him the logistics intelligence he needs to make his decision, but he cannot tolerate a ponderous, time-consuming process.

In the end our task force's recommendation on the establishment of logistics commands was rejected. Every country, including

---

*I especially recommend the following volumes: Roland Ruppenthal's *Logistical Support of the Armies, Volume 1: May 1941–September 1944*, and *Logistical Support of the Armies, Volume 2: September 1944–May 1945*, and Robert Coakley and Richard Leighton's *Global Logistics and Strategy, 1940–1943*, and *Global Logistics and Strategy, 1943–1945*, all published by the Center of Military History as part of its U.S. Army in World War II series. I would also recommend that students consult my own *Logistic Support* (Washington, D.C.: Government Printing Office, 1974).

the United States, objected to the term "logistics command." We pointed out that the NATO major subordinate commanders lacked any logistics resources to command and argued that some sound logistics command structure had to be established. The task force had to settle for the term "coordination." As a result, today there is a NATO Multinational Coordinating Center at each of the major subordinate commands to perform the logistics command mission for each region. The centers should provide a basis for real logistical commands in case of crisis. The agreed national resources would be integrated into an optimum support plan by the center.

The NATO governments also approved a recommendation in the final LTDP report requiring SACEUR and his major subordinate commanders to establish agreements between NATO commands and the NATO nations governing the actions to be taken by the NATO commanders in a crisis to establish priorities for use of national resources. This agreement process has been under way for almost ten years. It must be accomplished, both as a deterrent to war and for the current military effectiveness of NATO. Such an agreement in NATO itself could be used to integrate all the bilateral agreements now being negotiated between individual allies in other parts of the world.

## Interoperability in NATO

The term RSI is used throughout NATO. "R" stands for rationalization which means, as I interpret it, do whatever you can to do better. "S" stands for standardization, a very important part of NATO objectives, especially with respect to equipment, policies, and procedures. I believe it entirely unlikely that we will ever attain a high degree of standardization of equipment, but more likely we will agree to some extent on common weaponry, such as the F–16 tactical aircraft and some missile systems, to which certain nations have already agreed.

The most useful and essential of those three letters—the "I"—stands for interoperability. Simply put, interoperability means the knowledge and skill to use the weapons and equipment of allies, as well as the procedures, forms, and logistic language that would make it possible to facilitate alliance assistance to one another. It does not impose the need to standardize equipment but recognizes that in a multinational army it is imperative that units of the ally on your flanks can use your equipment in an emergency. We've talked about interoperability for years in NATO, but it has never been imposed across the alliance. From time to time local commanders have sought interoperability with nearby allied units. Maj. Gen. George Patton III, as a division commander, was a leader in this effort. The Army has translated some of its equipment manuals, and in the 1970s the ammunition people at Aberdeen Proving Ground began publishing information that explains what American ammunition can be used in what foreign guns and vice versa.

In our task force's opinion NATO could not deter war or wage successful combat without interoperability among the allies. There is still no basic plan or organization for establishing interoperability. It really is left up to the various agencies of the various nations to take whatever interoperability initiative they think advisable. In fact, it is at the lower levels of military organizations, such as combat divisions that are located close to other allied divisions, where initiatives have been taken to work out some local agreements on interoperability. This is good but not good enough. We need to establish mutual agreements at a national level that reflect a full understanding of the term "coalition logistics."

The task force strongly supported interoperability and the necessity to strengthen its implementation. For example, we recommended that NATO have a materiel management agency and suggested that the NATO Maintenance and Supply Agency (NAMSA), already in operation, could do the task. We recommended that NAMSA report directly to SACEUR—as it does in wartime—and serve as the nucleus for materiel management. NAMSA would be the library of knowledge and catalyst for utilization of standard logistic practices, procedures, and operations. There was some worry among allied ministers as well as the U.S. representative that our task force was aiming at establishing NATO stocks of materiel which would be run by NAMSA, such as a commodity command does in the United States. Actually, this was a misunderstanding. We did not envision a NATO stockage. We did foresee an agreed NATO control "string" on certain critical stocks that could be used to reallocate them among NATO nations in accordance with allied commitments. These stocks would not be moved from the inventories of the nations that owned them except in a crisis.

We really wanted NAMSA to maintain an information center concerning the various types of equipment and materiel as a reference source on interoperability for all NATO allies. It could also coordinate agreed-upon standard procedures such as the current automated logistics system called CALS. We further recommended that critical materials and weapon systems be earmarked for NATO control in case of combat. Nations would be committed to helping one another, which would create the need for interoperability to enable exchange and allocation of national resources between nations.

To a limited degree this latter recommendation was included in NATO's LTDP. Since the LTDP was finalized in 1978, there have been movements to recognize the need for follow-up to improve further the provisions for the allocation and reallocation of these critical weapons and supplies. But the proposal to establish NAMSA as a center of interoperability was tabled for further study. It is still being considered, at least in part, twelve years later.

## NATO's Transportation Capability

My experience as an ordnance officer and logistics commander underscored the truth of Winston Churchill's words in *The River War*: "Victory is the beautiful, bright coloured flower. Transport is the stem without which it could never have blossomed." Even if you have all the other logistics you need, if you lack adequate transportation capability, your logistics remains at a standstill. In speaking before logisticians, especially during presentations at the Transportation Center school at Fort Eustis, Virginia, I have always called military transport the spearhead of logistics. In time this phrase became the motto for the U.S. Army Transportation Corps. Our NATO task force understood the truth of this motto, and we pushed hard for a reform in the management of transportation in NATO planning.

In NATO, as in any other military alliance, the military command must strive to set up a coalition transportation movement agency. The command must understand that the various complex transport movements needed by the various allies competing for a limited number of lines of communications require careful coordination. In any contingency involving NATO nine nations would be using the same line of communications in central Europe alone. Many senior officials focus on the stockpiling of war reserves and tend to ignore transportation planning and allied agreement on lines of communications. Our task force tried to make clear that it was the lines of communications and the staffing of the communications zone that make it possible to transport war reserves to where they could be used effectively. But agreement was essential that someone must be in charge, namely the NATO commander under allied agreement.

In Vietnam U.S. transportation management was controlled by the Transportation Management Agency (TMA) under MACV. At the time I argued against this strong centralized control because

MACV headquarters at Tan Son Nhut Air Base had limited communications available, making it impractical to coordinate the transportation in all four "island" commands running the length and breadth of Vietnam. We succeeded in getting regional TMAs established under MACV headquarters. This gave us the key to successful management of transportation because each of the remote "islands" could operate independently to do what the local support command commander needed while remaining technically under the supervision of the Transportation Management Agency at MACV.

The task force's emphasis on the role of transportation and transportation management also reflected several specific instances of transport problems in wartime that I have observed over the years. The most recent example occurred during the Yom Kippur War in Israel in 1973. I accompanied a GAO representative to survey logistical problems during that war and its aftermath. One of my first questions to the Israeli joint commander, Lt. Gen. Mordechai Gur, was, "How did you control movement?" His immediate reply was, "We had MPs on every corner." That was the beginning of several weeks of questioning about movement control (as differentiated from traffic control). The Israeli transportation movement agency was made up of reserves, and it did not even have a muster at the outbreak of the Yom Kippur War because of the difficulty in getting to assigned stations in the first few days of the war. They were not fully operational for almost a week after the war started, even though they were fully trained. When I asked about retrograde, I learned that there was no return flow from the forward area. The roads, once you left the Tel Aviv area, were not good. Traffic often had to go only one way, carrying men and supplies to the forward battle areas. The Israelis had to fix whatever they could on the battlefield where the equipment had become inoperable.

I was concerned about NATO's lack of planning for retrograde of materiel and personnel during combat and passed my concerns along to my task force colleagues. I emphasized the tendency to disregard the return flow of civilian refugees, in spite of the fact that population movements can greatly inhibit combat action. In Germany we were told that German law prohibited refugees from moving unless they were within 35 kilometers of the front line. I respect German law, but human nature being what it is, it would be a serious mistake to count on recognition of such a law when people are under fire. We may say, "Well, if they don't obey the law, that's a Federal Republic of Germany problem." That's true, but it's also NATO's problem if it happens to take place in the combat zone and blocks our tactical movement. Refugees can stop an army in its tracks as they did in Korea. NATO must recognize this in its planning and training.

Our task force realized that, in case of a crisis in central Europe, the best plan would be to assign the U.S. Transportation Movement Activity under USAREUR now located outside Frankfurt to AFCENT as a U.S. contribution to NATO, just as combat troops are now designated as a contribution in case of emergency. With this unit under its control AFCENT could then serve as the basis on which to create a full-scale transportation movement agency to support war plans including those under the command and control of the U.S. commander in Europe as well as other commanders.

In our long-term defense program for NATO the task force recommended that a logistics command—in today's parlance, a logistics coordinating center (LCC)—be established in NATO with a transportation movement agency responsible for coordination of transportation in each of the major subordinate commands. This LCC transportation agency has not yet been created, but the beginnings of such a structure—a joint transport coordinating agency—exist in the NATO subordinate commands.

## The Task Force Report

At the end of our LTDP study each of the ten directors had the opportunity of presenting his task force's recommendations to the Council of Ministers. When my turn came, I noticed that the attention of many of the ministerial groups immediately slackened when I began to talk about logistics. Once again, the mistaken principle of logistics as solely a national responsibility tended to cause each nation, including our own, to want to hear little about coordination and certainly nothing about integration of logistics in NATO. They forgot that when the NATO charter made each nation responsible for the provisioning of its forces, much of this provisioning must be through a coalition of logistic support, such as host nation support.

I was upset by their attitude. They asked, "General, as a logistician, what kind of war are you preparing to fight? Is it going to be short or long?" Such questions implied that logisticians didn't really know what war was all about. As a consequence, they found little of interest or of meaning in our recommendations. In an informal meeting with the ministers, and subsequently in a meeting of senior NATO logisticians, I referred to the question of a long or short war. "You've asked me what kind of war we're fighting. I tell you that we have to be prepared to fight whatever war the enemy decides to engage in. Otherwise, we will lose, because he will pick out the kind of war we cannot support. If you people do not agree on following the recommendations of our task force, then I can assure you that the war we will fight will be a short war. It will last three to five days, and we will lose." Although my comments didn't win approval for our recommendations, they certainly won the ministers' attention.

I suppose I should have been heartened by the fact that, although the ministers rejected or tabled for further discussion many of our recommendations, not one raised a question about the appended NATO logistics principles on which they were based. In working on the Logistics Task Force of the LTDP I personally pulled together those logistics principles that all of NATO had agreed to, but which were now generally ignored. I appended them to our report and later published them in the *Defense Management Journal*. The principles are as follows:

1. Economy of logistics force is the basic logistics principle.
2. Cooperation and collaboration are required for more efficient and economical use of logistics resources.
3. Logistics interdependence requires "guaranteed satisfaction" of other national force logistics requirements equivalent to one's own.
4. Provision of logistics resources to meet NATO operational plans is a national responsibility.
5. Determination of logistics requirements is a NATO responsibility.
6. Multinational logistics is a NATO responsibility.
7. Logistics practice must be the same in peace and war.
8. Standardization of materiel and services should be attained.
9. Interoperability must compensate for any lack of standardization of materiel and services.
10. Logistics information will be fully and reliably exchanged within NATO.
11. Constant satisfactory logistics readiness must be maintained.
12. Logistics plans must be based on updated combat operational plans and immediately convertible to combat logistics requirements at the moment of enemy attack or threat.
13. Mobility and dispersion must replace voluminous static storage of combat supplies and equipment.
14. NATO logistics facilities must be configured for passive defense in peacetime to assure survivability in war.
15. Duplication of common logistics functions must be minimized within the Alliance through specialization and single management.
16. Logistics procedures must be standardized and harmonized to provide flexibility between nations in logistics support of NATO forces.

All of these principles have since been included in the *NATO Logistics Handbook*. NATO is slowly making progress by getting them adopted. Now they must be put into practice.

In the end our logistics task force got better support from West Germany and NATO Deputy Secretary General Rinaldo Pitriani of Italy than it did from the American representative. General Haig and my military colleagues at SHAPE supported us 100 percent, but their representatives did not want to speak openly in the ministerial meeting about this support. Others, like the Secretary of Defense's special NATO assistant Robert Komer, stressed strategic stockpiles with far less emphasis on other logistics improvements such as standardization of weapons, transportation, and interoperability. In at least one wire to the U.S. Ambassador to NATO, Komer indicated that it "was not necessary for Heiser to repeat his SHAPE report for the third time." I did not take kindly to such comments, nor did I think that Komer gave the logistics task force adequate support in selling our recommendations.

Komer did a very valuable job in emphasizing the importance of NATO and the actions needed to be achieved to strengthen it. He was primarily responsible for the progress made as a result of the LTDP. However, Komer and others in DOD seemed to misunderstand that the logistics thrust of the LTDP underscored the fact that standardization of weapon systems could probably be achieved to only a limited degree and that interoperability and coalition logistics therefore had to be implemented to the highest degree practicable.

Komer and I disagreed about the recommendations that should be contained in the task force report. For example, he was strong on increasing war reserves and sought NATO agreement on that objective. But he didn't want me to emphasize the necessity for having a fully coordinated line of communications. He didn't seem to understand that having war reserves but not being able to put them where they were needed when they were needed was worse than not having the war reserves at all. As a result he failed to support me on other recommendations. Our task force did emphasize the necessity for war reserves and the need for nations to support one another logistically if one nation was short of something that was essential. No one nation could carry the burden alone, especially the United States. To deter war in the first place or to fight if deterrence failed, each nation had to play its part to support NATO agreements.

In spite of this difficulty with Komer and the sometimes indifferent reception from the NATO Council of Ministers, I believe that our task force accomplished a great deal. We won approval for creating the position of Assistant Secretary General for Infrastructure, Logistics, and Civil Emergency Planning, the first change in the senior level of NATO since 1950. We got logistics coordinating centers established throughout NATO (even though they do not yet operate in the way they were designed). We also won an agreement at a meeting of the heads of the NATO nations in Washington in 1978 that SACEUR and the NATO subordinate commands would establish guidelines on the wartime uses of national resources. Finally, we got the ministers to increase NATO's war materiel reserve and to establish or beef up existing logistics staffs at the various NATO headquarters.

## NATO in the 1980s

The third and fourth phases of my NATO work occurred in the 1980s. In 1980 General von Senger and his Deputy Chief of Staff for Logistics, Brig. Gen. (now Lt. Gen.) Claude B. Kicklighter, asked that I return to Europe to review logistics work being undertaken at the AFCENT headquarters in the Netherlands and to provide advice on how to achieve greater readiness. Accompanied by Harold Denny, then vice president of LMI, I spent several weeks reviewing logistical operations in this major NATO subordinate command. Many of the actions recommended in the 1978 LTDP had not yet been acted upon or completed in their command. We were able to help them set up an AFCENT program to implement those actions within their authority and to seek approval of other actions requiring higher echelon approval.

In March 1988 I participated in an examination of issues "related to the balance of forces of NATO and the Warsaw Pact" at the request of the Comptroller General of the United States, Charles A. Bowsher. Because of State Department and White House emphasis on obtaining agreements with the Soviet Union on arms control and reductions in nuclear weapons (which was certainly supported by public opinion across the country), the strengthening of our conventional capability was absolutely essential. I once again had the opportunity to stress some of the important logistical issues affecting NATO conventional forces. I felt this was a fine opportunity to stress again those things that needed to be done within NATO to give it an effective and efficient logistics organization to support the combat forces of all the NATO allies, including the United States. Many of the matters that I proposed to Bowsher were items which we had included in our recommendations for the Long Term Defense Program but which had not yet been implemented by NATO. One of the most important unresolved items was the command and control problem. I once again emphasized that the idea that NATO logistics is a national responsibility is dangerous. I pointed out that in 1977 the Secretary General of NATO, Joseph Luns of the Netherlands, had labeled as "fallacious" the perception that logistics is a national responsibility. In fact he called such thinking "the achilles' heel of the NATO organization." I also warned that while the major subordinate commands of NATO, including AFCENT, were responsible for directing NATO defensive combat operations in the case of enemy attack, the AFCENT commander could not write a logistics annex to his operation order because he had been given no logistics resources or authority with which to support his operation.

This issue of responsibility for logistics in NATO had been forcefully addressed by Senator Sam Nunn in the Nunn-Bartlett Report to the Senate Armed Services Committee in January 1977. At that time Nunn warned that "ultimately, progress [in NATO defense] will require discarding of the notion that logistics should be exclusively a national responsibility." The irony is that, from the very beginning of NATO's existence, the allies have all agreed that unity of effort in logistic support was essential for combat success of the NATO alliance.

I prepared a paper for Bowsher to be presented to congressional representatives for possible use in their review of treaties with the Warsaw Pact–Soviet representatives. I presented this paper to congressional representatives on 12 April 1988. It contained the sixteen NATO logistics principles we had included in our report to the NATO ministers. The paper also discussed mobilization. I argued that it is foolish for the United States and its allies to attempt to carry out unilateral mobilizations when the real strength of the free world lies in its alliances. For example, the western European nations possess the greatest industrial complex in the world. Add this strength to that of the United States and its Asian allies, such as Japan and Korea, and you have a coalition that should discourage any large-scale aggression. However, there is much to do before coalition efficiency and effectiveness will be achieved. Arms control negotiations may provide the spark needed to really get people to forget their sovereign rights, at least to the extent necessary to provide adequate coalition planning for any possible attack.

Another point focused on the agreements between the United States and its allies in western Europe covering host nation support for American forces in peace and war. This host nation support is based upon bilateral agreements between the United States and the individual countries owning the resources involved. But those nations with limited resources also have bilateral arrangements with every other reinforcing country. They also assign the highest priorities for support to their own civilian and military needs in the event of a crisis. It is absolutely essential that these bilateral agreements be tested in peacetime so that mutual collective problems involving host nation support can be discovered. So far there has been no test to determine if all bilaterals, made in good faith, would be compatible if invoked all at once during an enemy attack.

I pointed out that host nation support must be arranged but that this support should supplement a minimum military capability on the part of the United States and each of its allies to support their own forces in the event of attack. This order of precedence would provide field force commanders with the flexibility necessary to meet contingencies when the best-laid plans for host nation support, with all its inherent problems, do not work out as envisioned.

Finally, the Bowsher report examined the logistical choke points and bottlenecks bound to occur in the event of attack on NATO forces. NATO should identify the choke points and bottlenecks, and it must determine alternative courses of action to be taken in the event of their occurrence. I pointed out that resolution of logistic support problems could not be delayed further in light of the apparent forthcoming agreements with the Soviet Union. NATO needed a coherent coalition logistics plan and a commander in charge of all war-fighting capabilities, including logistics, in the event of attack. This does not mean the United States and its allies must relinquish their sovereign rights in peacetime. It does mean that they must plan, in the event of any military contingency, for the best NATO logistic support organization possible. It also means that they must be willing to sacrifice some of their sovereign rights to assure victory by their troops, who would be committed to battle by NATO commanders, not national commanders.

In summarizing the NATO–Warsaw Pact balance of forces in 1988, I reported that NATO can have all kinds of plans, procedures, policies, and doctrine to implement in time of war, but it must recognize that for many reasons its plans will never be fully implemented. For example, the logistics planners would like to throughput resupply from the point of production to the point of use. That would cover the entire pipeline from CONUS or elsewhere to the soldier in the combat front line. Theoretically, this should work, but in fact it never works because of those forces—some man-made, some not—that tend to interfere. NATO, therefore, must be prepared to handle interferences in such a way that the objective will still be attained even though not as planned. It must have flexibility in its structure and in its systems to cope with wartime interferences. While planning operations, setting doctrine, and rehearsing procedures, NATO must spend at least equal time seeking out the choke points and bottlenecks that are likely to occur when plans go wrong. It would be foolish for us logisticians to base our structure and our procedures on the idea that anything like 100 percent of resupply could be throughput from point of production to point of use. We've got to have control points along the way, especially where interferences are likely to occur, so that when they do occur, those at the control points know in advance what the alternative courses of action should be. But we must have the logistics general support capability to allow the necessary flexibility.

The ability to improvise is vital, especially in war when a commander often must respond quickly to acts of God (think of the storms during the Normandy landings) or unexpected moves by his enemy or allies. A sure knowledge of his logistics capabilities and limitations should give him the ability to improvise plans and procedures to achieve his objectives despite the changing odds. This is the *art* of logistics, which differs considerably from the *science* of logistics. Both are important, and neither should be neglected.

CHAPTER 13

# A Point of View

My forty-eight years' experience in logistics has imbued me with some strong convictions about the state of logistics in today's Army and Department of Defense. I want to leave my reader, especially those young officers who will be the Army's future leaders in logistics, with my considered thoughts about current logistical organization and the readiness of our logistical functions—the good points and the bad—as well as some of the lessons I have learned about leadership in logistics, which I consider at the heart of our task of supporting soldiers.

## Logistics in the Department of Defense

"Everytime we want something done in a hurry and want it done right," Deputy Secretary of Defense David Packard told a congressional committee in 1970, "we have to take the project out of our system." He revealed the department's standard practice: "We give a good man direction and authority and let him go—and it works." But then this most perceptive deputy secretary—to my mind one of the best—went on to report the downside: "When we are not in a hurry to get things done right, we over-organize, over-man, over-spend and under-accomplish."*

There has been much progress in the establishment of standard policies and procedures within the Defense Department in the last generation—much progress compared to the various systems of the early 1960s. But there is much room for further improvement. It is a complex task; many solutions have been proposed, but none of them is simple. The problems faced in the Office of the Secretary of Defense by such senior staff as Packard in the 1970s and Richard

---

*U.S. Congress, House, Hearings by Committee on Government Operations, *Policy Changes in Weapon System Procurement*, 91st Cong., 2d sess., November–December 1970.

P. Godwin in the 1980s reveal the difficulties in carrying out the necessary standardization of logistics in the services. Godwin's efforts at standardization might well have been correct, and perhaps the services should not have opposed them. However, the problem is larger than service opposition; it really centers on logistical organization. Without a strong, working organization, approaches to problems change as personalities change.

I must emphasize that experience in combat teaches the necessity of $C^3I$ (command, control, communications, and intelligence) within combat service support at least as much as within combat and combat support echelons. This $C^3I$, especially the ability to create integrated logistical operations both horizontally and vertically (covering hundreds of miles in places like the plains of Europe or the deserts of Saudi Arabia) must be based on commodity know-how, especially for ammunition, POL, and transportation. The greater the mobility and maneuverability, the more the know-how becomes essential because there will not be a wide range of capabilities to choose from. (This is another important example of the application of the "art" of logistics.)

Difficulties with standardization of logistics that began with the 1962 Reorganization Act continue to exist. The combined efforts of Dave Packard and those of Tom Morris and Barry Shillito, two outstanding Assistant Secretaries for Installations and Logistics, were unable to solve all the problems. Their unattained objectives indicate just how difficult standardization is to achieve among the services as well as centralization of authority and responsibility. Some of this difficulty is based on parochialism, but much on the fact that the services and their logistics requirements are genuinely different. The closer you get to the actual aircraft in the Air Force, the ship in the Navy, and the soldier and his weapon in the Army, the more you recognize essential differences that require unique logistics structures. At the same time we must concede that much of the disagreement is based upon the fact that each service remains responsible for the combat readiness of its force, and, therefore, each wants to retain its own capabilities to ensure that combat readiness. Standardization and centralization would reduce that authority.

Standardization and centralization also affect service budgets. These are the basic reasons for the continual objection to putting more and more common responsibility into the Defense Logistics Agency. (The other is that span of control is easily lost in an agency that big.) One of the usual opposition statements is that "because DLA has no direct responsibility for the readiness of the airman, the sailor, or the soldier, each service has to retain its responsibility." This

A POINT OF VIEW 237

is not one of those black-or-white situations where the services are wrong and OSD is right, or vice versa. Unfortunately, there are many gray areas that make final decisions very difficult and often tenuous.

Some think that the commanders of the services' materiel commands—Joint Logistics Commands (JLC)—can solve such problems informally. However, history demonstrates that while logistics commanders reach informal agreement on things easy to solve, they cannot solve the more difficult problems that must be solved in order to achieve the efficiency and effectiveness of standard DOD systems. In part this is because JLC membership is restricted to commanders of the major subordinate commands of the services. The services' deputy chiefs of logistics, the senior policy and doctrine officers in each service, are not only excluded from the JLCs, but at times are not even kept informed of what the JLCs are doing.

I believe that reviving the Logistics System Policy Council (LSPC) is still the best answer. This organization, established in 1970, was a means for OSD and the services to cooperate in working out practical approaches to standardization. Such arrangements take time. If there were easy answers, they would already be implemented. The LSPC should be reestablished under strong leadership and with suitable assurances from the services and OSD that they will cooperate fully to expedite solutions to problems.

I also believe that the now-dormant Defense Logistics Advisory Board, which was established in 1982, should be reactivated to support the Assistant Secretary as well as the Secretary himself by recommending solutions to logistics problems. Its advice, from experienced logistics people, can be expected to be less subjective than that coming from those officials actively responsible for logistics in the services. We tend to let policies and procedures creep into place in peacetime that then become problems in time of war. Thus in peacetime the advice of combat-experienced logisticians—not only those soldiers who served in the combat zone, but those soldiers and civilians who served at a time when the logistics structure and system were geared to react to combat requirements—is particularly pertinent.

The Defense Department must reach the point where its logistical structure can effectively and efficiently support combat units. We have never done this before. We did make a beginning at the end of the Vietnam War, but there is much more to be done in order to ensure that this objective is reached before any future crisis. This includes such things as mobilization planning, especially today, when sustainability is given a backseat. While readiness looks good, the fact is that sustainability depends upon an immediate mobilization capability that simply does not exist today. This is a tremendous logistics task that must be faced soon. In fact, lack of sustainability could be the "achilles' heel" of the Army's military strength.

What is true for standardization is even more applicable to weapons acquisition. And here I must offer an amendment to the idea advanced by two logistics experts. I have already quoted Secretary Packard, who chaired the presidential commission on defense acquisition in 1986, and I admire the contribution made by J. Ronald Fox in his writings and in his service in the Defense Department.* Both men are well versed in acquisition in the Defense Department as well as in commerce. I strongly support their efforts, but I must caution against overemphasizing some aspects of acquisition at the expense of efficiency and effectiveness in the life, use, and support of existing weapon systems, especially in time of a combat crisis.

Another way of expressing my concern is to pass on the conclusions of a congressional committee which studied the problem in 1970. The House Committee on Government Operations noted that the Defense Department was directing considerable attention to management of the procurement process. Convinced that many cases of cost overruns and defective equipment stemmed from the dynamics of rapid technological change and the resulting uncertainties in weapons development, DOD had sought closer control of technical development. But the committee urged DOD to look beyond the procurement process to the management of supply systems, since it was just as important in achieving economy and efficiency. Supply management—that is, cataloging, standardization, and provisioning operations—often failed to get sufficient attention and resources, yet these activities were beset with the same pressures, rivalries, and controversies that nagged procurement.

The committee looked at each of these supply management elements. Cataloging, it explained, was the basic process in supply management, in the sense that it was the foundation of all other operations in the supply chain from procurement to disposal. Standardization was an associated process. Where cataloging sought to identify the universe of supply items, standardization sought to compress their number. The committee singled out provisioning, the flow of spare parts and repair kits to support end items of weapon systems, as the biggest problem. More than 90 percent of new items in the supply system enter through provisioning actions. Whereas the automobile of 1970 had about 16,000 individual

---

*See especially J. Ronald Fox (with James L. Field), *The Defense Management Challenge: Weapons Acquisition* (Boston: Harvard Business School Press, 1988).

# A POINT OF VIEW

pieces or parts, the F–111 aircraft had more than 300,000. Not all these parts should generate a new Federal Stock Number. It was imperative that only what was new, as against what was already cataloged and in the supply system, be identified through improved management techniques to avoid duplication. As early as 1970 this committee had isolated a major logistics problem. It called on the Department of Defense to "direct intensive high-level attention, comparable to that for weapons systems procurement, to the important technical programs which reduce lifetime support costs of military equipment."*

Twelve years later I wrote Deputy Secretary of Defense Frank C. Carlucci about the continuing problem of supply management. Specifically, I brought to his attention a contradictory element in his dual emphasis on shortening the acquisition cycle for new weapons while trying to improve the integrated logistic support (ILS) of weapon systems. I warned him that in shortening the former, the various elements of the latter are usually placed in such low priority that shortening acquisition time is achieved through reduction or elimination of integrated support. Seldom was ILS effectively executed prior to fielding a weapon system, and I estimated that over 30 percent of the cost of a weapon system came from "putting out fires" because a service lacked effective ILS prior to fielding the new weapon. The only solution, I argued, was that "strong *command* support be given by *commanders at all echelons*, beginning at the top of the Defense Department, to the essentiality of executing effective and efficient ILS prior to fielding any weapon system."

That letter was true in 1982, and it is even more true in 1990. It is absolutely essential that logistic command and control be exerted strongly and with telling effect not only in the acquisition process, but in the entire logistics process of research and development, production and procurement, and field support of weapon systems. The report of Packard's blue ribbon panel to the President in 1986 emphasized six underlying features that typify the most successful commercial programs. The first is clear command channels. The following five also apply as importantly and directly to other phases of logistics as to acquisition: stability, limited reporting requirements, small high-quality staffs, communication with users, prototyping, and testing.

---

*U.S. Congress, House, Committee on Government Operations, *Military Supply Systems: Cataloging, Standardization, and Provisioning of Spare Parts*, 91st Cong., 2d sess., 10 Dec 70, H. Rpt. 91–1718. For quotation, see p. 60.

Another important aspect of DOD's emphasis on acquisition has to do with the increased separation that exists between the people in the acquisition process and the people in the support process. There has always been a separation of thought, philosophy, doctrine, procedures, and the like between those involved in research and development, production and procurement, and those in field support. However, in the military there is a more direct capability to ensure the coordination of interrelationships between these logistics functions at the level of the commander of a major subordinate commodity command than anywhere else in the logistics structure. Simply put, a cardinal principle of integrated logistic support is "front-end analysis" of a weapon system throughout its life cycle. This has to be done especially in the conceptional and research and development phase.

The Chief of Ordnance presented a typical example of this model of coordination. The attached chart, put together in 1944, shows the time it took in that period to design a new weapon system and to standardize it in the hands of troops (*see chart*). Putting these weapon systems into the hands of troops from the date of project initiation required less than one year. Until 1962 this schedule generally held up. This occurred because it was facilitated by the organization of the Chief of Ordnance, who was responsible for R&D, procurement, production, testing, and field support, and was not obstructed by overdone and repetitious reviews and the resulting delays. One of the major delays in today's weapons systems acquisition can be blamed on the inordinate number of reviews demanded by current procedures.

Today up to 90 percent of the cost of most weapon systems over their 10- to 20-year life-span is spent in annual expenditures for operation and support. Only an estimated 10 to 15 percent covers the expenses pertaining to initial acquisition. Reflecting the great modernization program within the Defense Department since 1981, these figures illustrate what can happen when we separate field support from acquisition. We have in the field, and to the best of my knowledge we are still procuring, a large percentage of repair parts—something between 70 and 90 percent—that are not needed to support our weapon systems. The problems reported by the Committee on Government Operations in 1970 are thus even greater today. We are spending something over $30 billion a year in procurement of initial spare parts. Over half, and this is a very conservative estimate, are not only unnecessary and wasteful, but are interfering with the combat readiness of our troops because they cannot move the sheer weight of parts that have been pushed

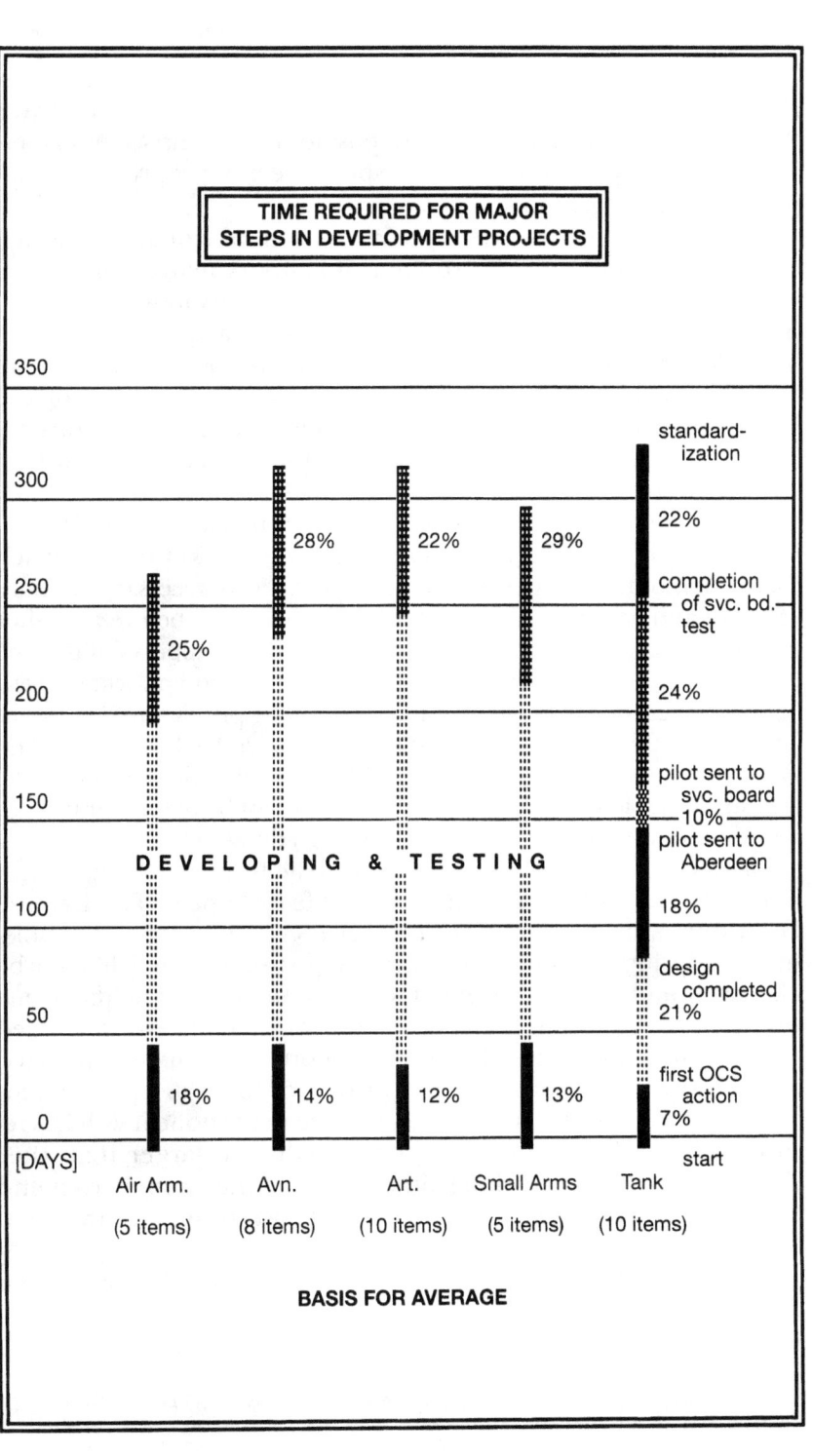

on them. This excess of parts also interferes with training. This is also true in the other services. A recent test of the Air Force's War Reserve Stocks, or "WRS Kits," pre-positioned for crisis support, revealed that only 10 percent of the spares were appropriate for support of the Air Force mission.

In the wake of the Vietnam War a congressional committee again took a look at the problem of support management and called on the services to involve their logisticians more directly in procurement planning and weapon systems acquisition so that basic designs and specifications could take proper account of the logistics aspects.* The committee concluded that, in view of the great cost of acquisitions as well as maintenance and operations, integration of logistics and procurement considerations must be done on a systematic, carefully planned basis.

Integrated logistic support is recognized in the Defense Department, as in commerce and industry, as the process through which those composite management and analysis actions necessary to assure effective and economical support of a product both before and after fielding are accomplished. DOD requires logistic supportability to be considered as a principal design parameter equal in importance with cost, technical performance, and schedule. The primary tool it uses to accomplish this balance is the Logistics Support Analysis (LSA). The goal of this analysis is to obtain a reliable, maintainable, transportable, and supportable materiel system at the least cost by the integration of logistic support considerations with detailed design effort.

This effort, however, must begin with the front-end analysis mentioned earlier, rather than later in the life-cycle plan. The Defense Department, in fact, has directed that LSA will be formally implemented during the concept exploration phase. But this will never be effectively and efficiently done if we continue to separate the acquisition process from the logistic support implementation. The need to combine acquisition with logistic support has been demonstrated again and again throughout the history of logistics management and combat support. The fact that we have never done it well has resulted in operational and support costs much larger than they should have been for a long time. Without the proper front-end analysis we simply cannot tell what it will cost to support a weapon once it is fielded. Very few weapons systems have met support requirements prior to fielding. The B–2 and the Apache aircraft are among current examples.

---

*U.S. Congress, House, *Military Supply Systems: Lessons from the Vietnam Experience*, 91st Cong., 2d sess., 9 Oct 70, H. Rpt. 91–1586.

# A POINT OF VIEW

What is the practical solution to this problem we're all trying to solve? First of all, we must have functional management at the top of the Department of Defense, with specific managers or commanders at service commodity commands responsible for specified, highly expensive and highly combat-essential weapon systems. Then we must branch out into commodity centers so that each commodity area will be given the kind of logistics management required for that particular commodity. We need to give the command and control centers in the various commodity commands the responsibility and authority to do their job in each commodity area. The program managers need to report to that commodity commander (the CEO, in commercial terms). That official could then be made responsible for support of the combat troops for that commodity. He would be not only the single responsible commander for that support, but also the single source of information and support, so that the customer would know where to get the support required. The Air Force logistics structure is based on this idea; in the Army, our experience with the project manager (PM) system proved most effective.

As far as other aspects of acquisition are concerned, procurement and production management operations in the past have been well managed by military logisticians who specialized to some extent in these functional areas after learning a basic understanding of a commodity. This was the fundamental logistic base which enabled us to give such great support to the combat soldier in World War II. This also was the fundamental base which enabled us to recover from the classic case of unreadiness that characterized the beginning of the Korean War. Unfortunately, this expertise after the war tended to reside in Reserve personnel who retired in the 1950s and 1960s.

We need constantly to ensure that DOD organizations reflect practical combat experience. My observations of property disposal depot operations (PDO), for example, caused me to recommend twenty years ago that authorities within a theater of operations should retrograde appropriate property to PDO yards at points of exit from the theater of operations. At that point the Defense Supply Agency (DSA) should take over responsibility for international sales. As a result of this recommendation DSA's successor, DLA, is now responsible for property disposal. In my opinion, however, this control went too far. DLA is not only responsible for property disposal at points of exit from the theater, it is also responsible for PDO within the theater itself. This may work in peacetime, but in war, I would argue, PDO responsibility within a theater must shift to the Army theater commander.

## Logistical Organization in the U.S. Army

While the Army is generally well organized logistically for peace, it will likely again find itself hard pressed to carry out its logistical mission in a war or major contingency. Specifically, even though we have the highest levels of combat operational planning, training, and readiness, we will be severely limited by the meager sustaining logistic support we will be able to provide in time of emergency.

A good example of the basis for this unpreparedness can be found in the recent changes ordered by the Reorganization Act of 1986. This document provides improved means of research and development and procurement—or acquisition, the term now used—but it does not equip us logistically for war. In the Army all program managers now report to the Under Secretary of the Army directly. These men have been picked because of their outstanding ability to head the organizations that acquire new weapon systems, but if a major war should start, this whole reorganization dedicated to improving peacetime acquisition would have to change. The highly capable personnel involved in these acquisition organizations would, for the most part, be immediately moved to positions involved in combat support in order to gain the advantage of the best people in the priority positions. The civilian secretariat does not conduct operations in wartime; its job to provide political support for the Army is very special and important, but the Army staff supports combat forces in war.

The Chief of Staff of the Army must provide the command and control required so that the Army can give its best support to wartime field commanders. Priorities would immediately change. Acquisition of new weapons would no longer be the first priority. Support of combat forces with the weapons they are already using would be the first priority. The problem of command and control would quickly become apparent. For example, today the command and control of ammunition rests in the hands of the brigadier general who reports not to the Army staff but to the Under Secretary of the Army. The first question that will be asked by the Chief of Staff if an attack takes place is, "What's our ammunition situation?" He will ask it of his chief logistician, the DCSLOG. The DCSLOG will have to reply, "I don't know, sir, but I will find out." The fact of the matter is that, because of the peacetime organization, the DCSLOG does not have the necessary management information tools—even with all of our computers—to give the answer that the Chief of Staff needs at the moment. The best the DCSLOG can do is go to the ammunition Program Executive Officer (PEO), who reports to the Under Secretary, and ask to be told what the situation is.

A POINT OF VIEW 245

We tend to forget that the Chief of Staff does not command combat troops in combat operations. But in wartime especially he has specific responsibility to support the combat forces, and to carry out these responsibilities, he must have a logistics deputy in charge of all types of support. Actually, it is not clear who is in charge of logistics in the Army today. The DCSLOG has responsibilities that are vastly different than originally planned. He no longer is responsible for determining logistics requirements. Such authority is now in the hands of the staff of the Secretary of the Army as a result of the emphasis on acquisition. The AMC commander considers himself the Army's logistics chief, but even though he is a full general, he is only partially responsible for the wholesale side of logistics. General Abrams said it time and again: the logistics head of the Army must be the DCSLOG. But today the DCSLOG has very limited responsibility, particularly for determining logistics budget requirements. At one time he had extensive budget authority and influenced most Army decisions. The other extreme has now been reached: the DCSLOG sometimes is ignored on issues within the scope of Army logistics.

If the DCSLOG is not given direct responsibility for acquisition processes and their implementation, we will leave unanswered the question of who is in charge of the provision of weapon systems, materiel, and their support in the field. Besides the Secretary and the Chief of Staff, who are responsible for all Army missions, there should be a deputy chief of staff responsible for all logistics as defined by the Department of Defense.*

Logistics in the military sense is defined by the Joint Chiefs as the science of planning and carrying out the movement and maintenance of forces. In its most comprehensive sense this definition includes those aspects of military operations which deal with the following: (a) design and development, acquisition, storage, movement, distribution, maintenance, evacuation, and disposition of materiel; (b) movement, evacuation, and hospitalization of personnel; (c) acquisition or construction, maintenance, operation, and disposition of facilities; and (d) acquisition or furnishing of services.

Logistics is the system that integrates these elements. The greater the lack of integration, the greater the problem becomes of ensuring that what the combat forces get is what they need, when they need it, and in the condition needed. Though logistics responsibilities may be fragmented in time of crisis, both the Army

---

*JCS Pub 1–02, "Department of Defense Dictionary of Military and Associated Terms," 1 Dec 89, p. 211.

Chief of Staff and the Secretary of Defense need one Army logistician to inform them of the entire logistics picture. When war begins the DCSLOG, who is responsible for field support, becomes the key man. This transition in authority from peacetime to wartime should be avoided. Ideally, the DCSLOG should be responsible for logistic support in both peace and war as he was before the reorganization of logistics in 1962.

Today there is considerable emphasis on weapon systems management. Authorities in the Pentagon, Congress, and even the White House ask questions about specific weapon systems—the greater the expense, the greater their interest. As a result management systems have been devised to provide answers. These systems are pertinent to the low-density, high-cost weapons, but they either ignore the high-density, low-cost items or complicate their management by applying directives aimed at the high-cost weapons unnecessarily to all items.

The Army needs an integrated logistics structure to support all weapon systems. We need management of specific weapon systems within commodity groupings. The commodity commands that existed before the reorganization of 1962 and those that continue to exist are the keystone of the Army's logistics structure. In my debriefing after commanding the 1st Logistical Command in Vietnam I recommended that we consider disestablishing AMC. The action taken by Secretary of the Navy John F. Lehman to abolish the Naval Material Command is certainly a precedent that might at least justify an Army review of the status of AMC. The DCSLOG and the commodity commanders (major general positions) are capable of the budgeting, planning, and programming now performed by AMC, and consolidation would greatly reduce the logistical overhead.

Serious consideration must be given to determine where program and special weapons management starts and stops. In my opinion the program manager's control should stop at the production line. However, his responsibilities for exercising technical know-how should continue until other responsible agencies gain the experience of supporting the system. If the program manager is part of the commodity command, this would be a normal flow of responsibility through research and development, through procurement and production, to field service.

Once weapons and hardware are put in the hands of troops, they should fall under the standard logistics structure of the Army with appropriate items of each system covered by intensive management. For that reason support of front-end analysis under the Logistics Support Analysis program of DOD and the Army should be the responsibility of the logistics system beginning with the DCSLOG and extending into the AMC and field operations and support. This important issue needs timely disposition.

The Department of Defense and the services have been directed by National Security Review 11 to reorganize logistics, among other defense functions, with emphasis on the "procurement process and management." The Army's response in 1989 to this directive reinforces my conviction that the Army needs to review the changes that have occurred since the 1962 reorganization to see what needs to be done to achieve the improvements intended by that reorganization.*

## Logistical Organizational Echelons

Senior commanders must recognize that a natural and somewhat friendly antagonism exists between lower and higher headquarters. Lower headquarters generally do not think very well of higher headquarters. That's because they are sure that the higher headquarters doesn't understand the job that has to be done, either its complexities or its difficulties. This situation certainly existed in Vietnam as far as logistics was concerned. The 1st Log felt that USARV was an unnecessary impediment to progress in logistic support. I am positive that USARV felt the same, to some degree, about MACV. In Europe COMZ felt USAREUR was an unnecessary headquarters. Even today many in USAREUR and USAFE consider the European Command an unnecessary burden whose essential responsibilities could very well be handled by others. These attitudes are usually not out in the open. Although they are entirely normal, they do require command attention. As long as they are controlled, they will not affect unit performance, but if left uncontrolled, these dislikes can weaken cooperation and coordination. Special emphasis should be given to coordination and cooperation between echelons of headquarters, especially through frank communication.

In peacetime just about any type organization can be made to work. It might not be the most efficient or even the most effective, but it can be made to work because there is time to correct errors as they occur. In a combat situation this is not true; we need a logistics organization that can perform effectively as quickly as possible. We need experienced leaders, both military and civilian.

---

*The Army response is included in *Defense Management Report to the President by the Secretary of Defense,* July 1989.

During World War II the acquisition process was supervised by military personnel, but it was the civilian corps that supplied the expertise and did the greatest amount of work. A specific example was the tremendous task performed by the acquisition personnel in the ordnance districts spread throughout the United States. Expertise was recruited from industry and commerce. These civilian employees were supported, and in many cases fully trained, by the Army's arsenal system. Today that arsenal system no longer exists. Industry and commerce must now provide the know-how that then existed within the Army.

I believe this military-civilian mix is far preferable to the establishment of a civilian acquisition corps in each service or a peacetime acquisition corps of military officers. In the last analysis the acquisition process is an industrial-commercial function more than a military one, even though military advice and guidance are essential. As in World War II selected assignments of military officers to a basically civilian corps to provide essential understanding and cooperation between those in acquisition and those in military leadership would provide the optimum melding of resources.

I am not convinced that the logistics lessons learned in our recent wars have become ingrained. Early official reports from Saudi Arabia indicate that some of the lessons learned in Vietnam are being ignored and that similar logistics problems continue to plague our forces. This should serve to emphasize the necessity for logisticians to know and understand history. Logistical experience is withering away with time, and current personnel are so busy with peacetime problems that they are not taking the time to review these lessons from the past that form the road map to the future. We need to make history required reading for all civilian and military defense officials.

The requirement for manpower to support Army field combat units is a major concern. The effectiveness of our combat sustainability has been reduced in order to increase readiness. With a constant manpower ceiling recent increases in the number of combat troops have required a corresponding drop in the number of combat service support troops. The proponents of this approach usually justify it by calling for increased productivity in logistic support. But our combat service support resources were already stretched, and today we are regressing to the conditions that prevailed when I enlisted in 1942. In those days the Army had to place notices in the newspapers for civilian specialists willing and able to train quickly so they could support troops ready for combat. They were for the most part unreachable by the draft because they held skilled jobs or were over age with dependents. I don't think future conflicts will allow time for such a buildup. We cannot say we are combat ready with no more than a three- to five-day support capability. Our degree of readiness has to be measured by our ability to sustain wartime levels of troops and equipment, not only in terms of supplies but also of maintenance, distribution, and other logistic services.

Some experts recommend reducing combat service support troops also because of new technology and containers. I agree in principle, but we cannot depend on technology's operating successfully 100 percent of the time. We must plan for problems and delays caused by human error and the weather, for example. We must build in the flexibility to cope with these problems. Flexibility is possible only with combat service support troops who can provide general support. Direct support by combat service support troops satisfies most of the forward combat area requirements, but backup support is also needed at the corps level and in echelons above corps. Unless we have the flexibility provided by general support troops (including supply, maintenance, transportation, and other logistic services), the combat troops, both forward and rear, will suffer.

Much of the current reduction in combat service support is based on packing ammunition and supplies in containers and moving those containers all the way up to the forward echelons. Even if everything goes as planned, this technique may not be effective. But in my seven years of combat service support in the three combat zones things seldom went according to plan. The weather stopped support in Normandy for days. The enemy prevented our taking over the Brittany peninsula and the port of Brest. The port of Cherbourg was badly damaged. Patton's Third Army broke through and crossed France so quickly there was no way to support it with fuel and ammunition. Infantry outfits had to be reorganized as truck companies. There were many similar unforeseen support problems during our first year in Korea. In Vietnam we had too much mass support from the home front; it took several years of effort to gain reasonable control over what was sent us. Many thousands of similar problems were corrected by the improvisation of combat service support troops. But each improvisation took time. If the time, leadership, and support troops had not been available, combat support would have been disastrous.

My experience prompts me to agree that increased efficiency of support is certainly needed and can be achieved, but to support combat troops effectively, we must recognize that unforeseen obstacles will affect that efficiency. Our combat service support must have the flexibility to improvise so that our troops continue to be supported as required. Improvisation is the most important requirement for combat service support in any battle.

Performing combat service support in the dark, under constant air attack, or in chemical, biological, or radiological (CBR) warfare is a source of concern because we lack recent experience in a variety of circumstances. Since the days of World War II, we have never been required to consider performing logistic support operations under blackout, under maximum camouflage conditions, or in other constrained environments. We were not subject to enemy air attack in Korea or Vietnam. It is my understanding that the Army has lately stressed training under air and CBR attack and in the dark. However, in talking with various Army echelons, I am not sure that we have sufficiently increased our efficiency under these conditions. Increased training as well as reviews are required to assure that we have the necessary equipment to support combat readiness and sustainability.

A logistics unit that must provide its own security can do productive work only by recognizing in advance the security requirements (time and personnel) necessary to protect the unit and its resources from enemy attack. In heavy combat operations this drain can be very significant. In Korea when the 707th Ordnance Battalion was surrounded by North Korean forces, we had over half our soldiers on sentry duty along the perimeter of our area. Again, in Vietnam, in places like the ammo depot at Qui Nhon, we sometimes had half or more of our logistics forces on the perimeter. Needless to say, this diversion detracted from the work of the logistics units involved. The greater likelihood of this happening in future combat must be recognized as a result of modern doctrine and tactics. Logistics security must be given first priority in order to protect the primary mission of support of the combat troops. The greater the mobility and maneuverability in the future, the greater will be the need for unit security.

## Logistical Functions

An important logistical function is the control of unserviceables. The Closed Loop system put discipline into the return of unserviceables when it required that a replacement item be issued to match each item that was unserviceable, destroyed, or consumed. Unfortunately, this system now covers only a few end items and components. Proper use of Inventory in Motion will provide as complete a knowledge of unserviceables in retrograde as it does for serviceables going to a consignee.

Inventory in Motion integrated, for the first time, the logistics functions of transportation and supply, and, in dealing with unserviceables, it extended that integration into maintenance as well. Through proper management and control of items in transit, not just "measurement tons," static stocks are reduced and stock levels are minimized, among many other advantages. Most significantly, the logistician can manage an integrated system of functions rather than letting separate functions manage him.

I recently received a copy of a report that had been commissioned by AMC in September 1988 to study JIT (Just In Time) inventory practices and their possible applicability to AMC. To say the least, I was surprised to see that AMC had felt a need to commission this report, since Just In Time is merely a new name for Inventory in Motion, which was part of the Army's Logistics Offensive launched in Vietnam in 1969 and extended throughout the Army after I became DCSLOG. The Army has been using some parts of what is now called Just In Time ever since those days. Inventory in Motion is supported by such systems as direct support, Closed Loop, direct exchange, SIMS (Special Item Management System), and phased provisioning.

By now everyone in the Army should have been fully informed on the specific advantages inherent in this kind of logistics management. If anyone at AMC had analyzed the reasons behind direct support and the other initiatives carried out by logisticians in Vietnam in 1969 or for that matter had read the discussions in the *Army Logistician* beginning in January 1970, he would have known that the Army had already taken advantage of Inventory in Motion to some degree. For us to be studying Just In Time inventory management today to see if it can be adopted in the Army is stupid.

## Automation

Even when I was serving in Vietnam computer technology was changing so rapidly that it was difficult for the logistics operators to keep up. These changes continue to occur today, and the marketing of automation has come to determine the automation programs available. The salesmen know the equipment, and they know better than anyone the kind of programs that work efficiently with their hardware. However, they do not always know the logistics functions that need to be automated. If we are not careful, we can find ourselves accepting programs to automate logistics that do not meet our requirements. At times logistics programs are installed by the command data processing element in collaboration with the commercial manufacturer without the involvement of the logistics commander and manager and his staff. This approach requires program changes right after they have been installed. Such changes take time and are usually very expensive.

The users, in this case the logisticians, must have a larger part in design of logistics software so that the software can be used effectively. Not only dollars, but lives can hang in the balance. We are investing billions in less-than-efficient automation now. I am sorry to say that as recently as 1986 the standard system for logistics management was designed by data-processing experts, not logistics specialists. In fact, General Jack Fuson and I discovered this in 1988 while we were reviewing automation at the DCSLOG level. When we asked detailed questions about the programs, computer experts had to be brought in to answer us. This is not good. Every effort should be made to ensure that the logistics managers who will be using the programs participate in software development. They have to define the requirements of their standard system of logistics management. Logistics people must manage computers and not let computers manage logistics.

Finally, we must be sure to build into any system a red light or flag that requires eyeballing by a manager before that function, automated or not, is allowed to proceed automatically through the standard system. Logistics commanders and managers know where problems arose in the past, both in combat and in peacetime. We know where checkpoints are required. One of the important checks is the editing of requirements. One of the weakest points of the logistics system is that almost anyone can initiate a requirement. Very often a requirement is never assessed to determine if it exists at all or if it was authorized for the level at which it is being initiated. In automation only a proper edit of a requirement at strategic points in the process can prevent automatic delivery down the line or fraud.

A good example of this type of check was a project called Challenge, which was part of the Red Ball operation in support of Vietnam. In coordination with the Logistical Control Office, Pacific (LCOP), in San Francisco, we inserted challenges at various levels in the Red Ball system, with the final checkpoint at Travis Air Force Base, the point of exit. If an item about to be shipped from Travis did not pass the standard required for Red Ball items, it was set aside and questioned at the LCOP before it was shipped. Many millions of dollars and many ton-miles of aircraft were saved this way

A POINT OF VIEW 253

by stopping items that should never have been requisitioned under the Red Ball system in the first place. Time and space were saved for essential combat supplies instead of nice-to-have items that should not have been in the Red Ball system.

## Maintenance Engineering

Under the arsenal system that existed before and during World War II, trained military and civilian personnel at ordnance arsenals knew the weapon systems in their commodity areas and the maintenance required to support such systems. These experts in maintenance engineering determined the technical procedures and policies for support of weapon systems being developed and produced for field use. They used testing and facilities called mop shops (maintenance operating procedures), where newly developed systems were disassembled to determine where the wear and tear would occur in the field. This testing was a key factor of parts provisioning.

Today the Army, like the Air Force, depends solely on industry, under the direction of a military project manager for individual weapon systems. There is very little surveillance of the weapon system by Army or Air Force user personnel; therefore, the contractor and the PM determine repair parts requirements. The success or failure of a weapon system acquisition is not measured by inefficient and uneconomical excess of spare parts, but by whether or not there is a part on hand when it is needed. Because there is a penalty for a shortage of a part, the contractor and the PM make sure the field organization has all the parts it could possibly need. Obviously it is best to be on the safe side, but little criticism is leveled for the number of excess spares that accumulate because repair parts are provisioned that are not really needed. A revival of maintenance engineering expertise needs to be started as soon as possible.

The military modernization program that was started in 1981 has been a mixed blessing. New weapons systems create new problems for repair parts management. Today the Army is spending between 40 and 60 percent of total procurement on repair parts. Questions about pricing policy and whether to procure from the manufacturer or through contractors obscure the more basic question of the real need for the parts, regardless of price. Half the time the part is not needed at any price. We are submerging field commands with parts they cannot carry, store, move, or count. We are spending transportation money to move excess, unnecessary parts back and forth. Excess parts are being stocked today for the Apache and every other Army weapon system. If some parts are needed as insurance items, they should be retained in a wholesale depot or contractor's plant for distribution when needed, not distributed to units worldwide and then months or years later transported back to the United States as excess.

The modernization of the 1980s produced over 500 new weapon systems for the Army in a short time. Congress and senior OSD executives highlighted parts problems with several very expensive new weapons but not with the multitude of less visible weapon systems. Of the 6 million parts in our catalog system, only 26 percent are described. We pay contractors to provide descriptions, but we do not include much of this information in our catalog. In addition, many parts in the catalog are listed by incorrect titles. Not only are we unaware of what is in the catalog, we have different names for the same item. Air Force and Army studies indicate the annual cost to maintain a single National Stock Number (NSN) in the inventory is approximately $200. With 6 million NSNs in our inventory and in our catalog, billions of dollars are spent just to maintain these stock numbers.

We procure annually over $30 billion in repair parts for the Department of Defense. If you add to that the cost of transportation and keeping track of repair parts, their cost becomes enormous. If only 30 percent are unnecessary, consider the effect of reducing our inventory on total costs. But we must act fast. In 1989 the GAO found that parts inventory cost for weapons in the Defense Department between 1980 and 1988 increased from $43 billion in secondary items to $103 billion, with over half of that inventory being inapplicable to material which it was intended to support.

It is simply unnecessary to procure so many spare parts to ensure the readiness of a weapon system. Only those parts that are absolutely necessary to troops operating the weapon system need to be procured initially and transported with initial issue of the weapon. The occasional random part can be obtained from the wholesale inventory or from the contractor if and when needed, or controlled cannibalization can be used pending receipt of parts. Moreover, many parts are not unique to one weapon; at least half of all parts are common to several weapons, thus underscoring the need for adequate catalog information. Of course if the weapon is very low density and 100 percent combat essential—such as special weapons—then appropriate mandatory stockage is required. However, our general parts stockage policy for missiles is wasteful and interferes with readiness. Contract provisions for phased provisioning can create incentives for reasonably effective support and also levy penalties for inefficient and ineffective repair parts support.

We've made some progress. In World War II and in Korea ordnance units had watchmakers. We even supported them with air-conditioned vans in the days when air conditioning was scarce. Today there's not a single watch repairman in the Army because we adopted the throw-away principle for watches in a field army. At the same time I think that we haven't searched nearly enough to learn how to optimize support to the combat soldier. The aim of the Logistics Offensive in the early 1970s was to do actual repairs at the appropriate level of the five levels available to any system, i.e., the operator, the operating unit, the direct support, the general support, and the depot. In most cases this should be considerably to the rear. We should do little or no forward maintenance; generally we should replace modules. That way we can conserve the kinds of skills that we need. This would have a tremendous effect on the number of mechanics that we have to put in the forward area.

I believe that in our research and development and production we haven't given enough attention to products that require no maintenance. You don't usually repair forward in a combat zone under fire, you replace. General support rearward normally repairs components.

Talking about difficulties in motivating return of unserviceables, I should mention stock funds. I am convinced that stock funds that include consumables, like food, are very effective and economical for the Army to use in peacetime. In time of war I believe that stock fund controls should go out the window in theaters of operations. Such controls should be maintained at higher headquarters. Trying to apply peacetime accounting by using stock funds and consumer funds to cover transfers of repair parts and other items from the wholesale to the retail and within the retail structure down to the actual user or operator in time of war is foolish. It won't work.

At any time, I think, it is foolish to consider nonconsumables, such as most depot repairables, as part of stock funds. Requiring a unit to carry repair parts as part of its consumer fund assets is a serious mistake. It is one of the major reasons that we cannot obtain the return of unserviceables. The units that have paid for the parts now unserviceable do not want to let go of them, even though they can't use the component, because it represents assets, money, that they have spent. If the unit could get a reasonable credit for return of the unserviceable item, that might help some, but I believe that we should take quick action to remove repairable spares and any other true nonconsumables out of the stock fund.

Ammunition renovation is a very important requirement in the combat zone, and yet we have not allowed for this in any depth in our DOD structure. This requirement was proved in World War II when we actually formed entire ammunition renovation companies. It had to be repeated in Korea. In Vietnam renovation teams had to be formed to handle the problem. I would certainly stress that an ammunition renovation capability will be needed by U.S. and NATO forces in any combat zone where we may be involved in the future, especially where we want to conserve ammunition.

Packaging is an important element of maintenance. This applies to all materiel. For example, it is so difficult and time-consuming to unpackage ammunition that combat soldiers tend to unpack only what they think they are going to need. What is eventually unused becomes suspect and therefore unserviceable. It's considered unserviceable because, no longer packaged properly, its reliability becomes uncertain.

Shipping back materiel from a combat zone creates another problem. Psychologically, once something becomes unserviceable, we tend to treat it as if it's worthless. As a result a great deal of the equipment that was unserviceable, but repairable, that came out of Vietnam, Korea, and Europe arrived back home in an unrepairable state. The destruction that occurred during shipping was sometimes worse than the damage in combat. By the time many items got to the repair depot, they were in such a state that they should never have been shipped in the first place.

## Coalition Warfare

Negotiations presently under way between the United States and the USSR in Vienna, the Conventional Forces in Europe (CFE) agreements, focus on the immediate military future of Europe in terms of the mutual drawdown of forces and weapons. Nevertheless, any agreements that emerge from these negotiations are bound to impact on our long-range military position. I am convinced that if the NATO partners take advantage of the international situation and adopt some logical logistical planning concepts, they can solve many of the problems that have beset the alliance, problems concerning command and control as well as rationalization, standardization, and interoperability. The goal of strong deterrence at far less cost is achievable if we plan now. I propose that four long-range logistic objectives (incrementally applied) be considered during the immediate planning now under way in conjunction with the Vienna talks.*

---

*The following observations are a summary of my comments in a recent exchange with Senator Sam Nunn, Chairman of the Senate Armed Services Committee.

(1) NATO's primary objective should be a composite armed force composed of forces allocated by the partners based on each nation's individual military and economic capacity. It would be a terrible mistake to draw down our alliance as we built it, with each ally going its own way. NATO's current level of deterrent strength has been so costly because we never possessed a true composite force, but rather depended on a loose arrangement of contributions from sovereign nations, a system diametrically opposed to the objectives of rationalization, standardization, and interoperability.

(2) Weaponry to support such a composite armed force and the weaponry levels settled on under the Vienna negotiations should be based on what is best suited to meet the requirements of the forces finally agreed upon. By forces, I mean the new NATO composite armed force, not the forces of the individual NATO partners. The needs of the composite force would also apply to those weapons placed in reserve to provide NATO sustainability and would lead to a common approach to research and development. Such measures would help us finally achieve the rationalization, standardization, and interoperability needed for an effective deterrence.

(3) This composite armed force should be financed by some sort of common defense fund to which each partner would contribute according to its size and economic position. NATO should initiate a bookkeeping system of credits and debits for contributions made to and/or costs incurred against the common fund by each member nation. Such a financial system would provide for the contribution of weapons to the composite force's war reserve, for example, or the operational costs associated with maintaining the force during peacetime. (Of course, an adequate system of verification and adequate backup support of trained and ready reserve forces in each allied country is mandatory.)

(4) NATO should immediately initiate the organization of a composite line of communications, beginning with the army group in the north of AFCENT. This LOC would be based on an agreed allocation of logistics forces, and the NATO command should be allowed to draw on the common defense fund to pay for it.

These objectives are based on several assumptions. They presuppose that the Conventional Forces in Europe negotiations will produce a verifiable balance of conventional forces and that the NATO partners will quickly develop a dynamic industrial mobilization plan so that reductions in forces and weaponry could be speedily reversed if the USSR or some other force should violate the treaty. Finally, such planning would not neglect America's other allies such as Korea and Japan. Planning similar to that envisioned for NATO could readily be adapted to other alliances.

If asked to summarize the above, I would say that we should now take advantage of the promise of the 1990s. We have to recognize that the best way to defend our sovereign rights is to do so through optimum cooperation between us and the nations allied with us who have similar objectives of peace and freedom. By doing so, we will avoid the waste that has beset NATO since its establishment. This applies not only to NATO in Europe but also to all regions where we are allied to other nations to secure our mutual objectives.

## Leadership

This book, ostensibly about logistics, is in essence about military leadership and the needs of soldiers. I believe, based on my experience, that only after learning how to lead troops—in other words, after receiving a thorough grounding in warfighting—should an officer begin his logistics training in a specific commodity area. This training then can be accompanied by a general introduction to logistics functions. As he develops in experience and seniority he can then be considered for a broader area of responsibility in the logistics community, including most of the acquisition functions as well as the logistic support functions. I include most of the acquisition functions because, while everyone cannot hope to be an expert engineer in the research and development community, he can know enough about research and development to manage a research and development activity. In fact, experience has demonstrated time and time again that the best manager of research and development does not come from the engineering community. It is far better to have such an individual come from the military logistics or business community.

I want to stress my belief in the importance to the logistician of learning the combat trade first. It is during this combat training and service with the troops that an officer develops the techniques of leadership that will stand him in good stead throughout a logistics career. In my own case, I applied leadership techniques learned in my days with the troops by always establishing goals just beyond an "accepted reach"; then, as the goal was being achieved, I'd move the goal further away so that we seldom became too self-satisfied. This applied to all facets of my responsibilities. Persons with the right attitude would hustle toward the objectives. Some would set their own goals just a little beyond mine. If someone's attitude was wrong, it either changed for the better or someone else moved in. Less than 1 percent had a poor attitude. The primary leadership challenge for me was to communicate adequately so that all could pull the load together.

This brings up teamwork. Pushing teamwork is a most essential element of military leadership. I've often used a baseball analogy to demonstrate the need for teamwork in the Army. For example, a major coordination that wins most games is that between the third baseman and shortstop. A ball hit toward the shortstop, especially a slow-hit ball, is always intercepted by the third baseman if he can reach it in order to better chances of throwing out the batter. On the other hand, a shortstop must go behind the third baseman to catch a short fly ball, even those in foul territory, because he can field the ball more readily from an angle than a backpedaling third baseman. Like the ballplayers, we are often called on to help another soldier do his job. The leader must show that, in the confusion of war, teamwork is essential, and it isn't who does the job that's important, but rather that the job gets done well for the good of all.

Finally, I learned early in my career in logistics how to depend on the support of my associates. For my subordinates, I used a careful blending of a pat on the back for good work along with a kick in the pants for not being good enough to urge them forward.

# CHAPTER 14

# The Logistics Imperatives

Coming to the end of this account of a military career spent in supporting soldiers prompts me to summarize the lessons that I and many of my colleagues have learned about the policies and practices considered necessary to achieve optimum results in logistics. I believe that these lessons can be summarized in the form of ten logistics imperatives. I list them for my readers' consideration.

1. **Involve the commander in all aspects of logistics.**

    + Logistics is a command responsibility at all levels of command, and commanders cannot delegate their logistics responsibilities to logistics specialists. Personal contact between the combat commander and the logistic commander provides the best basis for cooperation and coordination and results in mutual understanding and confidence.

    + Commanders must ensure that economy of logistics force is the basic principle of their commands. The major objective of economy of logistics force is getting materiel and services from the source of support to the troops in the right quantity, in the right condition, and at the right time in order to gain optimum combat effectiveness.

    + Motivated, dedicated, trained, and disciplined logisticians must provide objective advice to commanders so that together they can make intelligent, well-informed decisions.

    + The guiding principle for all logistic commanders is: Support the troops as you would want to be supported. Troop response to such leadership will provide the highest degree of recompense to all involved.

    + A theater commander in chief (CINC) must control the support forwarded to his theater as soon as he and his staff are in position, and a control agency in CONUS, responsive to the needs of the theater CINC, must be part of any logistics system.

    + A command management controller, reporting directly to the appropriate commander at field levels, is needed to assure optimum logistic support at all potential choke points and/or bottlenecks.

## THE LOGISTICS IMPERATIVES

+ Logistics authority and responsibility must be placed at the lowest level having the logistics intelligence to know the answers required.

2. **Prioritize logistics requirements.**

+ Requirements determine priorities, and commanders, in consultation with their logisticians, must establish realistic requirements.

+ Commanders must enforce discipline on the logistics system by clearly establishing the priority of their requirements.

+ A commander's critical items list (CCIL) must be established, prioritized, and approved by the commander personally at every level of command to highlight essential logistics requirements at optimum periodic intervals.

+ Mobilization lead time—D to P (D-day to Production-day)—must be provided for the war reserves that will support requirements until increased production can fill them. Similar logic must be applied to availability of logistic troop support and services in all contingency planning.

3. **Ensure logistic support is consistent with requirements.**

+ Economy of logistics force must determine personnel and materiel requirements.

+ Discipline in establishing requirements ensures the optimum economy of the logistic support force to meet combat readiness and effectiveness.

+ Logistic support must be consistent with, but should not exceed, the optimum capability to use personnel and materiel in a campaign or theater.

+ Base development planning is essential; its supporting requirements, based on command standards, determine what must be included in providing timely logistic support.

+ Transport capability must be balanced against CONUS output of personnel and materiel and all necessary retrograde.

+ A combat environment is no excuse for logistics ineffectiveness and inefficiency.

+ Waste of resources reduces combat effectiveness.

4. **Train logisticians under wartime conditions.**

+ Training in logistics activities is a continuing responsibility and must provide for disciplined corrective action when necessary.

+ Logistics training and education in peacetime for both commanders and logisticians must emphasize wartime capabilities and limitations of the logistics system while adhering to approved policies, procedures, and established doctrine. Such doctrine is not sacred, however, and training should change as experience dictates.

+ Logistics training and education must recognize that civilians comprise a significant portion of the total support system and that their support must be included in all contingency plans and realistic training exercises.

5. **Organize logistics systems in peacetime so they will function in war.**

+ Wartime logistics policies and procedures must be applied in peacetime whenever possible.

+ Every operations and contingency plan must include a logistics annex to set forth logistical support actions and requirements.

+ Logistics processes should be established in peacetime to assure prompt support for critical items in war in order to minimize production lead times.

+ Materiel readiness and sustainability are a continuing responsibility of the logistics community in both peace and war and require that wartime standard operating procedures (SOP) be exercised regularly in a realistic, disciplined manner.

+ Industrial mobilization, including national reserve requirements for manpower, procurement, production capabilities, and strategic materials, is a mandatory element of a logistic system and must be capable of meeting the lead times set forth in mobilization plans.

+ Logistics processes such as the direct exchange of modules, closed loop controls, and inventory-in-motion systems should be in place to assure prompt support of critical items.

+ Fixed supply depots must be eliminated in objective areas and replaced by mobile logistics general support to back up direct support in supply, maintenance, transportation, and services.

+ An essential element of integrated logistical support—Logistics Support Analysis ("front-end analysis")—is a maintenance plan that organizes maintenance in appropriate echelons, emphasizing module replacement in lieu of piece repair in forward echelons.

6. **Incorporate commodity and functional capabilities into all echelons of logistic support.**

+ Commodity and functional expertise must be incorporated at every level of support.

+ Logistics units must be organized so that they balance in every phase of an operation the capability of the combat units they support.

+ Soldiers and units should have a single source of logistic support.

# THE LOGISTICS IMPERATIVES 263

+ The impetus for support must come from the rear in timely fashion.

## 7. Consider logistics constraints in establishing operational capabilities.

+ Military operations are limited by logistical capabilities.

+ Readiness and sustainability, including mobilization and production capabilities of the nation, will determine how much logistical support is available.

+ Probable bottlenecks and choke points for logistic support must be anticipated and alternative courses of action determined to facilitate improvisation.

+ In coalition warfare the constraints on logistics, and by extension operations, will reflect on the ability of allies to coordinate joint mobilization, interoperability, common logistics, and host nation support in all environments.

+ Ready war reserves must be available to cover the void between the beginning of conflict and the availability of material and services.

## 8. Determine requirements based on factual data.

+ Effective and efficient logistics decisions depend upon command judgments based on optimum intelligence, ascertained facts, and honest estimates with clearly defined sources.

+ Logistics requirements must be determined by actual consumption data, and estimates for future needs must take into account such factors as new technology (including artificial intelligence), objective environments, firing rates, and pipeline fill.

+ Responsibility for establishing logistics requirements should be placed at the lowest level of support which has the answers based upon best logistics intelligence available.

+ Logistics data used to establish requirements must be suitable for both manual and automated operations. Communications methods and automatic data processes at all levels must be optimized to achieve a paperless SOP to enhance responsive logistic support with minimum user tasks, but they must all be prepared for manual operations in case of power failure.

+ The "fog of war" may cloud a commander's estimate of requirements, but such uncertainty must be minimized and cannot justify a philosophy of "mass logistics" or "firstest with the mostest."

## 9. Be flexible in adapting capabilities to requirements.

+ If something can go wrong in logistics, to some degree at least it will. Providing essential support to combat forces depends on the ability of logisticians to rise above the fog of war—to plan optimum solutions for potential problems, to be flexible, and to improvise intelligently.

+ Good logisticians will always find the best way to solve a logistics problem.

+ An essential element of the dialogue between logisticians and commanders of supported units and a source of flexibility in logistics is the logistics contact team.

+ Contact teams must be established at all combat echelons to provide continuous liaison with supported units and with all other related echelons up, down, and across the organizational structure to organize logistical support and to solve logistical problems.

+ In Hannibal's time, supply by elephants represented "state of the art" logistics, a state replaced in our times by modern communications, automation, transportation, and intelligence. Commanders today must rely for the most part on a zone of interior–based supply inventory in motion and on an echeloned maintenance support system. Insurance items must be retained at the ready in rear echelons, usually in CONUS. Depot stocks of all supplies, except Class III and Class V, should be normally restricted to CONUS and inventory-in-motion principles applied to all supplies.

10. **Learn from history for "the Past is Prologue."**

+ Time and environment change, but basic logistics problems and human nature remain the same. The opposition will be defeated by our learning and implementing lessons from the past.

# EPILOGUE

# Polishing the Mirror

A Navy chaplain once told me about a patient he met while assigned to a military hospital. The patient explained that he had only a few months to live. One morning while looking into his shaving mirror he began to think about how his life was itself a mirror, but one now clouded by the mistakes he had made and hurts he had inflicted. He decided that day, he told the chaplain, to spend his remaining time making amends. He was "polishing the mirror."

In these pages I have discussed successes and failures in military logistics during the last half-century. I have done this mainly by reflecting on events in my own career. In this sense, I too have been trying to polish the mirror, on both the personal and professional levels.

My experience covers three wars—seven years in combat zones—in logistic support of American troops, the finest Americans who ever lived, as General Abrams often reminded us. I hope that I have adequately conveyed to those in my profession some of the important lessons learned in these three wars and in the many years of uneasy peace in between. But as I look back on my career, several points that transcend discussions of military logistics and leadership also come to mind, points that I would like to underscore for my reader, especially those young officers and enlisted men and women who make up our armed forces.

First, my own experiences have convinced me that our individual visions of the United States and its future, often expressed in a cacophony of conflicting opinions and ideologies, are, in fact, remarkably similar. We all want peace, love, and freedom. The basic point I would like to make is that these goals, so ardently desired, require from all of us, but especially from those Americans in the armed forces, a strong commitment to three values: duty, honor, and country. While busy with research early one morning, I stumbled across a photo essay called *Our Country*.* Its closing lines contain an optimistic thought that I consider worth remembering: "We [Americans] have much more in common with each other than we think, and we are getting together to change the things that need to be changed." I pray that our young people, especially those in the military, will devote themselves ceaselessly to these values and this type of vision as they shape our country's future.

My military career, when viewed in light of my childhood, also clearly demonstrates how in the United States a person can achieve success against considerable odds. I do not mean success in achieving high rank. High rank is great, but it's for a lucky few. Unfortunately, there are never enough positions open to promote all those deserving it. Each time a general officer list is issued, it's wonderful for those who have achieved the promotion list, but there are a great number of others as well, or better, qualified who for some reason did not make the list. In the last analysis a successful career should be judged not on rank or power but on how one helps others. The essay in *Our Country*, in discussing the basis of America's greatness, refers to two sources that I often quote—the great French writer Alexis de Tocqueville and the English poet John Donne. Both wrote eloquently of how a person's success, and by extension a nation's success, must be measured by adherence to the basic moral precept of duty to others.

Finally, the profession of arms deserves to be ranked equal in skills and value to any other highly regarded profession. If our servicemen and women retain their soldierly skills through training and study and preserve their dedication to duty, honor, and country, they will continue to provide our nation with that essential support that makes possible our leadership in the free world, leadership so urgently needed now and in the future.

A great American statesman and general, Maxwell Taylor, once said, "America will never be defeated from without. If it is defeated, it will be from within. We will have lost faith in one another." I want to reiterate his warning as a last but important thought. Our faith in the United States and in one another will survive only if we adhere to our shared values and ideals.

America's glorious past as the world's foremost democracy has already been written. Its future is being written by us now.

God bless America.

---

*Editors of U.S. News and World Report, *Our Country* (Washington, D.C.: U.S. News and World Report, 1972).

"Spreading the Word." The DCSLOG speaks on logistics management techniques at a CENTO Logistics Management Seminar, May 1970.

A DCSLOG field trip to an Army supply depot with Assistant Secretary J. Ronald Fox.

"Kicking Boxes." General Heiser applies his well-known hands-on investigative technique to the supply situation at Anniston Depot, Alabama, 1969, and visits Vietnam, 1971.

Retirement, 24 November 1972. The Heisers with U.S. Army Chief of Staff Creighton and Mrs. Abrams.

1st Logistical Command Vietnam Memorial, Fort Lee, Virginia, built on a field named in honor of logistics Medal of Honor winner Sergeant William W. Seay. Plans are underway to further dedicate this memorial to all logisticians who have made the supreme sacrifice for their country.

# APPENDIXES

*Editors' note:* Beyond minor deletions, as indicated, and the correction of obvious typographical errors, the articles reprinted in the Appendixes appear without any historical editing on our part.

# APPENDIX A

Economy of Force: Application in Combat Logistics

by

Maj. Gen. Joseph M. Heiser, Jr., and Col. Louis Rachmeler*

The war in Vietnam is being sustained today by the most responsive support base in U.S. history. The objective before us is also to make it the most effective, efficient logistical operation in any combat zone.

The economic and prudent management of resources in the combat area, while at the same time unstintingly meeting the soldier's battlefield requirements, may at first appear incongruous. But looking further, it becomes clear that the application of sound supply, maintenance, and transportation techniques and systems molds together the notions of responsiveness to combat requirements and efficient management of assets during war. Successful mission accomplishment depends upon the complete compatibility and integration of these techniques and systems.

Background

In 1965, the decision to commit major forces into Vietnam brought with it the need to establish a strong logistical infrastructure. Geographically, South Vietnam posed a formidable obstacle to the rapid establishment of such a support base. Over 10,000 miles separated the supplier and the user, while airheads and deep-draft port facilities and highways were either nonexistent or totally inadequate. Despite these major deficiencies, the difficult terrain and a hostile climate, the logistics system grew by bounds, to keep pace with the accelerated escalation of troop strength.

Since 1965, Army troop strength increased from relatively few to well over 350,000. Six deep-draft ports were completed. Through these ports some 800,000 short tons of material are handled each month. Depot complexes were built; many logistic activities are still in final throes of construction; monthly the depots issue 160,794 short tons of material.

During the early stages of the buildup, the Army was faced with increasing troop levels but had no established demand data base. Having to rely chiefly on automatic resupply or "push shipments" to maintain the required level of support, cargo flowed into Vietnam at an unprece-

---

*This article was written and published while the authors were serving in Vietnam.

dented rate. Support agencies such as the Army Materiel Command, Defense Supply Agency, General Services Administration, and others did a magnificent job of moving supplies to Southeast Asia. Unfortunately the logistical forces in Vietnam could not receive the supplies as fast as the CONUS agencies could ship. Inventories grew, some unrecorded.

Redistribution of Excesses

In 1966, a Department of the Army team was sent to South Vietnam to assist the Command in reviewing the logistical situation. Problems were recognized—in retrospect, *earlier* than in *any* previous conflict—and solutions were recommended. As a result, among the many initiated actions, decisions were made in early 1967 to retrograde supplies excess to the needs of the U.S. forces in Southeast Asia though not necessarily excess to worldwide requirements. Then in November 1967 the Secretary of Defense designated the Secretary of the Army as Executive Agent for the Department of Defense to assure that Southeast Asia excesses were identified and made available for redistribution (PURM).[1] Commander in Chief Pacific (CINCPAC), was given the responsibility for organizing and operating a Pacific Command Utilization and Redistribution Agency (PURA). CINCPAC delegated the responsibility to the Commander in Chief, U.S. Army Pacific (CINCUSARPAC) who in turn designated the Commanding General, 2d Logistical Command, Okinawa, to establish and operate the PURM.

The basic objectives of the system are:

a. To promptly identify geographical excess material within the Pacific Command (PACOM).

b. To screen and redistribute geographical excess material of all services to satisfy existing requirements within PACOM to the fullest extent possible.

c. To establish policies and procedures for screening, utilization, and redistribution of retrograde material from combat areas in the future.

d. To advise CINCPAC, departmental secretaries, and Defense Supply Agency when information and findings indicate ways and means of minimizing imbalances of supplies and equipment within geographical areas.

e. To preclude procurement of items in an excess posture and disposal of excess items for which valid requirements exist; and to preclude expenditure of funds to ship items when required materiel is in place and available as excess.

In order to begin utilizing and redistributing known excess assets and not wait for computer programs and procedures for operational PURA to be completed, an interim phase was initiated in March 1968. As a result, some $3.3 million worth of materiel was processed for redistribution. The

---

[1] *Project for Utilization and Redistribution of Material in Pacific Area (PURM)*, Headquarters, Department of Army, Apr. 15, 1968.

# APPENDIXES

operational phase of PURA is not in effect. PURA has received some 470,000 items as excess nominations from eight of the participating agencies. The dollar value of these assets is approximately $144 million. Screening of PURA assets is to be extended to CONUS inventory managers and the U.S. Agency for International Development thereby making it possible for the redistribution of assets from the Pacific theater to any other theater, worldwide. This Command automatically ships its excesses to Okinawa after making them available to all services in-country. In this vein, the 1st Logistical Command and the U.S. Marines in I Corps Tactical Zone have agreed to interface their respective supply systems to provide for the effective cross-leveling of stocks, particularly critical items. In fiscal year 1968, 93,068 short tons of stores were shipped to Okinawa. The 2d Logistical Command returned $135,263,000 of this stock to serviceable supply accounts after identification, minor rehabilitation, and repacking.

PURA is in the process of maturing. The success in accomplishing its objectives depends largely on how well each service is able to identify its local excesses. Identification of local excess is a function of physical inventories, the reconciliation of materiel due into the inventory and materiel due out to the customer, updating of stocks records, and validation of requirements. These are fundamental hard core features of a managed supply system which, in turn, requires the timely integration of resources and management procedures under the control of fully trained personnel.

## Closed Loop Support

The identification and retrograde of local depot excesses is but one facet of the entire retrograde program that is being aggressively pursued in Vietnam. Materiel for retrograde is also generated through maintenance channels. During fiscal year 1968, 166,177 short tons of reparables were shipped out of the country. A major portion of this tonnage represented our contribution to the Closed Loop Support Program (CLS).

In an effort to provide the optimum in logistical support to military forces in Vietnam, Department of the Army has established a program for the special management of selected critical items in the Army Logistics System. It is called Closed Loop Support. The fundamental principles of military supply and maintenance are clearly in evidence throughout this program. It is, however, unique in that it is a specialized management procedure wherein command and support elements are employed in a closely controlled network. Logistical functions, such as supply, retrograde, repair, overhaul, and return to Army supply channels are arrayed in a detailed schedule. This provides the means for insuring that critical major items and major assemblies are expedited through the logistics system back to an overhaul facility and return to the command through the supply system.

Closed Loop Support is defined as a totally integrated system of all echelons of maintenance wherein supply repair, retrograde, overhaul, and return of selected critical items are rigidly controlled in a clearly defined net. The objectives of Closed Loop Support are: to insure timely response to the needs of operational units; to exert more effective control of critical serviceable and unserviceable assets in the logistics pipeline; to reduce the backlog of unserviceables at all levels; to insure the timely availability of reparable assets at maintenance overhaul facilities; and to provide worldwide asset control of selected critical items in the Army logistics system.

In Vietnam using units generate unserviceable equipment. Those items of equipment beyond the repair capabilities of in-country maintenance units are evacuated to offshore maintenance facilities or CONUS. For example, Armored Personnel Carriers (APC), are shipped into Sagami, Japan, which has a theater repair/overhaul capacity to support U.S. Army, Vietnam. The overhaul of APC's in Japan reduces the supply system's cost of support of APC's by approximately 27 percent. Anything that is added to the system comes from CONUS procurement or redistribution of assets from elsewhere in the Army system. Once the system is filled with appropriate assets, the only leaks to the system should be combat and maintenance losses. In order for the system to sustain itself a loss to the inventory must be replaced in order to retain the status quo. In some instances, for example, tanks, assets must be delivered through the supply pipeline for the command to be able to retrograde unserviceables to the overhaul facilities.

The Closed Loop Support Program provides opportunities, among other things, to control selected assets and to improve the condition of equipment. In addition, economies result from being able to repair and reissue equipment, like new, at from one-sixth to one-tenth of the original acquisition cost of the item.

Improvement of Support Management

The retrograde program in Vietnam is part and parcel of an overall program to provide support to the user in a combat zone as effectively and as economically as is practicable. There is currently underway in the 1st Logistical Command, a comprehensive series of projects designed to analyze, evaluate, and improve, where possible, every aspect of the supply system. Among the most important areas being considered are the automated supply management system, management techniques and procedures, depot and direct support unit (DSU) operational procedures, and the maintenance of an informative and comprehensive data base which can lead to timely and effective management decisions.

Automation

When the Inventory Control Center (ICCV) deployed to Vietnam in January 1966, a limited supply management system based on automatic data processing (ADP) equipment was designed and implemented in the ICCV and the depots. As commitments continued to increase, it became obvious that the system did not have the capability required to control the enormous quantity of supplies being used in the country. It was decided in the spring of 1967 that computers were required for the ICCV

# APPENDIXES

and at each depot; namely, Saigon, Camranh Bay and Quinhon. The first computer became operational at the ICCV in October 1967; the last one is to be received in October 1968 at Qui Nhon Army Depot. Card processing equipment was used previously. The major systems effort has been in the form of an entirely new system designed to utilize the latest developments in automated supply management. The system chosen for implementation was the U.S. Army Pacific Standard Supply System (3S) which has been in operation for some time. However, the system was modified to meet unique Vietnam requirements. The programing of the system modifications has now been completed and testing is ready to begin. During the last 6 months management personnel have been receiving executive training in the system at the 2d Logistical Command in Okinawa. A program for the lower echelon supervisors and commodity manager personnel is now being established in Vietnam.

The system, to be completed by the end of the year, will provide for the absolute management and control of theater stock, the development of requirements, and the acquisition of additional materiel through completely integrated subsystems at the depot and the ICCV. Under the new system, the depot will maintain detailed stockage data on the computer pertaining to location, condition, and the history of the demand of each item, as well as complete files on outstanding customer backorders, scheduled receipts, and the status of each. Additionally, other detailed catalog type data such as substitutable items, item weight, size, cost will be available in the computer for use by the item manager. The ICCV will maintain essentially the same data with emphasis on that information which allows for overall theater supply management. The computers at all locations will exchange management data making the overall system completely responsive to any combat demand anywhere in Vietnam.

Item Management

The ICCV initiated a program to standardize all stockage items that were amenable to such action. The most notable example of results achieved relates to paint. Prior to the review, 1,040 different types, colors, and sizes were stocked. This now has been reduced to 187.

Action is being taken to insure that only fast moving items are stocked in the forward support areas; those that are required less frequently are to be stored at the depots. The slowest moving items will be keyed to a specific depot, such as Camranh Bay. Prime transportation will be used to speed these line items to the customer.

Order and Ship Time (OST) represents the actual time required from the placement of an order to the receipt of stock ready for issue under normal conditions. Much thought and study is being given to the proper computation of the OST to insure that excessive quantities of any stocked item are not being ordered. The overall objective is to reduce the OST to a minimum thereby reducing the length of the supply pipeline. Recently the OST for the Meal, Combat, Individual, formerly known as the "C" ration, was reduced from 180 days to 165 thereby saving, on a one-time basis, $2.4 million. Plans have been finalized for the use of Automatic Data Processing equipment in the computation of the OST for munitions. Presently it is being done manually. This transition may result in a reduction of 10 days (11 percent) of the OST for munitions. Likewise as our depots and DSU's become more efficient, reductions in OST between depot and DSU shall become more feasible. These are but a few of the many ideas being considered for implementation to streamline the system.

The hot and humid weather in Vietnam has had a very severe impact on the use of dry batteries. Life expectancy had been cut almost in half by the time they reached the user. This situation caused an increase in the demand for batteries. As a result, the requirement for refrigerated storage increased to the degree that exceeded the onhand refrigerated storage capacity. A new procedure has been developed to solve this problem and is now being tested. Depot stockage is being eliminated except for a small emergency quantity; the DSU and unit stock levels are being reduced to about a 12- to 13-day level. Action has been initiated to ship 10-day quantities of batteries in refrigerated boxes direct from the port to the DSU where the batteries are issued to the unit, as requested. When the refrigerated box is empty, it is returned and exchanged for a full one. In essence, dry cell batteries will be handled like perishable subsistence.

When a significant item comes to the attention of management as moving toward a critically short position or it appears that control of the item has been lost to the extent that shortages are developing and equipment is being deadlined for the lack of the items concerned, the item is designated as an Intensively Managed Item (IMI). Initially a complete inventory in all command depots is accomplished to assure the accuracy of the stock status records. This is followed by such appropriate actions as the initiation of additional requisitions, reconciliation of dues-in and dues-out, and the provision for special handling in the receipt and issue process to avoid any delays. These actions are supplemented by frequent and continual review of the item until it resumes a normal supply posture. In addition, this management "logistics intelligence" is fed back to all support agencies and to the National Inventory Control Points so that the entire logistical system can respond effectively.

As an adjunct to IMI, the Commander's Critical Items List has been instituted. Tactical commanders at brigade and division levels provide the Commanding General, 1st Logistical Command a periodic, semimonthly as a minimum, list of items that are particularly and peculiarly critical to them. These items then receive IMI treatment (at general officer level as far back in support system as is necessary to solve it) so as to minimize any impact upon the unit's combat effectiveness.

Depot and DSU Operational Procedures

Emphasis is being placed on the depots and DSU to follow correct procedures in the discharge of their responsibilities. Instructor training teams have been formed to act as advisers and instructors to the Com-

APPENDIXES                                                                     279

mand's supply activities. These teams are assisting the depots and DSU's in the receiving, storage, surveillance, issue, and stock control activities by determining where deficiencies exist and by training personnel on-the-spot in the correct procedures to be used. Training of military personnel in large-scale depot operations is being stressed more than ever. If our supply system is to interface with a sophisticated CONUS supply system without slippage, then the requirement for personnel with the requisite skills becomes extremely pertinent and their availability imperative.

Data Base

It is a well known fact that an automated system complemented with the best of manager personnel and procedures is no better than the accuracy of the data available to the system. The 1st Logistical Command has undertaken Project "Count," a wall-to-wall inventory of its supply activities' stocks. The inventory program was initiated on August 28, 1968, is to be completed by January 15, 1969, and is designed to ascertain with a great degree of accuracy the stock status of the command stocks. Temporary duty personnel from CONUS, augmented by 500 soldiers and civilians from various U.S. Army, Vietnam, logistical headquarters and activities have been organized into teams and trained in inventory procedures and techniques. *Project Count*, the inventory of approximately $1.8 billion worth of stock in such a short period of time, is truly a monumental task. Moreover, combat support will be provided while the actual counting is being done. There can be no "Closed Door" inventory. The anticipated results will more than pay for the required Herculean effort; they will help purify the available data base at the ICCV.

Coincident with Project Count, the 1st Logistical Command's direct support and general support units have been directed to review their stock records for accuracy under Operation Clean; the review is to be completed by September 19, 1968. Initial reports reveal the cancellation by the DSU of requisitions for materiel worth millions of dollars. Located excess stocks resulting from the review are to be nominated for redistribution or retrograded out-of-country for further redistribution.

Efforts to improve the data base do not end with stock status data. Emphasis has been placed on reconciling customer back orders and ICCV back orders with the CONUS National Inventory Control Points to improve the accuracy and agreement of the files. These reconciliations are made quarterly, as a minimum. In order to reduce the input of nonessential items into Vietnam, all CONUS supply sources were directed by the Command in June 1968, under PROJECT STOP, to cancel, divert, or frustrate certain USAICCV requisitions, some dating back prior to June 1, 1967. Preliminary information indicates that shipments worth $93 million were either canceled or frustrated in CONUS, a dramatic illustration of the dynamic integration now being realized all along the entire logistic system.

Summary

The situation in Vietnam is dynamic by nature. Yet the support situation has been stabilized to the degree that troop strengths have been stabilized. In this environment we shall continue to improve upon the best combat logistical support ever provided to the fighting soldier; concurrently we shall manage our logistical resources throughout the system to the extent that we will have applied to combat logistics, as never before, a basic principle of war—Economy of Force.

Reprinted from *Defense Management Journal*, Fall 1968.

# APPENDIX B

### DEPARTMENT OF THE ARMY
### HEADQUARTERS 1ST LOGISTICAL COMMAND
### APO 96384

COMMANDER'S LETTER 7–1                                              1 July 1969

SUBJECT: 1st Logistical Command Offensive

1. At a recent change of command ceremony of the Commanding General, XXIV Corps, General Abrams indicated to me that he wanted to have a briefing because, as a result of various indications from combat commanders, etc., he began to see the results of what he called the "1st Log Command's LOGISTICS OFFENSIVE." (As a result, General Abrams is visiting HQ, 1st Log Command, for a command update in the very near future.) The results of the efforts of the entire command will be displayed for his review.

2. It is interesting to note that the dictionary of the U.S. Army defines the term "offensive" as (a) the condition of a force when it is attacking; (b) attack; ready to attack; (c) attack, especially one on a large scale.

3. I consider the term "LOGISTICS OFFENSIVE," as used by General Abrams, to be one of the highest compliments a combat field commander can give to his logistic element because this definitely indicates that a combat commander, who is continuously associated with the need for tactical offensives, is recognizing that logistics requires a LOGISTICS OFFENSIVE and that our commander appreciates the fact that we have such an offensive in being. Thus, the Command and Control Improvement Program which we have completed as of 30 June will now be classified as Phase I of our LOGISTICS OFFENSIVE. Phase II begins today. We must build on what others did prior to Phase I, and based upon the greater capability resulting at the end of Phase I, we must assure continued progress toward efficiency and effectiveness at an even more rapid, mature, and sophisticated rate.

4. During Phase I, we have attacked the problems of depot excesses, large inventories in property disposal yards, large inventories in CC&S activities, excesses in the hands of DSU/GSUs, excesses in the hands of using

units, reductions in ammunition inventory, upgrading of maintenance standards on materiel of all types, security of logistical installatons, security of convoys, and phasedown of personnel as well as a host of other problems while at the same time maintaining combat service support at the highest level ever attained under combat conditions. Our weapons have included Projects Count I and II, Stop and Stop/See, Thru-Put, Repair and Return, Clean I through V, Manifest, Supply Control V, Condition, Challenge, Skills I through III, Prayer, Alert, Ready, Trim Down/Tuck In, Purge, Smart, and many others. In waging Phase I of the logistical offensive we have made significant gains. Inventories of all classes of supply are down to more manageable levels. Operational readiness rates for combat equipment are well above recognized standards. Church attendance for the command exceeds thirty percent. Millions of dollars have been saved through the cancellation of requisitions of unneeded supplies. Additional millions have been saved through carrying out a new concept of supply (with ammunition as a pathfinder) which utilizes knowledge of what is en route and where it is (inventory in motion) to preclude large stockages on the ground. This concept must be fully extended throughout all our commodity areas of management.

5. Appreciation for the ground gained through our logistical offensive has been expressed at all levels throughout the Army as well as in other elements of the Department of Defense. The credit belongs to the men who have used their brains and brawn, coupled with long hours, to get the job done.

6. As indicated above, we have launched Phase II of our LOGISTICS OFFENSIVE today. We shall continue to attack many of the same targets—depot excesses, operational readiness rates, reduction of unserviceable inventories, upgrading of security at all levels, reduction of personnel overhead, refinement of statistical data, increase of fill on unit requisitions, processing of requisitions on a real time basis, upgrading of machine capabilities, and others. An old problem which will receive more intensified concentration will be that of retrograde, and to force our attention, we have introduced a new weapon called Project Retro-Right. The details of this new offensive weapon will be announced separately. Likewise we are introducing Project Duty which is aimed toward focusing the attention of every logistical fighter toward getting the job done to the best of his ability, working as long as is necessary and doing so conscientiously. In addition, as we reach certain intermediate objectives we must move on through the establishment of higher standards which will continuously require us to "reach" beyond that already attained. This technique leads to progress. Certain projects will be added during Phase II, and others will become even more important than in the past. One of the latter is "Buddy." The Presidential decision concerning the 25,000 reduction makes it absolutely essential that we push Buddy to assure that the Free World strength in support of our cause in Vietnam does not falter, but rather grows stronger and stronger. Buddy is directly involved in

achieving this in the area of logistics support and its very impact on the economy of the US and South Vietnam as well as that of our allies.

7. I am confident that every fighter of this logistical team will do his best to assure that we successfully meet our targets and thereby continue to wage our offensive in a manner which can only mean victory. The 1st Log Command responsibility and the opportunity for good increase daily. We must meet this challenge and we will.

JOS. M. HEISER, JR.
Major General, USA
Commanding

DISTRIBUTION:
A, plus
AVCA SG(10)

# APPENDIX C

## DEPARTMENT OF THE ARMY
Office of the Deputy Chief of Staff for Logistics
Washington, D.C. 20310

LOG–XO                                                                29 October 1969

MEMORANDUM FOR: SEE DISTRIBUTION

SUBJECT: DCSLOG Guidance Bulletin #24

The Attached is published and distributed for the information and guidance of all concerned.

FOR THE DEPUTY CHIEF OF STAFF FOR LOGISTICS:

1 Incl  
Guidance Bulletin #24

ROBERT W. PATTERSON  
Colonel, GS  
Executive

DISTRIBUTION: B

APPENDIXES

## DCSLOG GUIDANCE BULLETIN NO. 24

ACTION AGENCY

1. General Betts requested our assistance in assuring that we fully utilize RAC's capability during the current work year—started 1 Sep 69. Their current program is considerably short. Review LDSRA projects to see if part of their planned/programmed workload can be diverted to RAC. Are there other critical studies or projects which could go to RAC in preference to outside agencies? Funding through reprogramming of DCSLOG funds or perhaps RDT&E funds of CRD?   ADCSLOG(DSR) in coord w/all

2. I was briefed on 23 Oct on the status of actions which have been taken to implement the Chief of Staff's decisions on the Brown Board report. Many of the problems which we are facing today were identified in that report and decisions were made which, had they been fully executed, would have largely corrected the condition. I want to get on with doing those things directed to us and take advantage of that effort. We must review those decisions which were assigned to us for implementation and:   All

   a. Reopen and proceed with those which have not been fully executed to satisfy the intent of the decision.

   b. Expedite execution of those which have not been addressed or which are still underway.

   c. Obtain decision on those which were deferred or held pending completion of some related action.

   N.B. I'm particularly concerned with those decisions which addressed the quality and quantity of logsitics personnel, weapons system/commodity grouping management, technical channels and supervision related to materiel, the rotation base, logistic unit readiness, the interface between CONUS and the overseas commands, cataloging and item entry control, design and development of the Army logistics system.

3. Specific decisions on the Brown Board report which are critical to the Army's overall control of its logistics system and the items which are supplied/used at the user level:

   a. Organization, location, and operation of the ACMSs. Get AMC to move out on this.   ADCSLOG(DSR)

b. Establishment of a Troop Support Commodity Command. Let's review the follow-on study and get something underway.     ADCSLOG(DSR)

c. Decision II–10 concerning long range cataloging. What have we done? Not done? Why?     ADCSLOG(SM)

4. Get out a letter for my signature to the Commandant, C&GSC, on the overall status of Brown Board implementations as an example of what happens to studies at the DA level.     ADCSLOG(DSR)

5. I want a complete review of actions directed as a result of the Brown Board, under some sort of committee or group, to ascertain the current status, effectiveness, and adequacy of actions taken. This should result in a presentation to the Chief of Staff to handle remaining implementation as part of "normal actions" rather than continuing the present quarterly report.     ADCSLOG(DSR) and all

6. Does the Army's Life Cycle Management of Materiel Concept as expessed in current directives *and* as it is *actually* functioning comprehend the sort of decisions at DOD which are reflected in Secretary Resor's memo to the Dep/SecDef, 2 Oct 69, subj: "Improvement in Weapons Systems Acquisition"? Do we need a new procedure or emphasis on currently prescribed arrangements and controls? (See Staff Memo 705–2.)     All ADSCLOGs

7. I want to keep General Hurlbut of the JLRB fully informed on all significant logistics actions, especially those raised by higher authority. We simply cannot wait for him to ask us for information. In this regard send him a copy of the current actions "Review of Army Organization and Functions" together with our input.     All

8. I want to emphasize to all that we cannot separate supply and maintenance; they are inseparable elements of the same logistics materiel function and must be considered together at all times.     All

9. Several ideas are currently being revived which affect the interface between CONUS and the oversea commands, e.g., LCO, Theater Oriented Depots or Supply Centers, direct deliveries to DSUs, etc. At least some of these infer direct response to sub-elements below the theater command level. This sort of thing is inappropriate; whatever we do     All

# APPENDIXES

along these lines must be responsive to the theater commander's stated requirements and be subject to overall in-theater control.

10. The ADCSLOG(DSR) has primary action on developing the concept for the logistics offensive in support of DCSOPS Dynamic Defense. This will be combined with development of the Principles of Logistics and a Conceptual Logistics System for the future and pursued by an Ad Hoc Study/Review Group under DSR chairmanship. I expect completion, to include necessary decision briefings and documents, within about three months. — ADCSLOG(DSR) in conj/w/all

11. The SOMISS decisions have resulted in establishing the CSC under the AVCof S with responsibility for ADPE programming and installation. Concurrently, the DCSLOG has expanded responsibilities for determining what logistics applications CSC should program and install together with the details to be covered and the priorities to be followed. I want to know how the DCSLOG tells them (and DMIS) what to do, when to do it, and assures that what they are doing is responsive to DSCLOG direction rather than their own ideas, for example. — ADCSLOG(DSR)

12. I understand TSG is conducting a study on how the medical function should be conducted and controlled worldwide (outgrowth from the Brown Board). In this connection I want: — ADCSLOG(DSR) w/all

   a. Cognizance maintained over their study effort to assure appropriate DCSLOG comments during the study and before any decision is reached.

   b. To re-establish DCSLOG control and influence over the logistics portions of TSG's responsibilities.

13. I understand a study similar to that of TSG has been completed on the engineer structure and responsibilities. I would like a briefing covering the content and current status of that study. — DI w/all

14. Action on HG #134 re DCSLOG role in personnel management should be held until after we have developed a basic package with DCSPER. — ADCSLOG(DSR)

# APPENDIX D

The Logistics Offensive

by

Lt. Gen. Joseph M. Heiser, Jr.

There is an Army LOGISTICS OFFENSIVE in the making. The LOGISTICS OFFENSIVE, in its broadest sense, is an Army-wide program designed to reemphasize logistics principles, update and refine techniques, revise systems, and more clearly define training and career management objectives.

In addition, the LOGISTICS OFFENSIVE is geared to support the broad objectives of General William C. Westmoreland's four M's—Mission, Motivation, Modernization, and Management.

General Creighton Abrams used the term LOGISTICS OFFENSIVE at Phu Bai, Vietnam, last Spring to describe what was required across the entire Army logistics system in Vietnam. He meant it as a compliment for the progressive improvement made in all areas of logistics. But in reality, he was issuing a resounding challenge to all professional Army logisticians when he, as the leading combat commander in the field, applied the term "offensive" to a military logistics operation. General Westmoreland, in the name of all Americans, both soldiers and taxpayers, is also demanding "efficiency in logistics operations."

Thus, the Army is launching a logistics program to meet this challenge, using the term General Abrams coined. We, as professional Army logisticians, must muster all of the good things we have learned over the last decade, especially those that have been tried and found true, and with the same dispatch that a combat commander associates with an "offense," we must reach intermediate and final objectives with deliberate haste. To do less will mean that we have missed our opportunity and have failed to meet the challenge.

Many segments of the logistics offensive program are familiar ones. Many have been the subject of studies and tests, and some fine experience has been gained through the utilization of the majority of them. The important thing to remember, however, is that the Army is going to explore all possibilities applicable to the program. Any new segment developed for this program must be one of offense, not defense. I do want to emphasize that the logistics offensive program is going to move at a highly accelerated rate. Past studies and proven concepts will be implemented with minimum delay. New segments will be incorporated as they

APPENDIXES                                                                                      289

are evaluated. The contributions of all Army professional logisticians are needed to make the LOGISTICS OFFENSIVE a success.

The United States Army is a highly mobile, hard-hitting combat-ready force that is quick to respond to any emergency in support of our national objectives anytime, anywhere it may be needed. A critical factor in the Army's combat readiness, and in its sustaining power, is the efficiency of its logistics system which has shown significant development and refinement in the past ten years.

In addition to internal logistics reorganization, the Army has experienced the implementation of the Department of Defense Military Standards System not only in a CONUS peacetime environment but in an oversea emergency environment brought on by the Berlin buildup in Europe and the war in Southeast Asia.

While we have made significant progress in improving the Army's logistics system, we have also isolated many areas which require improvement. Undoubtedly, the military logistician, and the American taxpayer alike, face the greatest challenge and opportunity yet provided—"Efficient and Effective Combat and Combat Readiness!"

The best and the most recent proving ground for testing the Army's improvements in logistics management is our experience in Vietnam. It might be said that the Vietnam operation is unique and therefore, we must be very careful in applying lessons learned from experience there. I would agree that, if the experience gained in Vietnam was the result of uniqueness, its general application would be improper. However, fortunately for those of us engaged in logistics, I do not believe that there is much that is unique about allied logistics support in Vietnam, at least not from the standpoint of the significant lessons learned.

## MISSION OBJECTIVE

To meet the challenge of providing efficient and effective combat and combat readiness, I believe we must get our "eye on the ball" and then keep it there. The Army's logistics mission is to provide the American soldier with what he needs, where and when he needs it, in the condition required for his use! The Army's logistics doctrine, organization, systems, equipment, and training must be integrated to reach maximum efficiency and effectiveness in accomplishing this objective in the shortest practical time. To do this, the Army needs to marshal the momentum implied in the term LOGISTICS OFFENSIVE.

## PROGRAM SEGMENTS

. . . A brief discussion of some of the more significant segments of the logistics offensive program and other objectives follows:

—INVENTORY IN MOTION, a revitalized supply management program, will minimize the requirement for large stock levels at immobile depot activities in the combat zone. Integrated supply and transportation planning, realtime assets control of in-transit stocks, and more intensified management will yield rapid resupply response with smaller inventories and with reduced static stocks on the ground.

—There will be greater reliance on mobile maintenance support teams capable of quick reaction for the accomplishment of critical repairs and component replacement. This will allow greater flexibility in the scope of maintenance performed at each level.

—Through the availability of improved communications and air transportation, the echelonment of supplies, typical in the past, will be reduced in accord with revised requirements. Logistics units will be designed with a degree of mobility comparable to supported forces.

—Adoption of simplified supply procedures and greater selectivity for stockage will reduce the amount of supplies in a theater. Controlled and standardized authorized stockage lists (ASL's) and prescribed load lists (PLL's) will contribute to efficiency. Theater authorized stockage lists (TASL's) will be limited to items consumed on a recurring basis. Other items used less frequently will be provided through rapid transport from sources outside the combat zone on an expedited basis similar to RED BALL procedures. Inherent in this system is the maximizing of module maintenance, replacing components rather than piece part repair up forward.

—Expanded use of CLOSED LOOP and direct exchange procedures, used successfully for Vietnam, will provide realtime visibility and control of all intensively managed items that are critical to combat effectiveness and economic utilization of resources. This will result in economic trade-offs that will provide for more effective balance in the allocation of funds for investment and operation and maintenance.

—Standard software and integrated hardware to meet command management requirements will provide realtime logistics intelligence for proper and timely decisions providing for maximum economy of logistics forces and resources.

—Balanced logistics philosophy and management at all levels of command is required. It is essential that we balance the horizontal functional logistics management with the vertical weapon system commodity—oriented logistics management. Doctrine, systems, and training, as well as logistics career management, are being renovated to achieve this organizational objective.

—Management of logistics careers must keep pace with these improvements. A qualitative upgrading of management skills is in order. Such actions include the maintenance of a peacetime logistics sustaining base in the CONUS and overseas by the assignment of individual and unit missions to logistics personnel and TOE organizations that they must be ready to perform during a defense emergency.

Most of what has been discussed is certainly not surprising. In fact, the reader will probably say "I've heard all this before. These are a bunch of logistics cliches." And he would be right. That's exactly the point!

Much of what is needed for improvement in the Army Logistics System is well known and rather simple, but generally surrounded by a "professional mystique" that clouds the problem of resolution and implemen-

# APPENDIXES

tation. We must establish an integrated logistics program that will allow us to set firm, definite intermediate and final objectives with time phasing that will force us to meet the targets established. This is the very essence of the LOGISTICS OFFENSIVE.

## INVENTORY IN MOTION

This article, as the first in the series, highlights the subject of INVENTORY IN MOTION. This phrase means that we have an inventory, composed of items of supply, both serviceable and unserviceable, that is in motion. Too often, in the past, we have not recognized this inventory that is intransit and yet, we have come to recognize the great cost attached to supply in the military pipeline. Because the logistics intelligence concerning specific items that might be in the inventory intransit, on board a ship or on an aircraft, was not good, too often the items were dropped from the shipper's inventory and not picked up by the consignee until he had the items in his firm grasp on solid ground. Once on solid ground, we often lost track of this inventory through poor storage and inventory procedures.

Although we may have justified this situation in earlier times, we have no defense today. Improved communications, improved transportation, and improved computer capability, all controlled by improved command management, can and must provide the logistics intelligence required so that the items in transit can actually be accounted for better, both as to time and space, than supplies that may be on the ground in the combat zone. For example, instead of placing several hundreds of thousands of tons of ammunition in open storage in Vietnam, where it presented a very lucrative target to the enemy, we subtracted the amount on the ground by the amount flowing through the pipeline into the theater from CONUS. When consumption went up or when the enemy destroyed stocks on the ground, the combat commander could still be supported, because logistics intelligence available to the logistics commander provided the flexibility he needed to meet the requirement of the combat commander. This same technique was used advantageously in supplying petroleum.

The question arises—"What if the enemy had sea power, such as submarines, or air power that could destroy ships at sea or aircraft in the air?" "Is this not a lesson learned in a unique fight which would be dangerous to apply across the board?" I do not believe so. In the first place, if the enemy has viable air power, he may more easily attack logistics inventories on the ground than on the sea. Further, the enemy has already proved that several "sappers" can destroy inventories that are stored in open storage in the combat zone.

INVENTORY IN MOTION does not and cannot mean a blind approach—it calls for a high degree of sophisticated logistics management. If the enemy has the capability for destroying INVENTORY IN MOTION, this capability must be assessed. Proper action must be taken to compensate for this aggressiveness. For example, that is the purpose of a safety level. Although the stockage objective is determined routinely, a "management level" must also be established that provides for an amount determined appropriate in static storage based upon the environment involved. (This management level should have its upper and lower limits within which the inventory posture will be maintained.) I really do not believe that one can honestly say that the experience gained in the use of INVENTORY IN MOTION in Vietnam is unique. To the contrary, I believe that we have not reached the full realization of the value of INVENTORY IN MOTION that should be possible in the immediate future. We have only really gained significant advantage of this technique in class III "bulk" and class V supplies. We are beginning to realize advantages of this in other classes of supply, such as I, II, IV, and IX. We must pursue this tenaciously to achieve the fullest practical advantage in all classes of supply.

Essential to this is continuous asset control through the coordination of the U.S. Army Materiel Command, particularly the command's Logistics Control Office, Pacific (LCOP), and the many logistics agencies in U.S. Army, Pacific including those in Vietnam. This essential continuous asset control is being established so that the item with its Federal stock number (FSN) tied in with transportation documentation can be followed from the time it enters the pipeline until it is received by the consignee, particularly at the aerial transfer points or seaports. The cooperation and coordination of such agencies as the Military Traffic Management and Terminal Service (MTMTS) and the Military Sea Transportation Service (MSTS) and the transfer management agencies involved play a most important part. The establishment of the 1st Logistical Command's intelligence file at the LCOP in San Francisco provided the keystone for this entire system. The maintenance of this logistics intelligence at every level of control has provided the logistics system with the tools vitally necessary to facilitate proper planning and, therefore, to operate the logistics system itself effectively and efficiently.

The facets involved are almost too numerous to mention. Too long have we tolerated lack of proper planning for the receipt of supplies through a port into a depot—too often have operators at a depot been surprised by what they found arriving in their receiving yard. With the advent of INVENTORY IN MOTION, this will no longer be the case. We will know at all times where the supplies are, and their arrival at the depot will not come as a surprise to the depot operator.

Another important facet is the control of unserviceables. Today, the CLOSED LOOP system has put some discipline in the return of unserviceables. Unfortunately, this system to date only covers a few end items and components. Proper use of INVENTORY IN MOTION will provide as complete a knowledge of unserviceables in retrograde as it does for serviceables going to a consignee.

I have been discussing the subject of INVENTORY IN MOTION in today's "state of the art." I believe it is clear that the use of this technique becomes even more essential when we talk about taking advantage of such future capabilities as the new C5A transport, which we talked about in the 1960's, but which is with us now in the 1970's!

APPENDIXES 293

In essence, INVENTORY IN MOTION integrates, for the first time, the logistics functions of transportation and supply and, in dealing with unserviceables, it extends that integration into maintenance as well. Through proper management and control of, not "measurement tons," but of items in transit, static stocks can be reduced, the echelonment of stock levels can be minimized, as well as many other advantages accrued. But most significantly, the logistician will manage an integrated system of functions rather than letting separate functions manage the logistician. Like a pipeline filled with water, INVENTORY IN MOTION will provide those responsible for control the necessary logistics intelligence to know when and how to turn the control valve to provide the user with what he needs, when he needs it, and in the proper condition.

In sum, it provides Army command management in logistics with a technique designed to increase significantly the efficiency and effectiveness with which to better serve the country and the soldier! We need to use it to the maximum degree practicable!

Reprinted from *Army Logistician,* Jan–Feb 1970.

# APPENDIX E

Answer to a Challenge—The Logistics Offensive

by

Lt. Gen. Joseph M. Heiser, Jr., in collaboration with
Lt. Col. Albert F. Boll

Supporting Combat Operations in a limited war while simultaneously conducting large-scale troop withdrawals; increasing combat support and combat service support of our allies as they replace U.S. combat forces; and achieving and maintaining a high state of combat readiness for both U.S. forces and those of our allies is the logistician's challenge of the seventies. This challenge must be met despite significantly reduced monetary resources. The actions required to meet this challenge have been termed the LOGISTICS OFFENSIVE. We have established objectives and we are attacking logistics problems with the same aggressiveness that a combat commander uses in an offensive. We must proceed toward our objectives of improving the effectiveness and efficiency of logistics operations at an accelerated rate. Delay will only compound our problems, since we will still have the same job to do later on, but then with fewer available resources.

The LOGISTICS OFFENSIVE is not a reckless program. It strives to sharpen existing management tools and to apply proven concepts and techniques with minimum delay. There is little in the LOGISTICS OFFENSIVE that is new or unique. For the most part, it applies worldwide many of the management techniques used successfully in the Republic of Vietnam (RVN) and elsewhere in the Army. Objectives of the LOGISTICS OFFENSIVE fully support General Westmoreland's four M program—mission, motivation, modernization, and management—and are consistent with the national policy of reducing forces overseas while maintaining a strong and viable base within the United States.

### Aims Publicized

During 1970 we made an intensive effort to broadcast the objectives and purpose of the LOGISTICS OFFENSIVE to commanders and logisticians throughout the world. Appropriate Department of the Army regulations and circulars have been published or revised. Articles on various aspects of the LOGISTICS OFFENSIVE have appeared in many publications. I have spread the word through staff visits to continental United States (CONUS) and oversea commands and through more than 50 speaking engagements

APPENDIXES 295

at service schools and colleges and joint civilian-military seminars and symposiums. At the end of 1970, the LOGISTICS OFFENSIVE was moving forward on all fronts.

It has been encouraging to me to observe the enthusiasm that Army logisticians and their commanders have shown by participating in the program. As a result of individual initiative and organizational resourcefulness, the Army can show cost benefits in excess of $2.3 billion in actual savings or cost avoidance after the first full year of operation under the LOGISTICS OFFENSIVE.

Logistics operations today are a complex business. Army logistics commitments around the world, in support of U.S. forces and the forces of our allies, are at their highest level since the Korean War. In addition, the logistics system supporting these commitments has grown increasingly complex because of the increasing sophistication of Army equipment and the Army's growing dependence on outside agencies for major support.

## Central Coordination Required

Thus, it is essential that the Office of the Deputy Chief of Staff for Logistics (ODCSLOG), Department of the Army (DA), serve as the central coordinating point for all major programs and objectives of the Army-wide LOGISTICS OFFENSIVE. It is imperative that we keep the logistics system operating at peak efficiency during a period of general austerity. All personnel involved must contribute to the program not only by vigorously executing the various tasks and projects but also by suggesting ways and means of reaching our objectives of better support to the combat soldier at less cost.

The LOGISTICS OFFENSIVE was developed as the prime management technique to integrate and coordinate the many aspects and functions of logistics operations. Because so much had to be done in so many areas, we first identified the major areas in which management improvements were required. We than divided the management improvement areas into projects and divided the projects into tasks. Each project was defined to show its scope, objectives, and time-phasing and was underscored with a sense of urgency. Thus, the LOGISTICS OFFENSIVE facilitated the evolution of the supervisory effort to progress from detailed control by project management to management by exception, based on periodic project reports.

At the end of fiscal year 1970, more than 75 LOGISTICS OFFENSIVE projects had been initiated. Projects are added as the need for high-level emphasis becomes apparent and are deleted as final objectives are reached. There are over 120 projects currently under the umbrella of the fiscal year 1971 LOGISTICS OFFENSIVE. To tie all the programs together and to inform each participant of his role in the overall effort, we publish an objectives document listing all projects in the program for the next fiscal year, stating project definitions, goals, and time-phasing.

## Target Dates Met

Our goals are ambitious but realistic. Actually, very few of our goals have slipped from their original target dates. Logisticians on the Department of the Army staff and in the major commands have been more than equal to accomplishing their tasks. On 21 September 1970, for example, the 1st Logistical Command, United States Army, Vietnam, received Presidential recognition for their outstanding accomplishment in reducing costs and improving management. While engaged in combat operations, the 1st Log Command significantly increased logistics responsiveness to the combat units in Vietnam and at the same time saved more than $353 million. Savings since 1968 have exceeded $1 billion. This is the first time that a logistics unit in a combat zone has received this award.

## Tempo Increasing

Momentum of the LOGISTICS OFFENSIVE built up rapidly during the first year and is increasing in tempo this year. I am provided a status report of each project in the LOGISTICS OFFENSIVE program monthly, or more frequently if needed. Some of the more significant, current programs are described below.

- **The Army Logistics System Master Plan (LOGMAP).** LOGMAP was started in March 1970 when we began to pull together into one document all those things we are doing that would give uniform direction to our efforts. LOGMAP is a refined approach to developing and maintaining a master management plan that announces the objectives and provides the methods, schedules, and interrelationships of logistics subsystem development efforts from the present to a future time frame. Several editions of LOGMAP have been published as draft documents, and as development continues, it eventually will be issued as the single source for logistics systems development planning. One facet of the plan is entitled "Project TURN-THE-CORNER." This project is designed to determine where we are in the development of systems, identify the best parts of each system, and apply them Army-wide. As a part of the effort to "turn-the-corner" and gain control over the vertical development of logistics systems, baseline requisites were developed and teams were sent to the field to compare ongoing systems to the requisites. The data obtained on these trips are being analyzed and after appropriate study and approval, the best of what we have today or under development will be used to develop a standard system or modify current systems. Follow-on evaluations and further refinement of the baseline requisites will be required until such time as there is developed a set of logistics requisites and standards by which the development of Army-wide vertical logistics systems can be controlled.

- **Inventory in motion.** This is a management technique developed a few years ago in Vietnam for managing ammunition supply. The concept now includes other classes of supply and has helped to reduce our Vietnam stockage lists from almost 300,000 Federal stock numbers (FSN's) to

90,000 FSN's. *Inventory in motion* is a revitalized supply management program that minimizes the requirement for large stock levels at immobile depot activities in the combat zone. Fewer supplies on hand mean fewer problems of in-storage maintenance, security, and inventory management. While continuing the high level of combat service support, oversea stockage lists during the 15 months of worldwide operation under this program were reduced from an aggregate of 1,063,000 to 459,000 FSN's. Based on recent experience, we have been able to revise the original goal for fiscal year 1971 downward from 360,000 to 180,500 FSN's. The *inventory-in-motion* concept is being applied in over 20 different LOGISTICS OFFENSIVE projects.

- **Project DA Clean.** This project was established as an integral part of the LOGISTICS OFFENSIVE under the *inventory-in-motion* concept to eliminate excess supplies from the Army Supply System by determining what supplies were on hand in the field but were no longer required for mission accomplishment and then to redistribute them to where they were required. During the first nine months of 1970, supplies valued at almost $835 million were eliminated from oversea areas. In fiscal years 1969 and 1970 the U.S. Army, Vietnam, alone retrograded over 750,000 short tons of supplies.

- **Containerization.** Containerization is a valuable shipping technique that reduces damage, loss, and pilferage of cargo while improving distribution capability. Army use of intermodal containers and intermodal container systems has been significant since fiscal year 1969. For example, 11.6 million tons of cargo was shipped from CONUS to oversea destinations in fiscal year 1969. Of the cargo shipped in fiscal year 1969 that could be containerized, only 28 percent of it was shipped by container. That percentage rose to 45 in fiscal year 1970. Military vans (MILVAN), 8- by 8- by 20-foot containers, are being used to ship supplies to the Republic of Vietnam and Thailand. These cargo containers are moved as far forward as the tactical situation and the ability of the units to receive and unload supplies permit. A limited test of containerized ammunition shipments last year indicated operational benefits as well as potential dollar and manpower savings both at the ports and within the theater. We will continue to expand the use of MILVANS in support of the *inventory-in-motion* concept.

- **Operation STREAMLINE.** This project is designed to eliminate unnecessary stocks and supply echelons, reduce the order and ship time, modify certain procedures to accomplish more maintenance at less cost, establish theater-oriented depot complexes, accelerate direct delivery from the United States to direct-support-unit (DSU) and general-support-unit (GSU) levels in combat areas, and improve logistics intelligence and asset control (particularly in-transit). STREAMLINE capitalizes on recent improvements in communications, heavy lift aircraft, and automatic data processing. This LOGISTICS OFFENSIVE project is divided into six subprojects, each similar but with local adaptations for the Pacific (PALOS), Europe (EURLOS), CONARC (CONLOS), Alaska (ALLOS), Southern Command (SOLOS), and the Army Reserve and National Guard (REGLOS).

Under PALOS we have, for example, released the Ikego Ammunition Depot, Japan, to the U.S. Navy. That eliminated over 50,000 short tons of ammunition stocks and reduced manpower requirements by well over 300 spaces. Similar actions are scheduled for other areas. The emphasis of Operation STREAMLINE is to improve the efficiency of the logistics system by eliminating the unnecessary rather than simply reducing costs. Any savings, however real and important, in reality are fringe benefits.

• **Troop Dining Facilities.** Of particular interest to the lower enlisted grades is our action to obtain authorization for spaces and funds to use civilian KP's in Army appropriated-fund dining facilities worldwide. Korea was converted in October 1970, and Panama, Okinawa, and Europe are scheduled to be converted in fiscal year 1972. Another action to improve food service during this fiscal year is a short-order menu to widen the variety of food offered in dining facilities. We are also preparing to test the feasibility of having civilian caterers operate Army garrison mess facilities.

• **Direct Supply Support (DSS).** Delivery of supplies direct from a theater-oriented depot complex in CONUS to oversea DSU's and GSU's, bypassing oversea depots, is a system designed to operate effectively in peace or war. The initial 120-day phase of the test of the system was conducted between CONUS and Europe from 1 July through 31 October 1970. The test objectives were to reduce from an average 95 days to 35 days the order and ship time from the wholesale system in CONUS to the consumer in Europe. Overall goals for the system are to provide effective support and improved asset visibility while reducing budget and resource requirements. Operation of the system will also shorten the distribution pipeline in oversea areas. The test is being expanded incrementally to include all of the VII Corps and class II and IV supplies for all issue priority groups and fringe items including VULCAN/CHAPARRAL and aircraft. The direct supply concept is also being tested in Korea. . . .

• **Selected Item Management System (SIMS).** A program for the intensive management and control of selected items of materiel, SIMS encompasses the functional aspects of logistics—procurement, supply, storage, distribution, transportation, maintenance, and retrograde. At the beginning of fiscal year 1971, we had 4,600 FSN's under SIMS. This represents approximately 50 percent of the annual demands for secondary items. Much remains to be done before the advantages of SIMS can be fully exploited.

• **Maintenance Support Positive (MS+).** MS+ is a hard look at the total maintenance concept to see how and where maintenance tasks can best be done. In view of the increased sophistication of equipment, shortage of skilled maintenance personnel, and reduced financial resources, we must devise more efficient maintenance methods. MS+ will exploit modular design in maintenance, make necessary changes in doctrine and regulations, revise the maintenance task allocations, determine organizational impacts, develop mobile maintenance concepts, revise the maintenance management process, and expand the advantages of direct exchange procedures in order to achieve an optimum balance of maintenance support.

# APPENDIXES

Through increased emphasis on modular replacement rather than piece-part repair and an improved use of diagnostic equipment and techniques, especially in the lower echelons of maintenance, we will be able to shift the emphasis of the maintenance repair functions from forward to rear echelons.

A few months ago we completed an initial revision of 40 maintenance allocation charts and 130 repair parts and special tool lists. This resulted in easing the maintenance burden at the organizational level and reducing the number of parts and tools required to be in the supply system.

- **The Army Maintenance Management System (TAMMS).** Formerly The Army Equipment Record System (TAERS), TAMMS is a system of recording essential data concerning equipment operation and maintenance. The transformation from TAERS to TAMMS, initiated in October 1969, preserved the standard recordkeeping system, but made major changes in the requirements to record and process data, especially at the national level. Under TAMMS we reduced reportable line items from 556 to 297 line item numbers (LIN). In September 1970, we further streamlined TAMMS by reducing the reportable items to only 40 LIN's, primarily aircraft, combat, and tactical vehicles. This action has virtually eliminated most of the reporting to the national level of the data submitted on DA Form 2407, Maintenance Request. Instead, a system of selective sampling will be used to gather the management data still required at the national level.

Conversion from TAERS to TAMMS eliminated millions of forms and reduced the overall workload. At the installation level, for example, processing maintenance data requires 25,000,000 fewer punchcards and 193 less man-years of key-punch effort. This alone represents annual savings of approximately $1.1 million in manpower and material. Converting to TAMMS Streamline has reduced the key-punch workload by still another 9,800,000 cards.

Further streamlining TAMMS will reduce the volume of data generated, received, and processed and will allow us to focus our attention on critical maintenance areas and provide for necessary improvements in the Army maintenance system.

- **Small Shipment Consolidation Centers.** Consolidation points were established during fiscal year 1969 to improve control over shipments, reduce transit time, and lower transportation costs. Test consolidation points—one in Philadelphia and one in Toledo—resulted in a savings of over $228,000. Additional points were opened at Atlanta, Memphis, and Chicago, on 1 August 1970.
- **Mechanization of DSU/GSU Supply Operations.** Mechanization of supply operations is proceeding on schedule. Over 140 NCR 500 systems have been installed, and by fiscal year 1972 installation of the NCR 500's will be complete.
- **The Closed Loop Support System (CLSS).** CLSS was one of the most successful intensive management techniques that we used in the Republic of Vietnam, achieving a high degree of asset visibility and control throughout the supply, maintenance, and transportation system. During fiscal year

1970, equipment worth $1.4 billion was put into the Republic of Vietnam, while reparables valued at $1.5 billion were retrograded under CLSS. The difference of $100 million represents equipment no longer needed as a result of better management of assets and of troop redeployments. It is currently planned that the CLSS will be expanded to include support of the Army of the Republic of Vietnam, and other allied programs.

- **International Logistics.** President Nixon has stated on numerous occasions that we must do what we can to help our allies help themselves. To supplement Military Assistance Program (MAP) funds and to obtain maximum use of any long supply or excess items, procedures have been established to transfer those items to MAP at no cost. Major items (MIMEX), secondary items (SIMEX), and property disposal items (MAPEX) transferred under these procedures totaled $231 million in fiscal year 1970. The MIMEX/SIMEX/MAPEX estimate for fiscal year 1971 is $270 million.
- **Personnel and training.** These are the keys to any successful logistics systems. In June 1970 a DA Review Board was convened to develop recommendations to improve the methods by which logistics doctrine, training, and military career development are formulated, coordinated, and accomplished. The Board studied structuring of Army logistics personnel into control-management groupings and suggested career progression and training patterns that will produce the kind of professionals required. Additionally, plans are being developed for establishing a professional logistics program for civilians.

## Logistics Intelligence Needed

It is rather obvious that the common denominator in each of the management improvement areas is logistics intelligence. Throughout my career, I have been hampered by the lack of good logistics intelligence. Although we have been making tremendous progress in recent years, we still do not have an adequate method for an accurate and timely determination of true requirements and conditions in all areas of logistics. Feedback of data and processing of logistics information through the reporting systems are still slow and deficient in many areas. Management systems, both new and existing, must be structured to include adequate provision for the free flow of meaningful and timely logistics intelligence.

As stated earlier, there is nothing startlingly new in the LOGISTICS OFFENSIVE. It simply is a management technique used to get a big job done in a hurry. The accomplishments of the LOGISTICS OFFENSIVE in the first year of operation have been remarkable.

Many LOGISTICS OFFENSIVE projects have softened the impact of funding limitations. Wholesale Army Stock Fund obligational authority, for example, has been cut from $1.4 billion in fiscal year 1968 to $0.7 billion in fiscal year 1970. During the same period, obligational authority for procurement of equipment and missiles, Army, secondary items dropped from $484 million to $187 million. Improved logistics management not only permitted us to absorb the cuts but in some cases prompted cuts by reducing materiel requirements and by effectively redistributing excesses. Other recent management improvements made throughout the logistics spectrum have resulted in estimated total cost benefits of between three and four billion dollars.

Congressman Chet Holifield of the House Committee on Government Operations complimented Army logisticians when he pointed out recently that the Army had mounted an impressive campaign to improve logistics and supply operations. It demonstrated, he said, an awareness of the need to learn from the Vietnam experience and to modernize its supply systems to exploit new computer, transportation, and communication technologies. Current Army programs singled out by Congressman Holifield for special mention were those to reduce oversea stockage, to control expensive repair parts, and to pare down the number of items stocked at posts, camps, and stations in the United States.

Despite the success of the LOGISTICS OFFENSIVE, there yet remains much more to be done. By no means is our job finished; we have only just begun. New ideas and individual initiative are needed as we continue to explore avenues which will assist in answering the challenge of the seventies. This will make up later phases of the LOGISTICS OFFENSIVE, preparing us for the 1970's and for the transition into the 1980's. We must continue with a sense of urgency to provide efficient and effective logistics support to the combat soldier.

Reprinted from *Army Logistician,* Jan–Feb 1971.

# APPENDIX F

## The Long-Term Defence Programme
## Crucial to Credible Deterrence

by

Lt. Gen. (Retired) Joseph M. Heiser, Jr.

For almost 30 years, the fallacy that logistics is a national responsibility has hampered attempts of the North Atlantic Treaty Organization to achieve a coalition of logistics efforts. Now, however, as a step toward discarding its erroneous notions about logistics, NATO has developed the Long-Term Defence Programme, a plan to coordinate logistics support, as well as improve NATO's capability in air and sea defense, reserve mobilization, electronic and nuclear warfare, communications and control, readiness, and reinforcement. The program provides an opportunity for substantial progress to be made toward credible deterrence.

Authorized by the NATO Heads of State and Government in May 1977 and developed during 1977 and 1978 by selected NATO task forces, the Long-Term Defence Programme was reviewed, debated, and amended by successive NATO councils, including the May 30–31, 1978, meeting of the Heads of State and Government in Washington, DC.

Among the items included in the approved program are thirteen pertaining to consumer logistics. In addition, there are many other logistics-related actions included in the "subsidiary and no cost/low cost measures" scheduled for follow-up by the Defence Planning Committee/Executive Working Group.[1] Summarized, the task force recommendations address the following areas:

- Improving war reserves
- Harmonizing the communications zone
- Strengthening NATO's logistics organization structure
- Bolstering logistics personnel staffing
- Establishing and maintaining a logistics master plan for meeting objectives
- Other specific actions required to provide the fundamentals of "coalition logistics" in the NATO Alliance

---

[1] The no cost/low cost items are calalogued in "Long Term Defence Programme: Handling of Subsidiary and No Cost/Low Cost Measures,"(AC/281 (L&P) N (78)8-NATO confidential).

# APPENDIXES 303

The NATO communiques of May 19 and 31, 1978, stress the significance of these programmed actions and call for "vigorous follow-through action to be taken by National authorities and at NATO and international military headquarters." Such actions can significantly improve minimum essential logistics support for approved NATO strategy; indeed, several approved actions, such as the establishment of an assistant secretary general for logistics, have already shown significant progress.

But the real test, of course, is whether the momentum can be sustained. Will NATO headquarters be able and willing to exercise the vigorous follow-through so essential to effective implementation of the program?

## Obstacles to Implementation

Unfortunately, certain obstacles must first be dealt with. Otherwise, despite its great potential for good, the Long-Term Defence Programme will become one more paper exercise. While some of these obstacles are national and need national solutions, others pertain to the Alliance as a whole and need Alliance solutions. The remainder of this article summarizes the most significant of these difficulties.

**National self-interest.** Parochialism, generally related to short-term sovereign self-interest, can restrain the will to meet mutual needs. But the development of the Long-Term Defence Programme demonstrated the willingness of national and NATO participants to counter this propensity. If this determination continues throughout the implementation phase of the program, its objectives should be realized. In fact, national self-interest will ultimately be served through execution of the Long-Term Defence Programme.

**Professional staffing needs.** The NATO logistics-management capability is constrained by too few logistics professionals and too many national and Alliance committees related to logistics. Until summit approval of the Long-Term Defence Programme, there was only one logistics professional in NATO headquarters. Now a new assistant secretary general, a director of logistics, and a small logistics staff are being recruited so that logistics improvements can be spearheaded at NATO's highest level. Also needed is action to shore up the small logistics staffs in the NATO military headquarters so that the many logistics improvements needed by the Alliance and identified by the Long-Term Defence Programme can be carried out. When this is done, the Alliance will for the first time in its history have a staff capability that will allow implementation of Alliance logistics planning and coordination.

**Materiel emphasis.** The philosophy within NATO is that logistics relates to materiel only, and that the "front end" of logistics, so-called producer logistics, should be emphasized. Consumer logistics (which NATO loosely defines as anything pertaining to materiel logistics not included in producer logistics) is paid little heed. In fact, until recently, the staff at NATO headquarters, including part-time personnel, accounted for less than five professional man-years of effort, mostly devoted to planning and organizing committee meetings concentrating on producer logistics. Other Alliance staffs are similarly limited.

The Long-Term Defence Programme should result in a more equitable arrangement for consumer logistics, but logistics definitions will need clarification, and effort should be redistributed. Also, such essential non-materiel logistic functions as medical and engineering planning and staffing will require support at all NATO levels, particularly within the major NATO command staffs.

**Assumed support for mobilization.** Within the Alliance there is an underlying, unofficial assumption that, in the event of enemy attack, the United States and Canada are the only sources for resupply. Yet neither country is prepared to assume this responsibility, nor have member nations presented their requirements to the Alliance. The Long-Term Defence Programme recommends a resupply plan so that the logistics requirements of resupply will be planned for in peacetime. If the North American countries are expected to support a mobilization, then resupply requirements must be specified.

## International Cooperation Essential

**Constraints on logistics cooperation.** Although Alliance members are evidently willing to cooperate, NATO's logistics posture is constrained by national economic self-interest in several functional areas. Coordination of the research, development, and production of weapon systems generally falls within this category.

However, there is another oft-overlooked constraint: the more productive nations are reluctant to provide resources to an Alliance pool under control of NATO commanders such as the emergency stockpile which could be used to bolster the less productive nations. Their reluctance is partially attributable to a suspicion that pooling resources will cause the less productive nations to depend on others rather than to make them contribute fairly to logistics support. But unless this constraint on Alliance readiness is resolved, the less productive nations will never be able to provide support. The alternative is bilateral arrangements, which are only a partial answer at best.

**"Teeth-to-tail" constraints.** In structuring a national military, the trend today is toward maintaining or adding combat units while concurrently reducing the active-force logistics structure. This means that in an emergency logistics support must be provided by mobilized reserves or by host nation support. But these alternatives can handle only part of the task, and without sufficiently detailed planning and testing even that will lead to failure. Instead, there must be far more recognition of the need for a minimal military support capability that is active in peacetime and can be reinforced quickly by reserve units. All three elements—active logistics forces, ready reserves, and host nation support—must be balanced.

The only effective way to support fighting units is to have a base of military logistics units ready. In peacetime it is difficult to accept economically

# APPENDIXES

and politically that logistics support is imperative, since it is so much easier to recognize the need for combat unit strength. Thus, when military planners are pressured to reduce logistics support and maintain combat strength, an unrealistic expectation results; in turn, this tends to be taken as a rationale for eliminating logistics structures. This objective is worthwhile if only unnecessary structures are eliminated. But most nations in the Alliance unfortunately have eliminated many necessary structures, including organic support in land corps and air wings. The Long-Term Defence Programme recommends that NATO commanders assess their national logistics structure, their counterpart reserve assets, and host nation support plans and agreements. Such a realistic assessment and appropriate action will assure a ready balance to support NATO operational plans.

**Selectivity in logistics improvements.** The Alliance tends to select those recommendations on logistics in the Long-Term Defence Programme which are most easily acceptable, and to table for study those actions requiring resources or pertaining to sensitive sovereign rights. Yet the logistics recommendations in the program encompass the minimum requirements of a strategic logistics plan which are considered vital to the support of the NATO strategy of flexible response. Like an integrated weapon system, an integrated communications network, or an air defense system, this logistics system must contain all of the basic ingredients; deletion of any essentials will render the system ineffective. This is particularly true in an alliance of sovereign nations wherein each must depend upon the whole or face disaster.

## Organizational Needs

**NATO logistics constrained.** Because of the top-heavy committee structure of the Alliance, there is a general aversion to establishing any new organizations, logistics or otherwise, that require more people and money. However, the NATO logistics organization has been constrained for too long, primarily as a result of the attitude that logistics is a national responsibility. Unless the situation is remedied quickly, other approved logistics actions will be endangered.

Fortunately, the Alliance has already achieved some success in fulfilling several recommendations of the Long-Term Defence Programme; for instance, it has established a multinational logistics coordination center at the Allied Forces Central Europe headquarters, the position of assistant secretary for infrastructure and logistics, and other staff positions referred to earlier. Moreover, the Senior NATO Logisticians Conference provides a forum for gaining consensus and implementing consumer logistics measures at the council level.

**Coordination of materiel planning.** Still, such actions alone are insufficient. Yet to be addressed are continuing problems such as the limited use of the NATO Maintenance and Supply Agency (NAMSA). The logistics solution recommended in the Long-Term Defence Programme is to convert NAMSA into a technical management agency, preferably under the Supreme Allied Commander Europe, so it could serve as a clearinghouse for standardization and interoperability related to consumer logistics.

Not expressed specifically in the report is a longer-range objective to convert NAMSA into a NATO Materiel Management Agency (NAMMA), which would coordinate materiel planning for NATO, especially the major NATO commanders. This will provide a structure for introducing and modifying new weapon systems and for planning and coordinating the necessary training within NATO and with member nations.

When separate agencies are established as program managers of common weapon systems in NATO, as for the F–16, system management would be coordinated and integrated as appropriate by the proposed Materiel Management Agency. This would provide a mechanism for maximizing effectiveness and efficiency in logistics support of weapon systems using common logistics resources. Thus, in spite of its current limitations, the NATO Maintenance and Supply Agency could become a most valuable organization.

Until the organizational recommendations of the Long-Term Defence Programme are fully approved and implemented, however, adequate logistics planning for wartime support will not be possible. Moreover, logistical standardization and interoperability will continue to be empty buzzwords, and NATO military commanders will be unable to implement their logistics coordinative management requirements.

**Command-national agreements.** NATO commanders must have effective agreements with all nations covering specific logistics support functions and emergency operations, with annual exercise to improve such agreements. NATO operational plans can succeed only if NATO logistics support is effectively planned and implemented. Otherwise, host nation support will remain a series of uncoordinated bilateral arrangements incapable of fully supporting NATO in war. There can be little doubt that this is a very serious flaw to credible deterrence.

**Determining logistics requirements.** There is one other serious organizational weakness not addressed in the Long-Term Defence Programme: the Military Committee, which is the highest military staff in the Alliance, does not provide a forum for unrestrained presentations of military logistics requirements. Rather, the committee is constrained by the same parochial economic and political pressures that later beleaguer the civil authorities of NATO. Even worse, some commanders do not intervene at councils in which they have seats because of the misconception that the Military Committee represents the final position of the NATO military authorities. If this organizational problem is not resolved, echelons above the major NATO commanders will not recognize the true extent of NATO logistics requirements, and readiness will be seriously compromised. The major NATO commanders must give a full and accurate picture of military logistics requirements; if they do not, then the economic and political leaders get a laundered list of requirements.

# APPENDIXES 307

## The U.S.–NATO Logistics Relationship

The United States, like other member nations, depends upon the Alliance for defense and deterrence. Unable to stand alone logistically, the United States must rely upon its NATO allies for support. As a principal in the Alliance, the United States must take the initiative to assure that the allies cooperate in coordinating all logistics support functions through the NATO commanders, based upon negotiated logistics agreements. Otherwise, logistics improvements will at best be piecemeal and will fail to meet objectives.

The NATO commanders, many of whom are U.S. military personnel, must be given authority and capability to coordinate logistic support. This coordination must involve "the integration of national logistic capabilities into an effective and efficient Alliance logistic system which can provide the logistic support required to deter war or assure logistics to provide the needs of NATO combat forces in war in accord with NATO operational plans."[2] The Long-Term Defence Programme substitutes the word "harmonize" for "integrate" because, even though the Alliance military community recognizes the absolute necessity of full coordination, member nations do not universally accept it under peacetime conditions. In fact, whenever such coordination involves any apparent invasion of sovereign rights, the reaction is negative, including that from U.S. spokesmen.

Until the initiation of the Long-Term Defence Programme in May 1977, the U.S. approach to NATO logistics was essentially a hit-or-miss proposition, with each problem being addressed in isolation. There was no formally recognized set of logistics objectives, and there were only limited programs for their accomplishment on a planned, disciplined basis. But an organized approach is crucial to the success of the Long-Term Defence Programme. Thus, in an effort to follow through, the Department of Defense logistics master plan for NATO, which was recently approved, incorporates the Long-Term Defence Programme logistics measures. DoD Directive 2010.8 sets forth Department policy for NATO logistics.

In addition, the NATO logistics functions within DoD must be recognized as an essential part of the armed forces' primary mission rather than something which is relegated to specialists in international logistics.

### Potential Achievements

Accomplishment of the Long-Term Defence Programme's objectives will provide a basic posture of logistics readiness that can support NATO strategy.[3] Such readiness is the basis of true deterrence.

If effectively implemented, the recommended and approved actions of the program will produce positive results. For example, specific logis-

---

[2] NATO Policy MC 36/2, Revised 1960.
[3] Full cooperation from France would, of course, significantly enhance NATO's logistics posture.

tics agreements will be made between each NATO commander and each country on which the commander must depend for operational support. These agreements must be made in peacetime, tested in practical exercises, and improved so as to be ready for disciplined execution in any crisis. In addition, effective logistics planning will be possible at all echelons of the Alliance, with particular emphasis on determining the logistic requirements for support of NATO strategy and operational plans.

Carrying out the Long-Term Defence Programme will also result in an improved, practical means of fully implementing standardization and interoperability in consumer logistics support functions, as well as in the establishment of an improved war reserve posture in munitions, fuel, and equipment. NATO logistics requirements will be expanded to include personnel logistics and other support requirements previously neglected. Finally, there will be a logistics test program which, when combined with the instituted review and analysis mechanism, will determine not only what achievements have been made in logistics readiness, but also what weaknesses still need corrective action.

The Long-Term Defence Programme is crucial to a viable deterrence. Its objective of creating a fully coordinated logistics support structure that meets NATO strategy requirements must continue to have priority attention throughout the Alliance.

Reprinted from *Defense Management Journal*, Jul–Aug 1979.

# APPENDIX G

## Spreading the Word

> Blessed are the peacemakers . . .
> Matt. 5:9

One of my important duties as a senior officer, an obligation I continue to shoulder in my retirement, is speaking before groups of soldiers and civilians about the technical aspects of logistics management, or just as often explaining or defending U.S. policy. Especially in those unsettled times during the Vietnam War, I was apt to encounter a hostile or, even worse, an apathetic audience. To do my best in these situations, I developed a number of speaking techniques, some of which I described in Chapter 10, above. What follows is a listing of some of the ideas and phrases I found particularly effective in carrying out my mission of "spreading the word."

I have always tried to provide every audience a thought-provoking conclusion to my remarks. Among the particularly effective ones I often used were the well-known words of the poet John Donne and the political philosopher Alexis de Tocqueville. Donne's "Never send to know for whom the bell tolls; it tolls for thee" and his "No man is an island, entire of itself; every man is . . . a part of the main" beautifully illustrated a cardinal point of almost all my remarks: we soldiers, and by extension all Americans, must depend upon one another; when one is hurt, all must share the hurt.

De Tocqueville had something very important to say about America, something that I have often paraphrased for my audience. "I searched for the greatness of America," he reported to his masters in the French government around 1830. "I visited its cities, but could not find it. I visited its oceans and mighty forests, but could not find it. Then one day I went into its churches, and there I discovered the greatness of America. America is great because it is good, and America will remain great as long as it remains good."

I also repeated the words of a senior Raytheon Corporation official I once heard at a Presidential Prayer Breakfast. His thoughts have greatly interested my audiences. He told his listeners that "we seem to be in the midst of a historic cycle which has been repeated over and over in nation after nation since the dawn of history." He went on to outline this national cycle:

From bondage to spiritual faith;
From spiritual faith to courage;
From courage to freedom;
From freedom to abundance;
From abundance to selfishness;
From selfishness to complacency;
From complacency to apathy;
From apathy to fear;
From fear to dependency;
From dependency back again to bondage.

I would close by asking my audience rhetorically where it thought America was located in the cycle, reminding them that less than half of our voters voted in the last presidential election.

I also repeatedly used a story about Lawrence of Arabia. At one point in World War I, Lawrence led a small force of Arab volunteers across the desert to attack a Turkish fort. The men would march through the cooler night, resting during the daytime. One morning they discovered one of their number missing. When Lawrence asked for volunteers to search for him, the soldiers all refused, saying, "It is useless, it is written, he is lost." Lawrence returned alone to find the lost man. About dusk he returned, half dragging, half carrying the Arabian soldier. There was much joy in the camp, but Lawrence stopped the cheering. "I asked for volunteers to get this man," he told them, "but you replied, 'It is written, he is lost.' I tell you it is not written; we write."

I also found that I could move an audience at the end of almost any kind of presentation with something that was once said in my presence as a sort of benediction. It goes like this: "God, you taught us to swim better than the fish. You taught us to fly better than the birds. Now God, please help us walk like a man."

Some find evoking the Deity before a general audience inappropriate or self-serving. I shared that inhibition until an incident that occurred in 1970 when I was DCSLOG. Having accepted an invitation to speak at a university, I was taken aback when an official from that institution called to ask on what Bible verse I would base my talk. My first thought was to refer the man to the Chief of Chaplains because the school had no doubt mistakenly thought me a member of the Chaplain Corps. It turned out that the talk was to be given in the university chapel, to mute any possible problems arising because of the students' opposition to the Vietnam War. In such a setting, the officials believed, a scriptural reference was appropriate.

Thinking about how to respond to this singular request, I stood at the window of my office on the Pentagon's E-Ring facing Arlington Cemetery, my right hand improperly resting in my uniform pocket, jingling several coins. Withdrawing one, I remembered the motto that appears on all U.S. coins: "In God We Trust." It occurred to me that, while I did not believe I should base my talk on a biblical verse, this ubiquitous phrase might well serve my purpose. With that in mind I decided to research the motto. The first answer from the Library of Congress was a "we don't

# APPENDIXES 311

know," but with persistence and a little southern charm I learned from one of the librarians that President Abraham Lincoln had added the words to our coins at the urging of a Pennsylvania clergyman. That man had convinced Lincoln that, given the chaos of the Civil War then raging, the world might come to forget that there had once been a United States of America founded upon a belief in God. Since coins often survived nations, he recommended that American coins be imprinted with the phrase, "In God We Trust." Thus the motto is on our coins because of the discouragement and despair of a man of God who thought that the end of our country was near.

I used this story as a basis for my talk, tying it to my usual theme that duty, honor, and country were values that must precede our goals of peace, love, and freedom. I also reminded my listeners that these values were associated with the founding of our country and that, as our coins indicate, we as a nation depend upon God no matter what our form of religion. The presentation was well received. The students seemed to take something from it for their future. For that I was thankful, for the purpose of all my talks was to leave the audience with something of value to remember. After the many speeches I have given, it is clear to me that quotations such as those that I have mentioned serve in a quiet, unobtrusive way to evoke a thoughtful response, which is the only true measure of success in spreading the word.

# BIBLIOGRAPHIC NOTE

### A Mandatory Reading List

The reader will find numerous volumes referred to in this narrative. Several of them, I believe, belong in the mandatory reading category for any serious student who seeks to understand the state of logistics in today's Army and how it came about.

James A. Huston's *The Sinews of War: Army Logistics, 1775–1953* (1966), is the essential source for a general overview of Army logistics from the Revolutionary War through the Korean War period. Although I take serious exception to Huston's extolling the idea of "first with the most" as a logistics principle, I nevertheless consider *Sinews of War* the finest general history of this complicated subject.

Both the logistical triumphs and failures of our World War II crusade in Europe are carefully documented by Roland G. Ruppenthal in his two monumental volumes on *Logistical Support of the Armies* (1953 and 1959). This work is key to the study of mass land warfare. I especially urge students to reflect on Ruppenthal's chapters on supply over beaches in support of a large invasion force and control and allocation of ammunition and other items in critically short supply.

James E. Hewes, Jr.'s *From Root to McNamara: Army Organization and Administration, 1900–1963* (1975), complements the Huston work by offering important insights into the organization of logistics in the modern Army. In particular, *From Root to McNamara* underscores the reasons for, and the consequences of, the abolition of the old tech services.

The information collected in "Report by the Department of the Army Board of Inquiry on the Army Logistics System," the multivolume survey by a review board chaired by Lt. Gen. Frederic J. Brown in 1966–67, is vital to a full understanding of the McNamara reorganization. With a wealth of detail it explains the effect on logistics of the advances in transportation, communications, and automation in the 1960s. I would especially urge readers to study volume I, "Introduction, Summary, and Guide to Implementation," which provides a historical setting for the important changes that occurred in logistics management in those years.

An understanding of logistical operations in Vietnam and the reaction to the logistical challenges of that war are central to any understanding of logistics in today's Army. I worked intimately with the authors of the seventeen monographs prepared by the Joint Logistics Review Board in 1970 and consider their work indispensable to a proper awareness of the problems encountered and solutions devised by Army logisticians during the Vietnam War. Similarly, I urge logistics students to read my own *Logistic Support* (1974), one of twenty-one monographs written by senior participants on various aspects of the war. In that monograph I emphasized the techniques employed in accomplishing the logistics mission. I also discussed in some detail the logistical lessons we learned from our Vietnam experience.

The so-called Holifield Hearings, the investigation by the Subcommittee of the House of Representatives' Committee on Government Operations at various times between 1968 and 1970, is a work of vital importance to an understanding of the Army's recent logistical evolution. Realizing this importance, I and other senior logisticians of the time offered extensive testimony at those lengthy sessions, which, I believe, transcended our immediate problems in Vietnam and provided a broad-gauge look at logistics in modern warfare. These hearings, and the summary report entitled *Military Supply Systems: Lessons From the Vietnam Experience* (Hearings, 90th and 91st Congress, various dates between 24 June 1968 and 4–5 August 1970, and House Report 91–1586, 8 October 1970), actually analyzed the changes that occurred in Army logistics in light of the Vietnam experience. The subcommittee's timely and useful summary and recommendations for reform in DOD organization are central to the points that I have tried to make in this volume.

Finally, I want to mention two authors, both U.S. Navy admirals, who like myself are interested in investigating the principles (or imperatives) that have emerged from our nation's experiences in military logistics. Henry E. Eccles' *Logistics in the National Defense* (1959) and Thomas R. Weachler's "Priorities and Emphases for Logistics 1976–78," an article in the *Naval War College Review* (Summer 1976) both enhance our understanding of these principles.

## A Heiser Bibliography

The following books, articles, and speeches, written by me over the last several decades, may interest those intending to pursue further the topics covered in this volume.

1. "Close Ordnance Support," in John G. Westover's *Combat Support in Korea* (Washington: Government Printing Office, 1955, reprinted by U.S. Army Center of Military History, 1987).

2. "Economy of Force—Application in Combat Logistics," *Defense Management Journal*, Fall 1968.

3. "More Praise for VN Reservists," *The Officer* (Journal of the Retired Officer Association), Jun 1969.

4. "Logistic Offensive," *Army Logistician*, Jan–Feb 1970.

5. "Logistic Offensive Moving," *Army Logistician*, May–Jun 1970.

BIBLIOGRAPHIC NOTE 315

6. "What's Behind the Logistics Offensive?" *Army Digest,* Aug 1970.

7. "Answer to a Challenge," *Army Logistician,* Jan–Feb 1971.

8. "The Logistics Five-Year Plan," *Army Logistician,* Mar–Apr 1972.

9. "The American Flag," a speech delivered at the U.S. Military Academy, Sep 1972, U.S. Army Speech File Service.

10. "Army Security Assistance Program," *Defense Management Journal,* Oct 1972.

11. "Army Views Common Logistic Support," *Army Logistician,* Jan–Feb 1973.

12. "Research of Department of Defense Inventory Posture," Report Prepared for the General Accounting Office, Mar 1973, files of the General Accounting Office.

13. *Logistic Support,* Vietnam Studies Series (Washington: Government Printing Office, 1974, 1984).

14. "Yom Kippur War Report to the Comptroller General," 1974, files of the General Accounting Office.

15. "Past Is Prologue," *Defense Management Journal,* Jul 1976.

16. "NATO Principles of Logistics and U.S. Readiness: A Changing Environment," *Defense Management Journal,* Mar 1978.

17. "Cambodia Report to President Jimmy Carter," 1979, files of the White House.

18. "Long-Term Defence Programme," *Defense Management Journal,* Jul–Aug 1979.

19. "Logistics Issues," Logistics Management Institute Talking Paper for the Reagan Transition Team, 2 Dec 1980, LMI Archives.

20. "Logistics Issues," Logistics Management Institute Talking Paper for the White House, 4 Jan 1982, LMI Archives.

21. "Mobilization: What it Means to Me!" *National Defense Executive Reserve 1983 Conference Report* (FEMA).

22. "Mobilization and Related Geography," *NATO–Warsaw Pact,* U.S. General Accounting Office, Dec 1988 (GAO NSIA SG–23B).

23. "Principles of NATO Logistics," *NATO Logistics Handbook,* Nov 1989.

# Index

Aberdeen Proving Ground, Maryland: 21–22, 34, 91, 92, 107, 112, 225
Abramowitz, Ambassador Morton I.: 214, 215
Abrams, General Creighton W.: 120–21, 127–29, 131–33, 135, 139–42, 149–50, 156, 161–62, 164–66, 168, 183, 201–02, 208, 245, 265
Adak, Alaska: 59
Adams-Millis Hosiery Company: 10
Addabbo, Congressman Joseph P.: 170
Aircraft
  AH–64 (Apache): 242
  B–2 (bomber): 242
  F–111 (fighter): 239
  UH–1 (helicopter): 136
Aircraft Materiel Management Center: 160
Almond, Lt. Gen. Edward M.: 68, 73, 74
Ammunition
  60-mm. mortar: 60
  81-mm. mortar: 52
  90-mm. antiaircraft: 40
  105-mm. artillery: 64
  accidents: 42, 47, 61–63, 75–77, 185
  Class V supplies: 52, 64, 156, 177, 264
  containerized transport: 33–34, 249
  proximity fuze: 66
  renovation and recovery units: 50, 255–56
  requirements: 34–35
Anderson, Jack: 142, 169
Anderson, General Webster: 105, 117
Andrews Air Force Base, Maryland: 134, 213
Antwerp, Belgium: 42, 48
Army Materiel Command (AMC): 102, 107, 117, 121, 131–33, 137, 145, 147, 157, 179–80, 222, 245–47, 251
Army of the Republic of Vietnam (ARVN): 154, 161–62
Arsenal system: 110, 248, 253
Athletics
  baseball: 6, 7, 9–13, 57, 78, 99, 122, 259
  basketball: 4, 9–13, 99, 121
  football: 116
  table pool: 118, 122
  tennis: 10–12, 99, 201, 212
Authorized Stockage List (ASL): 155
Automation: 251–52
AVCO T–53 engines: 136

Aviation Materiel Management Center (AMMC): 160
Aviation Systems Command (AVSCOM): 210–11

Baker, Lt. Gen. William C., Jr.: 105
Barr, Maj. Gen. David G.: 68
Bastogne: 139
Battle of the Bulge: 41–43, 47
Beach, General Dwight E.: 130
Becton, Lt. Gen. Julian W., Jr.: 116
Bell Helicopter Company: 211
Bennett, John J.: 210
Bennett, Norman: 77
Berg, Assistant Secretary of the Army for Logistics Eugene E.: 164
Berlin crisis: 113–14, 222
Besson, General Frank S.: 107, 131–32, 145
Bigelow, Maj. Gen. Horace: 121
Billingsley, Col. John D.: 67–68
Black market: 46, 130
Board of Inquiry on the Army Logistics System (Brown Board): 121
Bohlen, Ambassador Charles "Chip": 100, 118, 120
Borg-Warner Corporation: 93–94
Bowsher, Comptroller General of the United States Charles A.: 210, 218, 231, 272–73
Boy Scouts of America: 121–22
Bradley, General Omar N.: 44–46
Brest, France: 52, 249
Brittany, France: 47, 53, 249
Brown, Lt. Gen. Frederic J.: 120
Brown, Secretary of Defense Harold: 218
Brzezinski, Assistant to the President Zbigniew: 212

CALS (Current automated logistics system): 225
Cam Ranh Bay, Vietnam: 148, 153
Cambodia: 153, 212–16
Camp Drake, Japan: 59
Camp Jackson, South Carolina: 18
Camp Lucky Strike, France: 43
Camp Patrick Henry, Virginia: 21, 25
Camp Pendleton, California: 58
Camp Pickett, Virginia: 21
Camp Sutton, North Carolina: 10, 18

318        A SOLDIER SUPPORTING SOLDIERS

Carlucci, Deputy Secretary of Defense Frank C.: 239
Carter, President Jimmy: 212–16, 219
Carter, Rosalynn: 212–14
Central Intelligence Agency: 99
Charleston, South Carolina: 3–4, 6, 9–10, 12–13, 17
Chech'on, Korea: 75
Chemical, biological, or radiological (CBR) warfare: 250
Cherbourg, France: 48, 53, 249
Chesarek, General Ferdinand J.: 113 115, 116, 117, 132, 147, 179, 180
Chicago Ordnance District: 93
Chief of Ordnance: 56–57, 78, 92–93, 98, 101, 104, 107, 114, 121, 240
Chiefs of Technical Services: 101–02, 106, 108
Chosin Reservoir, Korea: 68
Citadel, The: 13, 17
Clark, General Mark W.: 91
Clements, Deputy Secretary of Defense William P., Jr.: 210
Closed Loop support system: 137, 138, 250
Combat service support: 21, 25, 103–04, 109, 111, 161–62, 236, 248–50
Combat Support of the Army (COSTAR): 103, 117
Command and General Staff College: 57–58, 92, 134, 176, 182
Command, control, communications, and intelligence (C³I): 236
Commander in Chief, Europe: 171
Commander in Chief, U.S. Army, Europe: 123, 177
Commanders' Critical Items List (CCIL): 138, 261
Commerce, Department of: 99, 117, 153, 238, 242, 248
Commodities: 61, 101–04, 108, 110–11, 117, 160, 181, 236, 253, 258, 262
Commodity commands: 106–07, 138, 225, 240, 243, 246
Communications zone (COMZ): 22, 42, 43, 49, 53–54, 105, 115, 116–18, 120–24, 127, 206, 221–23, 226, 247
Computers: 32, 110, 175–77, 244, 252
Conn, Billy: 29
Containers: 33–34, 249
Conventional Forces in Europe (CFE) agreements: 231, 233, 256–57
Cooke, Terence Cardinal: 163
Coronado Naval Station, California: 59
Corpus Christi Depot, Texas: 137
Cox, Dorothy: 11
Critical items: 47, 52, 112, 137–38, 151, 261–62

D-Day: 27, 30, 32–33, 35–37, 39, 48, 204
Da Nang, Vietnam: 148, 153, 160
Dahl, Sgt. Larry A.: 164
Davis, Brig. Gen. Benjamin O.: 27–28, 30
de Gaulle, President Charles: 118–20
de Tocqueville, Alexis: 266
Defense Logistics Agency (DLA) (formerly Defense Supply Agency): 103, 106, 236, 243
*Defense Management Journal*: 229
Denny, Harold: 231
Deputy Chief of Staff for Logistics (DCSLOG): 101–02, 109, 117, 124, 127, 133, 137, 145, 147, 165, 168–72, 174–85, 201, 210, 231, 244–47, 251–52
Deputy Chief of Staff for Personnel (DCSPER): 180
DePuy, General William E.: 176, 180, 201
Dillon, Col. Leo J.: 28, 29, 32, 33, 37, 56, 58
Dillon, Reverend: 7
Direct support: 34, 49, 98, 177, 222, 251, 255, 262
Distinguished Service Cross: 32
Distinguished Service Medal: 202
Donne, John: 266

Ehrlichman, John: 185
Eisenhower, General Dwight D.: 26, 31, 43, 48
Electronics Command, Fort Monmouth, New Jersey: 144
Engler, Lt. Gen. Jean E.: 139

Federal Emergency Management Agency (FEMA): 116
Federal Stock Number (FSN): 136, 144, 154, 163
Ferenbaugh, Maj. Gen. Claude B.: 70–72, 74, 77–78
Fish, Congressman Hamilton: 78
Forrest, Lt. Gen. Nathan Bedford: 150–51
Fort Bragg, North Carolina: 158, 222
Fort Campbell, Kentucky: 158
Fort DeRussey, Hawaii: 185
Fort Jackson, South Carolina: 213
Fort Knox, Kentucky: 92
Fort Leavenworth, Kansas: 57–58, 69, 72, 92, 134, 176, 180, 182. *See also* Command and General Staff College.
Fort Lee, Virginia: 109, 164, 169–70, 180, 182
Fort Meade, Maryland: 185
Fort Myer, Virginia: 54, 127, 202
Fox, Assistant Secretary of Defense J. Ronald: 179, 238
Franklin, Col. Joseph: 211
Froehlke, Secretary of the Army Robert F.: 140, 201
Fuson, Maj. Gen. Jack: 183, 252
Fyfe, Charles M.: 6–7, 9

# INDEX 319

Galvin, Bob: 93, 94
Galvin, Paul: 96, 97, 204
Garner, Vice President John Nance: 5
Gay, Maj. Gen. Hobart R.: 59
Gehrig, Lou: 8
General Accounting Office (GAO): 51, 150, 174, 208–10, 218, 227
General Asbestos and Rubber Company: 12
Godwin, Richard P.: 104, 236
Goodpaster, Lt. Gen. Andrew J.: 166
Gordon, Sergeant: 163, 236
Graham, Billy: 162
Graves registration and mortuary services: 109
Gray, Sgt. Isaiah: 116
Grothous, Brig. Gen. Donald G.: 117
Gur, Lt. Gen. Mordechai: 227

Haeundae, Korea: 63
Haig, General Alexander: 109, 218–20, 230
Haines, General Ralph E.: 147
Haldeman, H. R.: 185
Hammell, Maj. James P.: 56
Hansen, Maj. Gen. Floyd: 98
Harbert, John: 32
Harvard University: 91, 93
Heinsohn, Alvin "Rock": 12, 18
Heiser, Annette: 12
Heiser, Edith "Sug": 6–7, 12, 17–18, 23, 45, 56, 58–59, 64, 96, 115, 141, 146, 202, 204–05, 207–08, 213–14
Heiser, Joan: 6, 58
Heiser, Joel: 6, 12, 38
Highpoint, North Carolina: 10–12
Hinrichs, Lt. Gen. John H.: 107
Holbrooke, Assistant Secretary of State Richard C.: 213
Holifield, Congressman Chet: 150, 174, 209
Hope, Bob: 163
Hughes, Maj. Gen. Everett S.: 78
Hughes, Senator Harold E.: 213
Huntsville, Alabama: 56
Hurlbut, Maj. Gen. Oren E.: 132

Ignatius, Assistant Secretary of Defense (I&L) Paul: 136
Inch'on, Korea, invasion: 60, 66, 68, 73
Indiana Arsenal: 91
Industrial College of the Armed Forces: 98–99
Infantry School, Fort Benning, Georgia: 92
Inland Steel Corporation: 93–94
Integrated logistic support (ILS): 239–40, 242
International Harvester Corporation: 93–95
Interoperability: 112, 219, 224–26, 229–30, 256–57, 263
Inventory accuracy: 51–52, 178
Inventory control: 20, 25, 60–61, 103, 111, 131, 138, 153–54, 156, 176–78, 252–53, 260

Inventory in Motion: 152–54, 157, 250–51
Iran: 210–13
Israel: 212, 227

Japan: 59–60, 62–64, 68, 73–74, 98, 141, 158, 166, 222, 232, 258
Johnson, General Harold K.: 124, 139, 141, 168
Johnson, Maj. Lebus C.: 33
Johnson, President Lyndon B.: 120
Johnson, Walter: 8
Juliana, Princess of the Netherlands: 26
Just in Time (JIT): 98, 153, 251

Kicklighter, Lt. Gen. Claude B.: 231
King, Admiral Ernest J.: 141
Komer, Robert W.: 219, 230
Korea: 22, 30, 32, 35, 44, 47–48, 50–51, 56–79, 91, 104, 108, 110, 112, 128, 138, 164, 206, 222, 227, 232, 249–50, 255–56, 258
Kornet, Lt. Gen. Fred: 202
Keyser, Maj. Gen. Robert C.: 124

Laird, Secretary of Defense Melvin R.: 185
Lancaster, Edgar W.: 107
Latta, Maj. Gen. William B.: 144
Le Havre, France: 42, 48
Leadership: 3, 6–8, 24, 28, 30–32, 93–94, 96, 115, 122, 139, 145, 148–49, 181–83, 185, 202–05, 235, 258–60, 265–66
Lee, Lt. Gen. John Charles Henry "Court House": 26–28
Leeper, Capt. Donald: 60
Legion of Merit: 30
Lehman, Secretary of the Navy John F.: 246
LeMay, General Curtis: 115, 117
Lincoln, Lt. Gen. Lawrence J. "Big Abe," Jr.: 127–29, 131–32, 139, 141, 146, 202
Lines of communications (LOC): 220–23, 257
*Logistical Support of the Armies*: 35, 39
Logistics Center, Fort Lee, Virginia: 180–81
Logistics Control Office, Pacific (LCOP): 154, 157, 252
Logistics Doctrine Systems and Readiness Agency (LDSRA): 180–81
Logistics Executive Development Course (LEDC): 182
Logistics Imperatives: 260–64
Logistics Intelligence File (LIF): 154, 156
Logistics Management Institute (LMI): 178, 179, 218, 231
Logistics Master Plan (LOGMAP): 172, 174
Logistics Offensive: 150, 152, 162
Logistics Support Analysis (LSA): 179, 242, 246, 262

Logistics System Policy Council (LSPC): 171, 237
Long Binh, Vietnam: 142, 166, 222
Long Term Defense Plan (LTDP): 219–20, 224, 226, 228–31
Louis, Joe: 29
Luns, Secretary General of NATO Joseph: 232
Lynch, Col. James: 72
Lynde, Maj. Gen. Nelson M., Jr.: 71–72, 98
Lynn, Maj. Gen. William McGregor, Jr.: 69

Mabry, Maj. Gen. George: 143, 165
MacArthur, General Douglas: 9, 68, 73
MacBean, Madeline: 213
McCormick, Brooks: 93
McCormick, Cyrus: 94
McCullough, Hugh: 218
McGuire, Jack: 99–100
McHugh, Maj. James: 31
McNamara, Secretary of Defense Robert S.: 99, 102–03, 110, 117–18, 122
Maintenance Support Positive (MS+): 179
Management: 12–13, 17, 102, 106, 117, 131–32, 137–38, 155, 172, 185, 238, 246–47
  career management: 180–83
  logistics management: 47, 110–11, 120, 145, 149, 154, 157, 169–70, 175–76, 225, 239, 242–44
  maintenance management: 147–48, 179
  training: 93–98
  transportation management: 35–37, 53–54, 65–66, 153, 155, 156, 226–28
Management by objectives: 152
Marshall, General George C.: 54, 55, 141
Medal of Honor: 164, 166
Medaris, Col. Bruce: 44
Meeks, Col. John Abner: 29, 36
Meloy, Maj. Gen. Guy S., Sr.: 92
Messmer, Pierre: 119
Mildren, Lt. Gen. Frank T.: 142–43, 150, 166
Miley, General Henry: 117
Military Airlift Command: 157
Military Assistance Command, Vietnam (MACV): 130
Military Sea Transportation Service (MSTS): 130, 141–42, 149, 153, 157, 161–62, 166, 183, 226–27, 247
*Military Supply Systems: Lessons from the Vietnam Experience*: 112. *See also* U.S. Congress, House Government Operations Committee.
Military Traffic Management and Terminal Service (MTMTS): 157
Monroe, North Carolina: 18–21
Montgomery, Congressman C. V. "Sonny": 11
Mop shops (maintenance operating procedures): 111, 253

Morris, Assistant Secretary of Defense (I&L) Thomas D.: 134–35, 209, 236
Motorola Corporation: 93–94, 96–98, 204, 223
Movement control: 53–54, 65–66
"Mr. Sheridan": 145
Munitions and Missiles School: 61
Muscaro, Gus: 7
Mytinger, Mr.: 62–63

Napper, Col. Frank: 37
National Automobile Dealers Association: 17
National Defense University: 100
National Inventory Control Point: 178
"National Security Review 11": 247
National Stock Number (NSN): 254
National War College: 98–99, 113–15, 140, 218
*NATO Logistics Handbook*: 217, 230
Navistar International Corporation: 95
New Cumberland Army Depot, Pennsylvania: 180
Nixon, Colonel: 44
Normandy beachhead: 30, 33–37, 39–41, 48–50, 52–53, 61, 151, 234, 249
North Atlantic Treaty Organization (NATO): 22, 36, 49, 109, 119–20, 212, 217–34, 256–58
  Allied Command Europe (ACE): 218
  Army Forces Central (AFCENT): 218, 228, 231–32, 257
  Council of Ministers: 228, 230
  NATO Long Term Defense Program: 219–31
  NATO Maintenance and Supply Agency (NAMSA): 225–26
Notre Dame University: 184
Nunn, Senator Sam: 232, 256
Nunn-Bartlett Report: 232

Office of the Chief of Ordnance: 56, 78
Officer Candidate School: 10, 19, 21–23, 57
Okinawa: 118, 131–32, 135, 142, 158, 166, 222
O'Meara, General Andrew: 123–24, 206
Ordnance Hall of Fame: 32
Ordnance School: 38
Orleans, France: 117, 222
Ostrom, Col. Charles: 38, 67, 74
Overseas Supply Division: 157

Pace, Secretary of the Army Frank: 91
Pacific Architects and Engineers Corporation: 159
Pacific Utilization and Redistribution Agency (PURA): 135–36
Packard, Deputy Secretary of Defense David: 105, 171, 235–36, 238, 239
Palmer, General Williston B.: 123
Paris, France: 30, 42, 46, 54, 99, 118, 120

# INDEX

Partin, Maj. Walt: 30, 31, 32
Patton, Maj. Gen. George S., Jr.: 17–18, 39, 44–47, 139, 249
Patton, Maj. Gen. George, III: 145, 225
Personnel and Finance Center, Fort Benjamin Harrison, Indiana: 180
Pitriani, NATO Deputy Secretary General Rinaldo: 230
Planning, Programming, and Budgeting System (PPBS): 99, 103
Pleiku, Vietnam: 153
POL (Petroleum, Oil, and Lubricants). *See* Supplies, Class III.
Prescribed load lists (PLLs): 155
Presidio, San Francisco, California: 185
Preventive maintenance (PM): 91, 92
Project manager (PM): 243, 253
Projects
  Project 170: 112
  Project Buddy: 161
  Project COSTAR: 117. *See also* Combat Support of the Army.
  Project Count: 133, 135
  Project DA Clean: 172, 173
  Project Stop See: 144
Property Disposal Office (PDO): 146–47, 243
Providence College, Rhode Island: 8
Proxmire, Senator William: 134–35
Pueblo Army Ordnance Depot: 31
Pusan Perimeter, Korea: 58, 63, 65–68, 73, 128, 222
Pusangin, Korea: 60–61, 65

Quartermaster General of the Army: 103, 105
Qui Nhon, Vietnam: 144, 148, 153, 250

Race relations: 28–30
  racial incidents: 27, 115–16
  racial integration: 74
Ramsey, Maj. Gen. Lloyd: 149
Rationalization, standardization, interoperability (RSI): 224, 256–57
Raybestos-Manhattan Corporation: 12
Raye, Martha: 163
Reagan, President Ronald: 116
Red Ball Express: 23, 46, 54, 139, 155, 252–53. *See also* Management, transportation.
REFORGER: 223
Reorganization Act, 1986: 244
Resor, Secretary of the Army Stanley R.: 133, 139–41, 168, 171–72
Retrograde movement of men and equipment: 49–51, 72, 219, 227, 243, 251, 261
Rhee, President of Korea Syngman: 64
RHIP (rank has its privileges): 204

Richmond, U.S. Surgeon General Julius B.: 213
Ridgway, General Matthew B.: 74
Rivers, Congressman L. Mendel: 17
ROTC (Reserve Officer Training Corps): 184
Rumsfeld, Secretary of Defense Donald H.: 218

Saigon, Vietnam: 22, 129, 142, 148, 153, 166, 202
St. Charles College, Catonsville, Maryland: 7
St. Joseph's Academy, Convent Station, New Jersey: 6
San Francisco, California: 58, 143, 154, 157, 252
Saudi Arabia: 110, 236, 248
Schultz, Secretary of State George: 78
Schwalenburg, Rev. Martin: 92
Scott, Brig. Gen. Terry: 163
Sears, Roebuck and Company: 93, 95
Seay, Sgt. William W.: 164
Seese, Mr.: 62–63
Seitz, General Theodore: 218
Seneca Ordnance Depot, New York: 23
Services of Supply: 26
Shah of Iran: 211–12
Shaughnessy, Thomas: 93
Sheen, Bishop Fulton J.: 7
Shillito, Barry: 171, 236
Siegfried Line: 39, 45, 53
Simon, Col. Leslie: 34
SIMS (Special Item Management System): 251
Singapore: 146
Single source support: 158–59, 160
Sink, Lt. Gen. Robert: 68
Slaughter, Brig. Gen. Willis: 92
Sloan, Capt. Medwyn D. "Red": 21–22
Sloan, Col. William N., Jr.: 93
Smith, Maj. Gen. Homer D.: 22, 32
Soissons, France: 30–31, 41, 76
Soldier's Medal: 30
South Korean Railroad: 65
Southern Base Section (SBS): 28
Standardization: 104, 110, 224, 229–30, 236–38, 256–57
State, Department of: 99, 120, 146, 213, 231
Status of Forces Agreement (SOFA): 118–20
Stewart, Gloria: 163
Stewart, Jimmy: 163
Streckfuss, "Tante" (grandaunt) Anna: 3, 6, 9
Supplies
  Class III: 61, 177, 264
  Class V: 52, 64, 156, 177, 264
Supreme Headquarters, Allied Expeditionary Force (SHAEF): 31, 53–54
Supreme Headquarters, Allied Powers Europe (SHAPE): 68, 218–19, 230, 266

Taiwan: 146–48, 222
Tan Son Nhut Air Base, Vietnam: 227
Tank, Maj. Gen. Charles F.: 115
Taylor, General Maxwell: 266
Technical Services
 manuals and catalogs: 104, 111, 238
 reorganization: 105–06, 108, 180. *See also* McNamara, Secretary of Defense Robert S.
Tet offensive: 149
Texas City, Texas: 57
Thailand: 141, 213–16
Theater Authorized Stockage Lists (TASLs): 155
Thompson submachine gun: 59, 108
Thrasher, Brig. Gen. Charles O.: 31
Training: 23, 68, 162, 180–83, 227, 242, 244, 250, 258, 261–62, 266. *See also* Management, training.
Training and Doctrine Command (TRADOC): 180–81
Transportation Command: 157
Transportation Management Agency (TMA): 226–27
Transportation Movement Activity: 228
Troop Support Command: 109, 170
Truman Doctrine: 128
Tryon, North Carolina: 12
Turner, Maj. Gen. Carl O.: 122

Underwood, Lt. Gen. George V. "Bud," Jr.: 172
United Auto Workers: 95
United Nations International Year of the Child: 213
University of Chicago Business School: 93, 98, 182
U.S. Army, Pacific (USARPAC): 130, 157
U.S. Army, Vietnam (USARV): 130, 165–66, 247
U.S. Army Logistical Commands
 1st: 142, 145–46, 148, 151, 158–61, 163–64, 222, 247
 2d: 67, 135, 158, 221–22
 4th: 113–14, 222
U.S. Army units
 Armies
  First: 44
  Third: 39, 44–45, 47, 249
  Seventh: 44
  Eighth: 66–67, 72–75, 91, 104, 222
  Ninth: 38, 44
 Corps
  X: 66–68, 73–74
 Divisions
  1st Cavalry: 159, 166, 242
  7th Infantry: 67, 69 (DIVARTY), 74, 112
  24th Infantry: 65–66
  29th Infantry: 27
  82d Airborne: 158

U.S. Army units—Continued
 Regiments:
  3d Infantry: 202
  11th Armored Cavalry: 145
  302d Ordnance: 21
  707th Ordnance: 71, 112, 250
 Companies
  699th Ordnance Ammunition: 23
U.S. Congress
 House Government Operations Committee: 144, 150. *See also* Holifield, Congressman Chet; *Military Supply Systems: Lessons from the Vietnam Experience.*
 Senate Armed Services Committee: 112, 232
U.S. Marine Corps: 17, 154, 203
 1st Marine Division: 60

Van Fleet, General James: 72
Vehicles
 DUKW (amphibian truck): 63
 M38 (jeep): 147
 M151 (jeep): 147
 M551 (Sheridan tank): 144–45
Verdun, France: 113
Vietnam: 11, 22, 32, 38, 44–45, 47–48, 50–51, 97, 103–10, 116–18, 121, 127–67, 171–72, 177, 184–85, 201, 209, 211, 222, 226–27, 237, 242, 246–52, 256
von Braun, Werner: 108
von Senger und Etterlin, General Frido: 218

Walker, Lt. Gen. Walton H.: 59
Walter Reed Hospital, Washington, D.C.: 58
War Department's Disaster Officer: 56
Ware, Maj. Gen. Keith: 166
Warsaw Pact: 119, 218, 231
Washington Boys' Club: 5–9, 19, 56, 59
*Washington Post*: 96, 161
West Germany: 49, 120, 230
Westmoreland, General William C.: 11, 128, 141, 168, 170–71
Westover, John G.: 112, 170–71
Wilhelmina, Queen of the Netherlands: 26
Wilson, Senator Pete: 112
WINTEX: 223
World War II: 10, 25–45, 49–51, 57–58, 61, 77, 94, 101–02, 104, 108, 110–11, 139, 141, 157, 164, 166, 221, 243, 248, 250, 253, 255–56
WRS (Air Force War Reserve Stocks) Kits: 242

Young, Mrs. Andrew: 213

Ziegler, Marion: 6
Zierdt, Maj. Gen. John: 93, 164
Zumwalt, Admiral Elmo: 167

# *Logistician's Creed*

★ I AM A PROFESSIONAL LOGISTICIAN SERVING IN THE U.S. ARMY.

★ I BELIEVE IT IS A PRIVILEGE TO SERVE MY COUNTRY IN PURSUIT OF FREEDOM AND PEACE THROUGHOUT THE WORLD.

★ I WILL PERFORM MY LOGISTIC DUTIES BY AGGRESSIVELY PROVIDING SUPPORT AND SERVICE TO THE LINE ON THE LINE.

★ I WILL ACCOMPLISH MY LOGISTIC MISSIONS BY CONTINUAL STUDY AND APPLICATION OF CONSTRUCTIVE INNOVATION AND CREATIVENESS TO PRODUCE MODERN LOGISTICS FOR A MODERN ARMY.

★ I WILL AVOID BECOMING STATIC IN THOUGHT, WORD, AND ACTIONS—LOGISTICS MUST BE PROGRESSIVE! COMPLACENCY WILL NOT BE CONDONED.

★ I WILL USE MY COMMAND / MANAGEMENT / STAFF RESPONSIBILITIES TO ASSURE ECONOMY OF LOGISTIC FORCES AND LOGISTICS INTELLIGENCE TO DETERMINE TRUE REQUIREMENTS.

★ I DEDICATE MY ENERGIES AND INFLUENCE TO THE CONTINUED IMPROVEMENT AND PERPETUATION OF A CAREER PROGRAM FOR DEDICATED PROFESSIONAL CIVILIAN, ENLISTED, AND OFFICER LOGISTICIANS.

★ I WILL ALWAYS REMEMBER THE ONLY REASON FOR LOGISTICS AND THE NEED FOR MY PROFESSIONALISM IS TO SUPPORT THE COMBAT SOLDIER SO THAT TOGETHER THE DEFENSE OF OUR FREEDOM-LOVING COUNTRY AND ITS NATIONAL OBJECTIVES CAN BE GUARANTEED.

★ I WILL SET AND MAINTAIN STANDARDS OF EXCELLENCE IN PERSONAL CONDUCT, LEADERSHIP, AND ALL LOGISTIC MISSIONS ASSIGNED.

★ MY GOAL IN PEACE OR WAR IS TO SUCCEED IN ANY MISSION. THEREFORE, I WILL NOT RESORT TO GUESSING AS I KNOW THAT CHANCE IS A FOOL'S GOD AND THAT I AS A LOGISTICIAN CANNOT DEPEND ON IT—I WILL BE SURE—ALWAYS!

www.ingramcontent.com/pod-product-compliance
Lightning Source LLC
Chambersburg PA
CBHW071652160426
43195CB00012B/1444